MW00812993

Making the
POEM

Making the

POEM

Stevens'
Approaches

GEORGE S. LENSING

Louisiana State University Press
Baton Rouge

Published by Louisiana State University Press
Copyright © 2018 by Louisiana State University Press
All rights reserved
Manufactured in the United States of America
FIRST PRINTING

DESIGNER: Mandy McDonald Scallan
TYPEFACE: Whitman
PRINTER AND BINDER: Sheridan Books, Inc.

Library of Congress Cataloging-in-Publication Data

Names: Lensing, George S., 1943– author.
Title: Making the poem : Stevens' approaches / George S. Lensing.
Description: Baton Rouge : Louisiana State University Press, [2018] |
    Includes bibliographical references and index.
Identifiers: LCCN 2018005619| ISBN 978-0-8071-6894-3 (cloth : alk. paper) | ISBN
    978-0-8071-6895-0 (pdf) | ISBN 978-0-8071-6896-7 (epub)
Subjects: LCSH: Stevens, Wallace, 1879–1955—Criticism and interpretation.
Classification: LCC PS3537.T4753 Z67446 2018 | DDC 811/.52—dc23
LC record available at https://lccn.loc.gov/2018005619

Chapter 2 makes use of material published previously by the author as "Wallace Stevens, Ramon Fernandez, and 'The Idea of Order at Key West,'" in *Something Understood: Essays and Poetry for Helen Vendler*, edited by Stephen Burt and Nick Halpern (University of Virginia Press, 2009). Used by permission.

The journal "Sea Voyage," kept by Mrs. Stevens, was first published in *American Poetry* (Spring 1986), vol. 3. It is used here by permission.

An earlier version of chapter 4 was published as "Stevens Prosody," in *Teaching Wallace Stevens: A Celebration*, edited by John N. Serio and B. J. Leggett (University of Tennessee Press, 1994). Used by permission.

An earlier version of chapter 5 was published as "Wallace Stevens in England," in *Wallace Stevens: A Celebration*, edited by Robert Buttel and Frank Doggett. Copyright © 1980 by Princeton University Press. Reprinted by permission.

The paper in this book meets the guidelines for permanence and durability of the Committee on Production Guidelines for Book Longevity of the Council on Library Resources. ⊗

To my brother, David Lensing

CONTENTS

ACKNOWLEDGMENTS

As someone who has been reading and studying the poetry of Wallace Stevens for many years, I find it difficult to "acknowledge" the many teachers, colleagues, students, and others who have shaped my appreciation of the poet. Reading Stevens' poetry today, I find his work as fresh and engaging as I did as a graduate student at Louisiana State University and through my career at the University of North Carolina at Chapel Hill.

In the case of this particular book on Stevens, and my two previous ones as well, I wish to thank the Department of English and Comparative Literature at UNC-CH, and especially the chairs under whom I have worked (the late Carroll Hollis, the late Jim Gaskin, Bill Harmon, Joseph Flora, Laurence Avery, the late Darryl Gless, Bill Andrews, James Thompson, and Beverly Taylor) for extraordinary and unfailing support. All academic scholars should be as fortunate as I. For nine years as Mann Family Distinguished Professor of English I am indebted to the Mann family for their generous support, and to the Chapman family for being named the recipient of the Chapman Family Teaching Award in 2011–12, during one semester of which I was a fellow at the UNC-CH Institute for the Arts and Humanities. To Davis Library and its splendid staff at UNC-CH I continue, year after year, to benefit from their diligence and patience in providing eager help with whatever issue may be at hand.

My years as book-review editor and reader of manuscripts for the *Wallace Stevens Journal*, especially under the editorship of Professor John Serio, have made me proud to have been a part of the single best source of Stevens studies, a claim to excellence that endures to the present. I owe a continuing debt of gratitude to the Huntington Library and Art Museum in San Marino, CA, where the papers of Stevens are housed and where I worked for four summers. In the years that have followed they have continued to offer friendly and prompt assistance.

This is my fourth book with LSU Press, whose faithful dedication to my work has been a constant inspiration. For this book I wish to thank Jo Ann Kiser, my copy editor; Lee Campbell Sioles, managing editor; James Long, literary editor who gave this book its birth; and MaryKatherine Callaway, director. The readers of the manuscript, Bart Eeckhout, John Serio, and Lee Jenkins, have made this a far better book than it otherwise would have been.

Stevens says in one of his "Adagia," "In poetry, you must love the words, the ideas and images and rhythms with all your capacity to love anything at all" (*CPP* 902). That of course is a large claim to make for the reading of poetry, but, in reading the work of many poets, but especially Stevens, I have come to recognize the truth of his claim. That is perhaps the most important "acknowledgment" of all.

ABBREVIATIONS

CPP   All quotations from *Wallace Stevens Collected Poetry and Prose*.
Library of America, 1997. (Standard source for Stevens'
poetry and essays.)

OP   *Opus Posthumous.* Ed. by Milton J. Bates. New York, 1989.

OP [Morse]   *Opus Posthumous.* Ed. Samuel French Morse, New York, 1957.

L   *Letters of Wallace Stevens.* Edited by Holly Stevens.
New York, 1966.

CS   *The Contemplated Spouse: Letters of Wallace Stevens to Elsie.*
Edited by J. Donald Blount. Columbia, SC, 2006.

SP   *Souvenirs and Prophecies* [Journals and Commentary].
Ed. Holly Stevens. New York, 1976.

SPBS   *Sur Plusieurs Beaux Sujects: Wallace Stevens' Commonplace
Book.* Ed. by Milton J. Bates. Stanford, 1989.

Making the

POEM

INTRODUCTION

In an age in which poetry, when it is read at all, is often defined by preferred ideologies, historical and cultural contingencies, and a certain impatience with the mere text of the poem itself, it is worth noting that Wallace Stevens himself was remarkably tolerant and eclectic in his response to readings of his own work. In a revealing exchange of letters to a business associate, Stevens endorses the idea that "[poetry's] measure is the variety of constructions that can be placed upon it: the variety of meanings that can be found in it" (in Lensing, "Wallace Stevens and Stevens T. Mason," 36). In another letter, to R. P. Blackmur, Stevens made the same point: "For the life of me, I don't, in any case, see why a poem should not mean one thing to one person and something else to another" (in H. Stevens, "Flux," 774). The poet, he insisted, was not the only arbiter of his poem nor his intention its final blueprint. To us, his readers today, he seems notably generous in inviting a promiscuity of readings.

In still another letter, he seems deliberately to open up the poem to all the circumstances by which it was conceived and constructed. A bibliographer of his work wrote in 1940 putting forth the view that the critic "rightfully and necessarily uses every mite of evidence accessible (autobiography, biography, letters by and to the artist, contemporary records and memoirs, collateral works of art, etc. etc.)"[1] In his response, Stevens agreed: "On the other hand, it is not the simplest thing in the world to explain a poem. I thought of it this way this morning: a poem is like a man walking on the bank of a river, whose shadow is reflected in the water. If you explain a poem, you are quite likely to do it either in terms of the man or in terms of the shadow, but you have to explain it in terms of the whole. When I said recently that a poem was what was on a page, it seems to me now that I was wrong because that is explaining in terms of the man [the poem]. But the thing and its double [autobiography, biography, etc.] always go together" (L 354). Stevens' poetry itself casts a long shadow upon the stream because it invites an ever-widening speculation about what constitutes its makings and meanings. Or, to put it slightly differently, we have learned in the years since his death in 1955 that the poems seem to accommodate a vast array of "approaches." Through the ebb and flow of theory and criticism, we never seem to get him whole, which, I believe, accounts for our endless fascination with him.

Making the Poem: Stevens' Approaches plots out a loose trajectory that traces this poet's "progress" in the making of his poetry: I. A Poem's Origins: "Sea Surface Full of Clouds"; II. The Poem Itself: "The Idea of Order at Key West"; III. The Social Context: Poetry and Politics; IV. The Music of the Poem: Style and Prosody; V. Publication and Reader: Stevens Abroad. The purpose is to see Stevens widely and from multiple aspects, and the format is one of latitude and pliability. For the newer readers of the poet, I hope that these pages can be of some foundational benefit in your own gradual "placing" of this poet; for his more seasoned readers, you will inevitably widen, rewrite, and debate this book according to Stevens' "approaches" as you know them. For the most part, I read Stevens sympathetically, a bias I willingly own; theory here is always subordinate to the poem. It is the rich tapestry of this modernist poet's work that most interests me, and I have never allowed myself to go too far afield from the selected poems themselves.

If, as Stevens professed, "the thing and its double always go together," this book attempts to trace a progression from a rare record of a journey made by Stevens and his wife that contributed to one poem's making; to a consideration of a seminal poem, one of the handful of his best-known works, "The Idea of Order at Key West"; to the consignment of his work through some of its very processes of creation—first politically and then stylistically; and finally to an international audience that has been slow to take his work seriously.

1. A POEM'S ORIGINS: "Sea Surface Full of Clouds"

"Sea Surface Full of Clouds" is an early, frequently anthologized poem by Stevens. Written after a cruise Stevens made with his wife in 1923, and on one of his few visits outside the United States, it is one of Stevens' most impressionistic poems. I have reproduced here Mrs. Stevens' brief day-by-day account of the trip from New York, down to Cuba, Panama, through the Canal, and a return to California. I edited her *Sea Voyage* and published it in the periodical

American Poetry in 1986; it has never been subsequently reproduced. The specific connections between Elsie Stevens' diary and Stevens' poem are remarkable: they afford the rare opportunity to observe a context and background in a broader biographical narrative out of which the poet transferred his personal experience into "that November off Tehuantepec."

2. THE POEM ITSELF: "The Idea of Order at Key West"

This chapter, focusing on "The Idea of Order at Key West," is the fullest treatment of that poem yet to have appeared. In the first sentence of the chapter, I call it "among the most admired poems by Wallace Stevens," even as it "has also most perplexed us." Instead of a man walking along a riverbank, we have here a woman walking along the seashore singing and a man who hears and describes her song and then voices his own songlike account of the reflected lights of fishing boats in the nearby harbor. Both woman and man make "words of the sea," and the speaker singles out in the final lines those "Words of the fragrant portals" through which, I suggest, rise up in the poem's variety of modalities words of the sea that are examined as imitations, orderings, incantations, performances, and manifestations of the human "spirit." In the poem "sea" and "she" come together and then move apart repeatedly until such a point where word, song, and "idea of order" converge to allow us, as hearers and audience, a passageway through such portals. I am particularly interested in how the presence of the French aesthetician Ramon Fernandez, who is named in the poem, performs our role, that of hearer-audience, but also permeates the poem through the background of his own essays and books. A small part of this chapter appeared in *Something Understood: Essays and Poetry for Helen Vendler,* 2009, under the title "Wallace Stevens and Ramon Fernandez, and 'The Idea of Order at Key West.'"

3. THE SOCIAL CONTEXT: Poetry and Politics

Stevens constructed his oeuvre during a time in which America went through a major economic depression, two world wars, the Korean conflict, and the Cold War with the Soviet Union, as nuclear weapons became instruments of constant international threat. Much attention in recent decades has been given to Stevens' "actual world" and how it is reflected in his poetry and how it influenced the poet. At one extreme, some have disdained his work as effete, irrelevant, and even decadent in the face of urgent social cataclysms, while, at the other, some have strained at times to ascertain political "subtexts" in his poetry. In truth, Stevens himself, even as an undergraduate at Harvard at the end of the nineteenth century, wrestled with a definition of beauty as a service, a food, a strength, even, he insisted, as it "must be part of the system of the world" (*SP* 38). In this chapter (a previously unpublished work) I am interested in how those contrary pulls weighed upon him throughout the ensuing decades and mark his poetry in the face of the crises, national and international, that he could not ignore. His poems of war, for example—introducing soldiers, bloodshed and death, etc.—refuse to succumb to brutal realism or ideological fixities. In the aftermath of World War II, Stevens could not escape the conclusion that, in the face of the sufferings of war-torn Europe, his poetry could seem "academic and unreal"—but he went on to add, "Yet to live exclusively in reality is as intolerable as it is incomprehensible" (*L* 525). In the end, Stevens struggled to create a poetry that was transpolitical but not unpolitical in that it could assimilate the shocks and suffering and pathos he saw around him but also reconfigure them in such a way as to give strength and sustenance for those who live in their aftermath. For this poet it is not so much how we can reform or heal a destabilized world as how we can survive and endure it. Stevens wrote many more political poems than is sometimes recognized, and many of them are considered in this essay. He is a political poet, but on terms that were uniquely and rigorously his own.

4. THE MUSIC OF THE POEM: Style and Prosody

What for a poet, one might ask, is the ideology of *sound*, the content of *rhythm*, the extrarationality of *words as objects*? Stevens' poems could be portentous and hortative, but they could also be rollicking and impertinent as they tickle our metaphorical ribs. Both such "styles," as I attempt to show in this chapter, possess versatile and original traits of rhythm, rhyme, and especially diction, all of which give them their characteristic *élan*. Even in his letters, essays, and *adagia*, the poet seems constantly to be reminding us, because we somehow need reminding, that poems must be one with a "buzzing world and lisping firmament" (*CPP* 301). Before ideology and content there is sound in all its registers upon our attuned ear, and before we can "understand" Stevens we have to learn to "hear" him. This chapter began as an essay that appeared in a collection called *Teaching Wallace Stevens* (1994) in which I proposed prosody as a means to teach young people to read poetry and to read Stevens in particular by connecting their own generational love of music to the variety of musical riches in Stevens' unique utterances. That essay, now revised and widened, is directed to a more general reader. For all of Stevens' readers, it remains to share with the poet a common love: "In poetry, you must love the words, the ideas and images and rhythms with all your capacity to love anything at all" (*CPP* 902).

5. PUBLICATION AND READER: Stevens Abroad

In 1980, I published an essay entitled "Wallace Stevens in England" in which I laid out some of the publishing history of Stevens' poetry in that country—a somewhat complicated narrative that included the publication in 1952 of a pirated edition of his poems, followed a few months later by a legally sanctioned edition of his *Selected Poems*. The pirated edition was suppressed and its copies ordered to be confiscated. The authorized edition was published by Faber and Faber with the aid of T. S. Eliot and Marianne Moore. That unfolding story, peopled by ambitious young publishers in England; Alfred A. Knopf, Stevens' publisher in New York; and Stevens himself, eager to have a British audience, reads today like an improbable comedy of errors and entangling rivalries that developed over some eight years of increasingly testy impatience and impenetrable barriers from both sides of the ocean before the appearance of the Faber volume two years before Stevens' death. In the years leading up to that publication, only a few of his poems had appeared in English anthologies and independent magazines. In that earlier essay, I also examined the early critical response to Stevens in England, a response that for the most part begrudgingly acknowledged his powers, even as it often tended toward dismissive accusations of finicky dandyism and impenetrable obscurity. Nonetheless, I concluded the essay of 1980 by noting the rising sales of his Faber edition in England and confidently predicted an ever-expanding and appreciative British audience. That estimation was overly optimistic. In 2004,

I published a follow-up to the essay entitled "Wallace Stevens and the Curious Case of British Resistance." For a long time, British attention has been almost invariably limited to favorite anthology pieces like "Thirteen Ways of Looking at a Blackbird," "Sunday Morning," "The Snow Man," and "The Idea of Order at Key West." This chapter builds upon those earlier essays, making up now the largest essay in the book. Stevens has had his champions in the United Kingdom and Ireland, including names like Denis Donoghue, Frank Kermode, Philip Hobsbaum, and Michael Schmidt, but many other critics have continued to find the Frenchified and arcane poet–insurance vice president difficult to take seriously. Although it cannot reckon with every essay and review in which the name of Stevens is invoked, this essay now examines in detail some of the reasons for this prolonged resistance. It also, in its third part, reckons with a surprisingly large number of British and Irish poets who have acknowledged a variety of Stevensian influences in their own work. Among others, these poets include Hugh MacDiarmid, Norman MacCaig, Charles Tomlinson, David Gascoyne, Peter Redgrove, R. S. Thomas, and Derek Mahon. I have also noted the responses to Stevens perhaps not so much as influence but as a discernible force duly and variously recognized by W. H. Auden, Dylan Thomas, Geoffrey Hill, and especially Seamus Heaney. The increasing interest in Stevens is then measured in the early years of the twenty-first century. Today Stevens as a major modernist is no longer ignored in the United Kingdom, but he remains to be fully absorbed and confidently placed by these readers.

In describing the poem as a man walking beside a riverbank, with his accompanying shadow on the water's surface as all the ancillary underpinnings and overpinnings surrounding the text itself, Stevens insists that both poem and its shadow are essential: "You have to explain it in terms of the whole." In saying that, Stevens did not mean that one reader or critic could appropriate poem and shadow in a complete or whole assessment. At the same time, he suggests, such an amassing inclusion can enable a reader to draw as much relevant material as he can into his focus upon the given poems. In a small way and through a holistic approach, it is toward that aim that *Making the Poem* aspires.

1

A POEM'S ORIGINS

"Sea Surface Full of Clouds"

O n October 18, 1923, Wallace Stevens and his wife, Elsie, sailed from
New York aboard the Panama Pacific liner *Kroonland*. Their destina-
tion was California via Havana and the Panama Canal. The cruise
itself continued for about two weeks, but the total journey was considerably
longer because of a leisurely trip overland from California to Hartford, Connecticut, their home. The couple visited Los Angeles, San Francisco, San
Diego, the Grand Canyon, Colorado Springs, and Pike's Peak. Stevens indicates in a letter that he returned to his office on December 10, about two
months after sailing from New York. It was probably shortly after the completion of the long trip that the poet composed his first draft of "Sea Surface Full
of Clouds" (*CPP* 82–85). The poem appeared seven months later in the July
1924 issue of *The Dial* and made up one of the fourteen poems added in 1931
to the second edition of his first volume, *Harmonium*.

Each of the poem's five sections begins with the phrase "In that November
off Tehuantepec" and proceeds to juxtapose a series of images and colors that
pattern a phantasmagorical reflection upon and under "that Pacific calm."
Tehuantepec, in fact, indicates the name both for the gulf and for the city
located in southern Mexico more than a thousand miles north of the Panama
Canal. There is no evidence that the Stevenses' liner docked at the city, and,
in an explanation to Ronald Latimer twelve years after the voyage, Stevens
explained that "all I know about the place is that one crosses the Bay or Gulf
of Tehuantepec on the way to California, so that being 'off Tehuantepec' is
not merely something that I have imagined" (*L* 288). Surely it was the sounds
of the Indian (Zapotec) word itself (plosives softened by the stressed glide of
"huan") that appealed to him. In any case, the 1923 *Kroonland* voyage occa-
sioned the writing of the poem, as well as Mrs. Wallace Stevens' *Sea-Voyage*,

a journal she kept between October 18 and November 1 and the contents of which make important connections with the poem.

In his letters, Stevens frequently provides a context for the writing of a given poem. He once insisted to Ronald Lane Latimer that all his poems had some kind of "actual background": "While, of course, my imagination is a most important factor, nevertheless I wonder whether, if you were to suggest any particular poem, I could not find an actual background for you" (*L* 289). The only other instance that I know of where Mrs. Stevens herself provides such a background is a postcard to her mother in which she briefly describes the setting for parts of the poem "Variations on a Summer Day": rocks, spruce trees, gulls and other sea birds, all of which made their way into her husband's poem.[1] In 1939, Wallace, Elsie, and their daughter, Holly, were visiting Christmas Cove in South Bristol, Maine, and traveled by boat among the surrounding islands.

Surviving written impressions of any kind by Elsie are notably rare. We have 272 extant letters from the poet to Elsie, mostly written during the years of their courtship when he was living in New York and she was back home in Reading, Pennsylvania. For whatever reasons, we have not a single letter written from her to him, and only five postcards and one telegram remain among Stevens' papers (*CS* xi). In later years, she shared an interest in family genealogy with her husband. In an extant typescript entitled "A Branch of the Bright Family," she traces both sides of her own family, perhaps aided by one of her husband's genealogists. Her interest in the project had surely been heightened by her reflections on the death of her father, Howard Kachel, who had died less than a year following her birth. It remains that there are many impressions *of* Mrs. Stevens but almost none *by* her—all of which make the survival of *Sea-Voyage* of added interest.

Sea-Voyage, in spite of its rather clipped and apparently hurried entries, is keenly observant: changes in weather, vistas from the deck of the *Kroonland,* and changes in the surface of the sea itself. Reading the journal, we have the opportunity to stand between the author of the journal and poet of "Sea Surface Full of Clouds" as the latter compiles his own observations of the same scenery, weather, and even events aboard the *Kroonland* for the sake of his poem. Dramatic re-creations of those scenes in the poem's own "fresh transfigurings" and what they "made one think of" (*CPP* 85, 84) transform tourist into poet. Such glimpses in general of the sources of Stevens' works are uncommonly rare.

The journal, consisting of about eight hundred words, is recorded in pencil in a small (3"x 6"), dark red, paperbound notebook. It contains entries for twelve of the fifteen days and was discontinued as the liner drew near California. The remarks for October 23 appear to have been erased, and there are none for the following day, October 24, or for October 27. *Sea-Voyage* is reproduced here in its entirety:[2]

• • •

Thursday [,] October 18. After a good luncheon at the Commodore, our hotel in N.Y. since the previous Sunday, we taxied with our four suitcases to the dock and entered the boat—the large steamship "Kroonland." We were taken to our cabin which is the front end one on the starboard side, having two portholes and a door which we leave open and outside of which is a screen-door opening on a deck. I met the steward and stewardess of our cabin[,] a young English man and an Irish girl. Unpacked the necessary things while apprehensive of seasickness, especially after the boat was on its way an hour or so. The stewardess said "There are little white horses on the waters now." I felt dizzy and went to bed early after a cup of broth.

Friday, October 19th. Do not remember whether I had breakfast but stayed in the cabin all day. My nice Irish girl brought me orange juice, and broth, and fruit.

Saturday, October 20th. Rose at 7:15, bathed, breakfasted in my cabin on orange juice, dry bacon and graham rolls and coffee[,] and then went up on deck and met W. promanading [*sic*]. In the afternoon, late, it was very rough off the coast of Cape Hatteras.

Sunday, October 21st. A beautiful calm day along the coast of Florida. With the aid of glasses which some passengers loaned us, we could clearly see the Casino and the Flamingo Hotel at Palm Beach, and other large white buildings in a bright green setting. Had breakfast, lunch and dinner in the dining-room. Saw porpoises and flying fish.

Monday, October 22nd. Up before seven—bathed. The steward rapped on our door before we were dressed saying the doctor was on board and on deck to inspect everyone. Dressed hurriedly, but could not find the doctor—nor could any one else so it seemed. Had breakfast and managed the exciting adventure of going down the gang-plank to the launch which took us over to the Havana dock. We left the party and walked through the interesting narrow streets by ourselves, noticing the iron balconies and the tiles on these old stone houses, many having a pink stone base about three feet high. Saw many interiors with archways and winding stairs and took a number of snap-shots.

Went around to an office where a Mr. Marvin, who W. met before, introduced us to a Mr. Whitman, the chief. Then Mr. Marvin went about with us in a Ford.[3] We stopped to buy some cigars opposite the Presidential Palace, and went into a shop to buy a scarf—and arrived back at our launch before twelve. Must not forget to mention the pina-fria at the Lafayette Hotel[,] a delicious drink made of pineapple juice. There are no windows—only openings with shutters to close them. Saw palm trees for the first time.

Thursday, October 25th. Entered the Gatun Locks in the morning and all day went through the Panama canal, with the thickly foliaged bank on either side. Saw some straw huts of the natives—and the many wooden shelters for the employees on the canal. The day was said to be exceptionally cool, having had rain in that location for three days before. I sat up on the bridge with some others and could see on both sides as well as in front of us. The most changeable weather I have ever experienced. Rain for a few minutes—then bright hot sunlight—then rain again and sun again all afternoon. I had my umbrella and we used it for both. Arrived at Balboa in the Canal Zone at six o'clock. Quickly had dinner and went ashore. Drove through the Canal Zone and Panama City. Many interesting old Spanish churches. The women and little girls wear black scarves over their heads[,] the children looking delightfully demure with them and little black slippers and white stockings. A band stand in every green square. English is taught in the schools in the canal zone and Spanish in Panama. Our colored driver spoke English as well as any ordinary darky in Hartford, having gone to school two years and working with Americans. The doorways are very wide and we saw family groups, one after another sitting right in off the sidewalk[,] some sewing, some playing cards and other games, other[s] just talking. Saw the prison and heard some prisoners singing together. Caught glimpses of the Pacific ocean at the end of some of the streets. Large shopping district. The larger shops close at eight. The smaller ones remaining open until ten. We had to be back on ship-board by 11:30[,] the ship leaving dock at 12 o'clock.

Friday, October 26th. A calm beautiful day. Everyone resting after yesterday's standing on deck all day to see our course through the canal. Saw the spouting of whales.

Sunday, October 28th. The sea as flat and still as a pan-cake, before breakfast. Started reading Carl Van Vechten's "The Blind Bow-Boy."[4] The wind blew up after sun-down—came through a mountain pass from the Gulf of Mexico. Dizzy, so had dinner in my room and went to bed.

Monday, October 29th. A bright calm morning. Finished "The Blind Bow-Boy" on the deck when not dozing. Quite the warmest day so far. Saw many dolphins.

Tuesday, October 30th. Warm—but calm. Had our chairs brought to the front of the deck where there was a fine breeze. Mrs. Manning and I talked about housekeeping, interior decorating and her husband's family and his business.

Wednesday, October 31st. This was a sunny calm day spent mostly in my steamer chair. A Halloween party in the evening—nearly everyone en masque.

Thursday, November 1st. Cool this morning. Still plowing through the Pacific—just now near lower California. We have turned a little more northward—the sun setting directly opposite the port side, instead of forward deck.

• • •

Despite her problems with seasickness, Elsie Stevens emerges through these brief pages as an eagerly alert reporter. Her descriptions of Havana and Balboa, the city at the Pacific end of the Panama Canal, are sharply vivid, her eye capturing verbal snapshots as precise as those she mentions snapping with her camera in Havana. The domestic life of Mrs. Stevens is reflected in her topics of conversation with Mrs. Manning on October 30. It may be from this exchange that she received the recipe for the frosting of a cake which is recorded on one of the back pages of the journal. Her rapid reading of Carl Van Vechten's newly published novel, *The Blind Bow-Boy*, gives the lie, at least in part, to the commonly held notion that Mrs. Stevens took no interest in her husband's literary acquaintances.[5] Briefly editor of the magazine *Trend*, Van Vechten had published poems by Stevens as early as 1914 and had become acquainted with the poet and his wife on social occasions before their move from New York to Hartford in 1916. Van Vechten had been instrumental in urging Alfred A. Knopf to publish *Harmonium;* Stevens had sent the manuscript to Van Vechten, who, in turn, had passed it on to Knopf. Only a month before the cruise, the grateful poet had sent a copy of his newly published volume to Van Vechten: "I am sending you a copy of Harmonium—since you were its accoucheur" (*L* 241).[6]

One regrets that more detailed information about her husband is not forthcoming in Mrs. Stevens' *Sea-Voyage*. The poet's celebrated penchant for walking is recalled by her mention of "W. promanading" *[sic]* on the decks of the *Kroonland* the third day out. It is easy to imagine his assuming the role as guide for his wife when they sailed past Palm Beach on October 21. He had visited the city on one of his business trips to Florida in 1916. More recently, he had spent a long weekend in Havana the previous February, having sailed over from Key West after bidding farewell to his business companion for the many Florida visits, Judge Arthur Powell. From this earlier visit had come the poem "Discourse in a Cantina at Havana" that would appear in *Broom* at the very time of the *Kroonland* voyage.[7] He must have retraced some of his steps taken eight months earlier now at his wife's side. One wonders if the Halloween party toward the end of the voyage, "nearly every one en masque," included the diarist and her husband.

It is unknown whether Stevens consulted *Sea-Voyage* in the process of writing "Sea Surface Full of Clouds," and of course many of the reactions of his wife to the places and episodes of the passage may have differed considerably from the poet's own. Even so, there are singular similarities between Elsie's notebook and the language of her husband's poem. More importantly, the journal helps us to ground the poem's self-indulgent and surreally impressionistic images, where "loyal conjuration trumped," into Stevens' own unique and independently constructed world. This is important because the poem might well be called his most "Symboliste" work,[8] and, for all the poem's shifting and metamorphic "sea surfaces," they are nonetheless founded in a real time and a real place. The journal, for example, identifies various vantage points from which Stevens enjoyed vistas of sea and clouds. From the private cabin, "two portholes and a door which we leave open and outside of which is a screen-door opening on a deck" gave the poet a private but limited prospect. Stevens' pleasure in promenading the deck itself, however, suggests the wider view, and from the bridge where Elsie sat going through the Panama Canal on October 25, it was possible to see "on both sides as well as in front of us."

The six tercets that make up the five parts of the poem (*CPP* 82–85) are carefully structured in parallels of imagery almost on a line-by-line basis. No other poem by Stevens employs this technique so rigorously, and if it weren't for the elements of surprise, the use of reversals, and the poem's constant exotic and dramatic imagery, these orderings and parallels might appear to some as excessively mechanical. On the contrary, it is these very images that give the poem a firm structure and, in effect, hold it together. Each section presumably represents a different morning as seen from the deck of the *Kroonland*. Apparently unaware of the insights of *Sea-Voyage* but ironically pointing toward it, Kay Harel concludes: "When he focuses on the objects that accompany him each day—-the deck, the ocean, its green—they are irrevocably different because of his experiences during the intervening 24 hours of existence" (5). I want to summarize briefly that structure of the poem as each section, comprising eighteen lines, reflects the same setting and plot as the other four. Few poems are more overtly—indeed, even self-consciously—framed.[9]

In each of the first two lines of each section, and in nearly identical language, we are placed "off Tehuantepec" as night falls and the "slopping" sea is stilled. Morning follows and the speaker's pleasure in observing the sea causes him to think of varying kinds of chocolates and varying kinds of umbrellas. In each section, the color green, in differing applications and settings, is then introduced immediately following the umbrella images. The reflections of "blooms" upon the sea surface are introduced and described variously as they appear in the first four sections, omitted only in the fifth.

Each section then poses the question (twice in Sections I and II) as to "who" creates the imagined reflections of the clouds on the surface of the sea (in the fifth section, the "who" is rephrased as "What pistache one?"). The answer to the question is boldly given as the speaker's own interior and subjective self, but in a sentence that is rendered in French and placed in line 12 of each section. The emphasis should be applied to the possessives (*mon, ma*) as this moment of self-awareness and self-revelation is presented in exclamatory and intensely personal endearments—until, that is, we come to the fifth and final section:

PART I: *C'était mon enfant* [child], *mon bijou* [jewel], *mon âme* [soul].
PART II: *C'était mon frère du ciel* [heavenly brother], *ma vie* [life], *mon or* [gold].
PART III: *Oh! C'était mon extase* [ecstasy] *et mon amour* [love].
PART IV: *C'était ma foi* [faith], *la nonchalance divine* [the divine nonchalance].
PART V: *C'était mon esprit bâtard* [bastard spirit], *l'ignominie* [the ignominy].

The dramatic climax of each section, occurring in the final four lines, involves the disturbing of the ocean's placidity as the billowing clouds displace the surface and undersurface of the sea through the observer's own power of imaginative redefinition. An "enormous undulation" of fleeing "ocean-blooms" concludes Section II, while the "rolling heaven" of Section III "Deluged the ocean with a sapphire blue." A similar rolling and heaving of the ocean marks the culmination of each section, as the poet's eye coaxes to life the various activities of the clouds working upon the surface, its impediments overcome. In the final lines of each section, including the final one, the poem introduces the color of blue, replacing or absorbing the earlier green, as these lines capture the final triumph of the speaker's rousing inventions. In many ways, these enchantments anticipate the reflections upon the sea of "emblazoned zones and fiery poles" creating "enchanting night" (*CPP* 106) in "The Idea of Order at Key West," as we will see in the next chapter.

Each section of "Sea Surface Full of Clouds" is a rewriting of what came before and will come after. The poem unfolds as an experimental workshop instead of a crafted art work on final display. Seeing the world, at first superficially, as reflections of clouds on the surface of the sea, unleashes a congeries of eccentric, multilingual and sometimes incompatible inventions. We enter a verbal fun-house, not for belly laughs, but for the serious business of seeing how language and its tropes and variations within repetitive frames create a gala of surprises, not unlike a birthday party of a child.

Our interest in "Sea Surface Full of Clouds" does not dwell for long in the poem's outline for each of its sections or in the mere repetition of images one to the next. Rather, its power derives from the way Stevens renegotiates them—through startling modifications, qualifications, and wordplay. Anyone reading the poem knows at once that his account is hardly literal, even as the poem clings to the bones of the literal structure underlying each section. As Stevens himself said of the poem, "It is obvious that the repetition of a theme and the long-drawn-out rhythm that results from the repetition are merely mechanisms" (L 390). Nonetheless, in order to register the poet's delight in the final lines in each section, one must first work through the processes as I have outlined them in the poem's parallel image structures and, in so doing, discover what John Crowe Ransom calls the "most magnificent poem, technically" ("The Rugged Way of Genius," 162) of *Harmonium*.

The poem represents something more complex than an aesthete's surrender to a solipsistic world made of his own interior predilections as defined in the various lines-12. One can hardly overlook the fact that his perceptions of the scene before him and the pleasures they afford him are not without qualifications. The machine-ocean (in lines 6–7 of each section) is described as "perplexed," "tense," "tranced," "dry," and "obese" respectively. (Stevens here imbues the ocean as pathetic fallacy, not without humor but also not without disorientation.) The color green is described in Part I as "Paradisal" and "swimming," but as "sham-like" in Part II (like the "sham umbrellas" in the same line), as "uncertain" in III, and "too-fluent" in IV: "A too-fluent green / Suggested malice in the dry machine / / Of ocean, pondering dank stratagem." The ocean itself in Part II lies in "sinister flatness." Instead of pleasure only, the beholder senses fakery, surfeit, uncertainty, and even malice. The scene of placation is destabilized and disrupted, however briefly and inconclusively.

Sources of his interior powers are further undercut in the startling French line of Part V: "*C'était mon esprit bâtard, l'ignominie.*" This line is a sharp reversal from the rhapsodic wonder by which he defines his inner powers in the preceding French lines. What exactly is a bastard spirit and why does it engender shame? In a letter to the Yale undergraduate John Pauker—written sixteen years after composing the poem—Stevens responded to the student's own speculations about the poem:

> It is very easy to say that the poem, starting with the discovery of one's own soul as the thing of primary importance in a world of flux, proceeds to the ultimate discovery of *mon esprit batard* as the final discovery. In that sense the poem has a meaning and the final section represents a summation. You appear to regard this, or some substitute for it, as giving the poem a validity that it would not possess as pure poetry. (*L* 389)

But far from being a "summation," the "ultimate discovery" of the interior bastard spirit momentarily undermines all of the other previously defined sources within himself as described in the other lines-12.

Why would Stevens interject such a reversal? One cannot escape the presumption that such grandiose powers within the self can become *too* self-enveloped, *too* absorbed in the fancies of the unreal, *too* illegitimate. As Stevens would write in one of his "Adagia" many years later, "Eventually an imaginary world is entirely without interest" (*CPP* 912). As he concluded his depictions of "the imagination's life" (*CPP* 322) in "Credences of Summer," that life collapses at the end of the poem, "A complex of emotions falls apart, / In an abandoned spot" (*CPP* 326). "Sea Surface Full of Clouds" has already presented the clouds in the heavens as a "sham-like greenery" in their reflection upon the sea surface, but the poem then further removes them from their reality (as natural clouds) by calling them inventions of his own romantic "*extase et mon amour,*" his own "*nonchalance divine.*" Clouds in the heavens remade as surface reflections on the sea, and then relocated again within the poet's own interior reconstructions, are pushed toward a condition of being too removed from clouds-as-clouds. As later poems iterate, especially in his poems of autumn and winter, the imagination and its necessary illusions can become an agency of ultimate delusion if allowed to continue unchecked. This poetic caveat is, however, a caveat—as the concluding lines of the poem return to the rhapsody of human creation. Having established the dangers of excessive romanticism, the poet can now affirm a "clearing opalescence" and the "transfigurings" that playfully but also potently define the poem in its final lines:

> The sovereign clouds came clustering. The conch
> Of loyal conjuration trumped. The wind
> Of green blooms turning crisped the motley hue
>
> To clearing opalescence. Then the sea
> And heaven rolled as one and from the two
> Came fresh transfigurings of freshest blue.

In short, the poem demonstrates the power of the subjective eye by its very ability to transform calmness into undulation, flatness into the reflections of "rolling heaven," and a "malevolent sheen" into brilliant iris and blue. As if glossing this aspect of the poem in his essay "Three Academic Pieces," Stevens cites the "extraordinary transfiguration" of clouds reflected on sea. Such instances, he insists, satisfy the human craving for resemblances: "We say that the sea, when it expands in a calm and immense reflection of the sky, resembles the sky, and this statement gives us pleasure. We enjoy the resemblance for the same reason that, if it were possible to look into the sea as into glass and if we should do so and suddenly should behold there some extraordinary transfiguration of ourselves, the experience would strike as one of those amiable revelations that nature occasionally vouchsafes to favorites" (*CPP* 692).

The poetic "transfiguration[s] of ourselves" in the poem itself, especially in "Sea Surface Full of Clouds," derive also from the musical echoings of rhyme and partial rhyme, alliteration and assonance, and Stevens' evolving penchant for interrupting soothing iambs with more robust trochees ("shrouding shadows" [III], "loosed girdles" [IV], "tossing saucers" [V]). The irruptions in this poem of so many protean shapes, colors, and surfaces notwithstanding, we hear as much as we see. One noteworthy feature is the rhyming or partial rhyming of French and English words centering on the lines-12 and certain English words surrounding them: *âme:* balm and calm (I); *or:* floor (II); *amour:* sure (III); *divine:* marine; (IV) *l'ignominie:* sea (V). In his letter to Pauker, Stevens insisted on the poem's quality as "pure poetry": "As a matter of fact, from my point of view, the quality called poetry is quite as precious as meaning. The truth is that, since I am far more interested in poetry than I am in philosophy, it is even more precious. But it would take a lot of letter writing to get anywhere with this" (*L* 389–90).

The qualities and varieties of Stevens' transfigurations in this poem have progressed far beyond the world that is witnessed in his wife's *Sea-Voyage.* But, as I have said earlier, it has everything to do with contextualizing the poem by providing the aid of a fellow passenger whose account of what she and other passengers observed exists as a separate and independent commentary. The journal has nothing to say about shams or a "turquoise-turbaned Sambo"[10] or "the sea's loosed girdles" and "nakedness," but it has much to say about the sea's flatness, umbrellas on the deck, and passengers masqueraded (becoming "Salt masks of beard" in Part IV).

Mrs. Stevens delights in the sight of "porpoises and flying fish," "the spouting of whales," and "many dolphins." None of these found their way into the poem. Her note, however, that the sea on October 28 was "flat and still as a pan-cake" is pertinent in an important way. In fact, the calmness of the sea is remarked by Elsie on four other occasions as the liner moved north through the Pacific: it is a "calm beautiful day" on October 26; like a pancake on October 28; "A bright calm morning" on October 29; "Warm—but calm" on October 30; and "a sunny calm day" on Halloween. Having made such an impression on Mrs. Stevens, the placidity of the Pacific waters seems to have been noted with equal force by the poet. As we have noted, it is brought prominently into the poem in the opening lines of each section.

In the poem, a sudden quickening of the wind itself momentarily discomposes the dominant complacency of sea-machine. It is a phenomenon duly noted both in *Sea-Voyage* and in "Sea Surface Full of Clouds." In Elsie's account, the "wind blew up after sun-down" on October 28, shortly after the liner had turned north, and, in spite of her repeated remarks on the calmness of the ocean's surface, she enjoys "a fine breeze" sitting on the deck two days later. In the poem, too, the "sinister flatness" described in the second section is also interrupted by "windy booms" as they "Hoo-hooed it in the darkened ocean-blooms." In the triumph of the poem's conclusion a similar process ensues: "The wind / Of green blooms turning crisped the motley hue // To clearing opalescence."

Besides the ocean's calmness and occasional gusts of wind the unseasonably warm weather that marked the *Kroonland*'s movement north through the Pacific denotes another parallel with the poem. In "Sea Surface Full of Clouds" it is "summer" that "hued the deck" in "that November," and, again, a "summer-seeming" that characterizes the machinery of ocean. Holly Stevens noted in her edition of the *Letters* the alteration between the November of the poem and the October when the liner actually sailed by Tehuantepec (*L* 241). A likely motive for Stevens' deliberate change to November may have been to provide a sharper seasonal contrast with the imagination's "summer-seeming." *Sea-Voyage* makes clear the extreme changes in climate that greeted the passengers' progress northward. Monday, October 29, is "Quite the warmest day so far," while three days later, as the cruiser approaches California, Mrs. Stevens finds the temperature "Cool this morning," just as it had been "exceptionally cool" while passing through the Canal a week earlier. Moreover, the abrupt alterations on that same day between rain and bright sunshine are remarked with some astonishment: "The most changeable weather I have ever experienced." The convergence of "November" and "summer-seeming" in the poem were likely prompted by these same noted alterations in weather as recorded by Stevens' wife.

Mrs. Stevens' mention of the use of her umbrella for protection from both sun and rain while passing through the Canal on October 25 introduces the possibility that other passengers as well may have found use for parasols. In any case, umbrellas, along with chocolates, as we have seen, are colorfully interjected into each section of the poem. Whimsically and playfully describing the impression of the sun-streaked deck that succeeds the still sea of the night before, the umbrellas help to define the variety of moods ("made one think of . . .") with which the speaker views sea, clouds, and air. They also contribute to the poem's larger effect, coming, in the words of R. P. Blackmur, "as near a tone-poem, in the musical sense, as language can come" (192): "rosy chocolate / And gilt umbrellas" in section I; "chop-house chocolate / And sham umbrellas" in the next section; "porcelain chocolate / And pied umbrellas" in III; "musky chocolate / And frail umbrellas" in a less dazzling impression in IV; and, finally, "Chinese chocolate[11] / And large umbrellas." One notes the synesthesia of "porcelain chocolate" and "musky chocolate." Phoebe Putnam observes the "gastronomic interests" (45) converging in Stevens' images: "breakfast," "jelly," "chop-house chocolate," "milk within the saltiest spurge," "obese machine," "pistache," "tossing saucers." She poses a question: "One wonders why sensory pleasures seem to be so much a part of what one might think would be a neutral, descriptive sequence" (46). With the aid of Elsie's notebook, one can trace those sensory pleasures to the breakfasts and other meals aboard the *Kroonland*. She refers to them on October 18 and 20, including fruit, bacon, orange juice, graham rolls, coffee, and pancakes. In Part II of the poem, "At breakfast jelly yellow streaked the deck."

The atmosphere of easeful hours in deck chairs, with Mrs. Stevens reading Van Vechten "when not dozing," has a counterpart as "A mallow morning dozed upon the deck" in the fourth section of the poem and the ocean itself "perfected in indolence" in the fifth. One speculates, too, about the influence of the Halloween masquerade party, "nearly every one en masque," while the poet was creating his own costumes of cloud and water in the poem. Especially in the fourth section, the "figures of the clouds" are paraded upon the water, first like blooms, but then as characters in a sexual extravaganza: "Like damasks that were shaken off / From the loosed girdles." What follows is indeed a masquerade: "The nakedness would rise and suddenly turn / Salt masks of beard and mouths of bellowing." (More than one critic of the poem has observed that the Stevenses' only child, Holly, born the following August 10, seems to have been conceived during the extended trip.) The poem's party of revelers is interrupted in midsentence as the "heaven rolled," dissolving the "masks" and transforming the "nakedness" back to "blooms."

The reflection of clouds upon the surface of the sea would itself make up a trope that Stevens employed in later poems, as "the outer voice of sky / And cloud, of the sunken coral water-walled" (105) in "The Idea of Order at Key West, " or "Instead of building ships, in numbers, build / A single ship, a cloud on the sea" (*CPP* 198) in "Life on a Battleship," or "This cloudy world, by aid of land and sea, / . . . produces / More nights, more days, more clouds, more worlds" (214) in "Variations on a Summer Day." Like Monet's scenes of haystacks or the façade of the cathedral at Rouen in their various impressions of light, Stevens' poem here and subsequent poems of his record similar variations and modulations fixing upon a single scene.

After completing "Sea Surface Full of Clouds" in 1924, Stevens stopped writing poetry for several years. Preoccupied with business interests and intent upon professional advancement, he discontinued the practice of sending out poems to the magazines. A decade later he was named vice president of the Hartford Accident and Indemnity Company. His interest in writing seems to have resumed shortly before. The completion of that poem now appears to have marked a boundary in Stevens' evolving career as a poet; he was willing to put poetry aside for the next nine years.

The poem itself seems always to have been a favorite, possibly because of its associations with the *Kroonland* voyage with his wife. He included it in a selection he made for an unpublished collection of his poems in 1950, and also for his *Selected Poems* published in England by Faber and Faber in 1953. He recommended the poem to Renato Poggioli in 1953 as a "good poem to help fill the space"[12] for an Italian edition of his poems. Over thirty years after the passage through the Gulf of Tehuantepec, Stevens fondly recalled "Sea Surface Full of Clouds" by designating its title for one of his recently acquired paintings by Jean Jules Cavaillès.

Mrs. Stevens preserved the small journal of the trip with her husband for the rest of her life. In its few pages, she possesses a personal versatility and serenity as Stevens' wife that may not have been typical of the rest of the couple's married life, especially in the years that followed; here her identity emerges as a keenly observant housewife, seemingly content with her life of domesticity (see her chat with Mrs. Manning), but one who is aware of and conversant with at least one of her husband's literary friends as she reads his newly published novel. We see her sharing many of their experiences and impressions by his side and with no evidence of estrangement between them. (The trip took place fourteen years into their marriage.) The remarkable parallels between journal and poem bring the wife and husband into an implicit collaboration in the creation of "Sea Surface Full of Clouds." For the nearly two months that the trip entailed, and especially from October 25 to November 1 when the *Kroonland* passed through the Panama Canal and sailed north approaching California, Mrs. Stevens composed her own kind of prose poem of varying sea surfaces, the weather surrounding them, and her own registers of astonishment and pleasure. We have few other complete poems by Stevens in which such complementary and, I might add, harmonious "collaboration" converges. Finally, *Sea-Voyage* discloses in its particulars how the many conjurations of "Sea Surface Full of Clouds" were rooted in a lived experience, allowing us to see how, in a significantly large part, the poem itself came to be.

2

THE POEM ITSELF

"The Idea of Order at Key West"

Among the most admired poems by Wallace Stevens, "The Idea of Order at Key West" has also most perplexed us. J. Hillis Miller calls it "one of Stevens's greatest ethico-topographical poems" (259), while James Longenbach calls it "arguably his finest poem to date" (165) and Mary Arensberg agrees, calling it "the great text of *Ideas of Order*" (34). Frank Kermode sees an even broader significance; the poem "may stand as a great, perhaps belated, climax to a whole age of poetry that begins with Coleridge and Wordsworth" (*Wallace Stevens* 58). Harold Bloom, however, concludes that "despite all its strength, [it] remains equivocal and perhaps impossible to interpret fully" (*The Poems of Our Climate* 104), though, more recently, he has said it is "the poem that most expresses the ideas that would emerge into Stevens' most fully expressed work in later years, the work that would set out his aims and thoughts regarding the role of poetry and its sources" (*Wallace Stevens: Bloom's Major Poets* 55). Angus Cleghorn finds it "one of the most critically elusive and contentious in all of Stevens' work" (37). Bart Eeckhout concludes that the poem makes its statements "sufficiently elusively . . . to require a responding creativity on the reader's part" (*Wallace Stevens and the Limits* 230). Helen Vendler discerns in the poem's conclusion a "relative crudeness of representation," because the poet's "powers of representation are being strained" (*Words Chosen*, 69). The poem is "that most equivocal of American shore lyrics," concludes Lee Jenkins, even as it is "an Atlantic portal through which the crisis-poem returns to its Old World origins" ("The Strands of Modernism" 28). Joseph Carroll finds a "vagueness in the intellectual substructure of the poem" (63).

On the face of it, the poem would seem no more intractable than other poems by Stevens. Like "The Idea of Order at Key West," for example, dozens of poems set up an interaction between a human perceiver and the seashore.[1] In this particular case, however, many issues continue to confound us. There is no clear agreement as to who the characters in the poem are. Is the singing woman who appears in the first part of the poem a muse, a symbol of the imagination, the poet's Lacanian mirror image, a Jungian anima of the male speaker, a suppressed or silenced female voice, or a literal woman? And if the latter, is she being exalted or denigrated or—male to female—willfully suppressed? Who is Ramon Fernandez and what is his role in the poem? What are we to make of Platonic-sounding words like "genius," "spirit," "ghostlier," and "idea"? What is the referent of the pronoun "it" at the beginning of stanza 4? Is it reference to "spirit," or "song" or something more inclusive? In the same stanza, Vendler has noted the indefinite quality of "[Stevens'] most common early device for the distinction of orders of magnitude, the comparative and superlative degree:

> It was *more* than that.
> *More* even than her voice, and ours, among
> The meaningless plungings of water and the wind. . . .
>
> It was her voice that made
> The sky *acutest* at its vanishing. [Vendler's italics.]" (*Words Chosen* 68)

What is "more than that" in the poem?[2] The same indefinite comparative mode is adopted again in the poem's conclusion: "ghostlier demarcations, keener sounds." Is the speaker a persona for Stevens himself or is the speaker's authority in any way undermined, thus distancing speaker from poet? Because it seems unlikely that we will arrive at a judgment of consensus in response to these questions, is the poem's efficacy thereby diminished?

As I hope to show, the poem does not unfold in logical discourse even though it possesses a chronology (a movement from a historical account of earlier events of the day, followed by an account of a scene at night, leading to a directive addressed to Ramon Fernandez in the present tense, "tell me [now], if you know / Why. . . ."). Because it is dramatic and not meditative and because it defines more than one method of creating orders and making worlds, the poem is one of great compression where the concrete and the abstract do not always inform and illustrate each other seamlessly. No other poem by Stevens of comparable length is "about" so many things.

In the chronology of Stevens' works, the poem marks the return of his powers as a poet after a roughly nine-year hiatus from writing a poem like "Sea Surface Full of Clouds." In the previous chapter, we looked at how that particular poem came to be written following a trip shared with his wife whose impressions were recorded by her. I want to proceed now by focusing in some detail upon a finished poem in its own right before continuing on to chapters on Stevens' social context, style, and audience.

Following the publication of *Harmonium* (1923), Stevens dedicated his attentions to the demands of family and career and, reluctantly but resolutely, put aside the composition of verse. Largely under the prodding of Ronald Lane Latimer, a young and somewhat mysterious man whose Alcestis Press would publish Stevens' next two volumes in limited editions, Stevens took up his poetry again in 1933. Alan Filreis makes a good case that Stevens may have written "The Idea of Order at Key West" as early as that year, when Latimer first asked for poems for his soon-to-be-published quarterly, also called *Alcestis*.[3] On June 1, 1933, Stevens promised Latimer that "I shall send you something not later than the end of July," though we cannot be certain that "The Idea of Order at Key West" was part of the fulfillment of that promise. Stevens was in Key West on his annual business trip to Florida with Judge Arthur Powell in the winter of 1933 (*L* 267) and again in February of 1934 (*L* 268). On February 19, 1933, Stevens sent a series of postcards to his wife and daughter from New Orleans, where he visited either before or after stopping at Key West. In the cards he describes the Mardi Gras festivities then underway. In light of the mask imagery in 1ine 8 of "The Idea of Order at Key West" it is interesting to note his description in the postcards of "parades *en masque*" and "false faces" (*L* 264).[4] (As earlier noted, he had also used the *mask* imagery of Halloween in "Sea Surfaces Full of Clouds.") The poem appeared in the first issue of *Alcestis: A Poetry Quarterly* in October 1934, along with seven other poems by Stevens, and in his second volume, *Ideas of Order,* published by Alcestis Press in the following year. Almost certainly with this poem and perhaps "Evening without Angels" in mind, Latimer singled them out in a letter as "as fine as he's ever done" (in Filreis, *Modernism*, 325).[5]

Did Stevens himself, walking the beaches near his preferred Casa Marina Hotel, where he always stayed in Key West, encounter a singing woman there or note the reflection of lights upon the waters of the inlets there? In a letter of 1935 he would write, "I have been going to Florida for twenty years, and all of the Florida poems have actual backgrounds. The real world seen by an imaginative man may very well seem like an imaginative construction" (*L* 289). The "real world" of Key West is without long and sandy beaches. (Sand, such as it is, is imported to the island.) The water at the beach below the Casa Marina Hotel and elsewhere is shallow and rocky, hardly a setting for "meaningless plungings" of the ocean's swells. Nonetheless, the poem's "sunken coral water-walled" is clearly visible in the inlet below the Casa Marina Hotel, just as the year-round tropical climate of Key West creates the sounds of the warm wind and air, "a summer sound / Repeated in a summer without end." Following its opening in 1920, the hotel attempted to make up for any deficiencies, as described by John Cole: "But if it's possible, the Casa Marina's grounds were designed to be even more stunning, for Louis Schutt's [manager of the hotel's construction and furnishings] first love was landscaping, gardening and horticulture. He knew what plants, grasses, flowering shrubs and trees would thrive in Key West. With the resources at his command, he created his own green paradise around the hotel he had built with such care" (18–20). By the time of Stevens' visits in the 1930s, the hotel had welcomed Presidents Harding and Hoover. Robert Frost was also a guest there and was photographed with Stevens as the two poets posed on the terrace fronting the sea and with the famed arches of the hotel in the background.

In any case, it seems that the visits to Key West and the Casa Marina had something to do with Stevens' reclaim of his vocation as a poet, especially with the writing of "The Idea of Order at Key West." The poem's speaker and his "Blessed rage for order" through the power of "words" cannot be dissociated from the passion of Stevens' own release from his years of suppression and silence as poem after poem emerged after 1933. He would iterate a similar "rage against chaos," for example, in "Winter Bells" (*CPP* 114), a poem written a few months later.

As an undergraduate at Harvard, Stevens had written an Italian sonnet beginning with the line "I strode along my beaches like a sea." The setting is early evening and here induces in the young poet only "a deep despair" (*SP* 29). In the famous exchange of sonnets with George Santayana, also written while an undergraduate, he submitted to the poet-philosopher "Cathedrals are not built along the sea." Cathedrals, the sonnet argues, would be no match for the majestic intrusions of the sea: "And through the precious organ pipes would be / A low and constant murmur of the shore / That down those golden shafts would rudely pour / A mighty and a lasting melody" (*SP* 32). A few years later but still more than thirty years before writing his Key West poem, Stevens recorded in his journal one of his walks along the seashore which includes many of the images that would become part of the later poem:

> I am not at home by the sea; my fancy is not at all marine, so to speak; when I sit on the shore and listen to the waves they only suggest wind in treetops. . . . The sea is loveliest far in the abstract when the imagination can feed upon *the idea of it* [emphasis added]. The thing itself is dirty, wobbly and wet. But to-day, while all that I have just said was as true as ever, towards evening I saw lights on heaven and earth that never were seen before. The white beach . . . ran along behind and before me. The declining sun threw my shadow a frightful length on the sand. The clouds began to become confused and dissolve into a golden mist into which the sea ran purple, blue, violet. The sun went down lighting the underworld and gilding a few clouds in this one. . . . Walking over the beach under this lowering sky was like stepping into a cavern. Two women—one dressed in yellow, one in purple moving along the white sand—relieved the severity of the prospect. (*L* 59–60)

In spite of Stevens' confession that he was "not at home by the sea," he would return over and over to that setting and its relation to the poet.

From the earliest commentaries on the poem, critics have connected it by allusion or echo to several poems by Stevens' Romantic predecessors, especially works by Wordsworth and Whitman. Milton Bates, however, detects a more unsuspected and indirect connection, some lines by his father, Garrett Stevens, that appeared anonymously in the *Reading Eagle* [Reading, Pennsylvania] long before Stevens began writing his modernist verse. The lines describe a girl plowing in a field as she is observed by the speaker and his male companions ("And as we passed slowly on I saw the little bonnet turn / Just far enough to shoot a smile at us that seemed to say: 'I'm glad you saw me, sirs,' and we raised our hats to her" [in Bates, *Mythology of Self*, 13]). Wordsworth's "The Solitary Reaper" invites an inevitable comparison with Stevens' poem, as critics have noted. Observed by the speaker, the "Highland Lass" is "Reaping and singing by herself." Although she does not walk along the seashore, "No sweeter voice was ever heard . . . / Breaking the silence of the seas / Among the farthest Hebrides" (*Poems* 184–85). Like Stevens' singer, the Highland lass sings in words, but because they are in Erse the speaker cannot understand them.[6] Whitman's "Out of the Cradle Endlessly Rocking" ("And thenceforward all summer in the sound of the sea, . . . I heard at intervals the remaining one, the he-bird" [248]) and "As I Ebb'd with the Ocean of Life" ("As I ebb'd with the ocean of life, / As I wended the shores I know, . . . [I] Was seiz'd by the spirit that trails in the lines underfoot" [253] have been cited in connection with Stevens' poem. Other linkings have been established with Wordsworth's "Tintern Abbey," Emerson's "Seashore," Coleridge's "The Rime of the Ancient Mariner," Arnold's "Dover Beach," Hardy's "On Stinsford Hill at Midnight," Frost's "Neither Out Far nor In Deep," Crane's "Voyages," Bishop's "At the Fishhouses," Ammons' "Corsons Inlet," Plath's "Point Shirley," and others.

"The Idea of Order at Key West" is a poem about sounds, how they are made by the world around us and by ourselves, and how through the crossings of the two they assume meanings. It is a poem about how sound shapes itself into cries, into speech, into word, into song, and into poem. The various modalities of sound in the poem thus assume modalities of art that build toward a climactic spirit, a "spirit that we sought," and one that emerges through some kind of "idea" of order.

In the fourth stanza of the poem Stevens considers the possibility that the cosmos at large possesses its own varieties of voice: it can be "voice of the sea," "voice of sky / And cloud," voice of "sunken coral water-walled" (with a play on the homonym "choral"), voice of "air" and "summer." But having posited conditionally such voices in the stanza, he seems to undercut them by dismissing them as an anticlimactic "sound alone." The sea itself, whatever we concede to its voices, remains "meaningless plungings of water and the wind." It is as if the poet has momentarily and conditionally embraced the possibility of pathetic fallacy by attributing "voice" to the sea, but then finding it wanting or even repugnant. If the poem is to address the nature of sound, it must go beyond "sound alone" and become "more than that."[7] It is not only the voice of the sea that is found wanting. Even our own voices, without an ear to hear them or a poem to give them order and form, are equally inadequate as "sound alone." The poet goes on to affirm that what is more than sound alone is also "More even than her voice, and ours." Even though the lines I have been citing occur midway through the poem, they nonetheless introduce its most basic dilemma: how to escape sound alone and discover what is "more than that." The world may possess its own voices, just as the singing woman and interpreting speaker do. But voice and song are no assurance that one transcends "sound alone." Where does the poem, then, take us beyond "sound alone"?

Mimesis

One possibility is to create sounds that imitate the world. I will call this the inventions of *mimesis*. The song of the woman in the first thirty-three lines of the poem appears to the speaker to be a kind of mimetic echo. Between sea and she there is a "mimic motion," he concludes, and allows that "It may be that in all her phrases stirred / The grinding water and the gasping wind." She is seeking to transform the disordered and unruly sound of the sea into her song, "word by word," by copying the defining characteristics of water and wind and then remaking them. In its first thirty-three lines, the poem suggests the idea of imitation, at least to the extent that each is given its separate individuality and the fact that "voice" is tentatively attributed to both.

Is Stevens suggesting that we, like the singing woman, create *our* own individual worlds, first in our responses to the antecedent world and then through the synthetic power of the imagination? And do these creations coalesce in some composite labeled "The Idea of Order"? Commenting on the poem in a letter to Latimer in 1935, just after its first appearance, he allowed that "It may be that every man introduces his own order into the life about him." He goes on to add, "But then, I never thought that it was a fixed philosophic proposition that life was a mass of irrelevances any more than I now think that it is a fixed philosophic proposition that every man introduces his own order as part of a general order." Here he seems to deny, or qualify, such a composite "idea" of "a general order." However, he goes on in the letter to add, "These are tentative ideas for the purposes of poetry" (*L* 293), and perhaps for the purpose of this poem.

In Kant's third major "Critique," *Critique of the Power of Judgment,* he speaks of the "purposeness" of nature, not as possessing its own independent voice or pathetic fallacy, but by manifesting its own causative teleological ends within the larger unfoldings of its dynamic life in the world. Kant states boldly the mimetic act: "A beauty of nature is a *beautiful thing;* the beauty of art is a *beautiful representation* of a thing" (189). For the great artist, however, "genius" or "spirit" [*Geist*] is essential: "for *producing* such objects [or representations], *genius* is required" (189). By the spiritual force within him, the artist transfigures nature by its "representation," but nature enjoys no such reciprocal power, as Stevens' poem seems to hint at. Human agency, according to Kant, must "be free and grounded in autonomy":

> That nature has the property of containing an occasion for us to perceive the inner purposiveness in the relationship of our mental powers in the judging of certain of its products, and indeed as something that has to be explained as necessarily and universally valid on the basis of a supersensible ground, *cannot be an end of nature* [emphasis added], or rather be judged by us as such a thing: because otherwise the judgment that would thereby be determined would be *grounded in heteronomy and would not, as befits a judgment of taste, be free and grounded in autonomy* [emphasis added]. (224)

I have been suggesting that, at its core, "The Idea of Order at Key West" is a poem about how the human spirit encounters, registers, but then redefines the world as witnessed along an open seashore and, nearby, a town harbor. Ultimately, that Kantian human spirit gives a human "voice" to the poem's multiple perspectives and modalities, and it does so by setting up a highly complex process of imitating that world (*mimesis*), imbuing it with form and order (*ratio*), singing that new world into existence (*incantare*), and disclosing it in a highly staged and dramatic genre with a special emphasis upon the role of a listening audience (*spectaculum*). In the poem's first thirty-three lines, the world itself also possesses its own mysterious "voice." Of course, all of these motifs in the poem are not laid out discretely, nor are they developed in some kind of logical plot. They overlap, complement, and even compete with each other throughout the poem, as we shall continue to see.

The first half of the poem (up through line 33) sets up terms of interaction between the woman's song of words and the "grinding" water of the sea, but it is an interaction that is fraught with dislocations, qualifications, and denials. *Mimesis* is proposed but then called into question. It is as if the poem must first put itself and the reader through a destabilizing process of relationship, one that is syntactically charted by such words and phrases as: beyond; and yet; although; even if; it may be; but; it was only; but it was more than that.

The poem's speaker knows that he seeks the "spirit" behind the relationship, and he desperately wants to bring the relationship into some kind of "order," but he must first flail about as he proceeds from competing hierarchies in the relationship of sea and song. He can even be self-contradictory, as when he says in line 2 that "The water never formed to mind or voice" but then concedes in line 21 that "If it was only the dark voice of the sea. . . ." Both she and sea enjoy their own autonomies, genii, and cries. Yet each, as imputed by the speaker, makes a claim upon the other and then retreats to its autonomy and independence.[8] It is worthwhile, I think, to examine more closely in this part of the poem how it is that she and sea constantly shift from *association* to *dissociation* in an almost vertiginous flux—especially since this aspect of the poem has often been overlooked by its various readers.

(1) She sang beyond the genius of the sea.

[*association* or *dissociation*]: The song may contain the sea or omit it.

(2–4) The water never formed to mind or voice,
Like a body wholly body, fluttering
Its empty sleeves;

[*dissociation*] As an illustration of the dissociation of line 2, water as "wholly body" has "never formed" to human body as "empty sleeves." (The use of the word "body," however, is common to both water and human, and therefore hints at an ironic *association*.)

(4–7) . . . and yet its mimic motion   [*association*]
Made constant cry, caused constantly a cry,   [*association*] by way of imply-
         ing a human cry

That was not ours,   [*dissociation*]
although we understood,   [*association*]
Inhuman, of the veritable ocean.   [*dissociation:* "cry" is of the
         "ocean" and thus "Inhuman"]

(8) The sea was not a mask. No more was   [*dissociation:* neither "she" nor
she.   "sea" masks the other]

(9) The song and water were not medleyed   [*dissociation*]
sound.
(10) Even if what she sang was what she   [*association*]
heard,

(11) Since what she sang was uttered word   [*association*]
by word.

(12–13) It may be that in all her phrases stirred   [*association*]
     The grinding water and the gasping wind;

(14) But it was she and not the sea we heard.   [*dissociation*]

(15–17) For she was the maker of the song she   [*dissociation*—except the sea as
     sang.   ever-hooded allows for a
     The ever-hooded, tragic-gestured sea   masking that was otherwise
     Was merely a place by which she walked   denied in line 8. Is the sea
     to sing.   concealing its association with
         song? Moreover, the word
         "mere" derives in part from
         "mare," meaning sea, which
         thereby associates place with
         song.][9]

(21–28) If it was only the dark voice of the sea
. . .
If it was only the outer voice of sky
. . .
it would have been deep air,
The heaving speech of air . . .
And sound alone.

[*dissociation* as "sound alone," although it does concede to the sea the possibility of a human-like "voice" that was earlier denied in line 2]

(28) . . . But it was more than that.

[*association?* The previous *dissociation* of "sound alone" is now judged insufficient and inaccurate: now it is "more than that."]

Why have Stevens and his speaker so forcibly and assertively flung us back and forth between the unity of the singer and the sea by which she sings, and then the repudiation of that unity? Pathetic fallacy, for example, continually intrudes, imposing its own field of force, one which the speaker struggles to resist: the body of water possesses "empty sleeves"; the sea "Made constant cry"; the wind is "gasping"; the sea may possess "voice" but it is the "speech" of air, etcetera. It is as if Stevens echoes Virgil in his final eclogue: "*non canimus surdis, respondent omnia silvae* (78). ("The listening woods are echoing all our music.") Or, Wordsworth's Boy in Book V of *The Prelude* who "Blew mimic hootings to the silent owls, / That they might answer him. And they would shout / Across the watery Vale, and shout again, / Responsive to his call" (*Prelude* 78).

In these lines the poem suggests that the song of the singing woman is both mimesis and non-mimesis. Or, in the words of Michael Riffaterre, a constant "variation and multiplicity" in the attempt to attain mimesis: "Now the basic characteristic of mimesis is that it produces a continuously changing semantic sequence, for representation is founded upon the referentiality of language, that is, upon a direct relationship of words to things. It is immaterial whether or not this relationship is a delusion of those who speak the language or of readers. What matters is that the text multiplies details and continually shifts its focus to achieve an acceptable likeness to reality, since reality is normally complex. Mimesis is thus variation and multiplicity" (2).

In a letter to his fiancée many years before writing the poem, Stevens himself indulgently made "mind" into "motionless sea": "From one of many possible figures—regard the mind as a motionless sea, as it is so often. Let one round wave surge through it mystically—one mystical mental scene— one image. Then see it in abundant undulation, incessant motion—unbroken succession of scenes, say.—I indulge in heavenly psychology—I lie back and drown in the deluge. The mind rolls as the sea rolls" (*L* 118–19). In later poems Stevens would even more assertively personify the force and power of the sea. The imagination triumphs "over the water wallows / Of a vacant sea declaiming with wide throat" in "Puella Parvula" (*CPP* 390), and, in "Notes toward a Supreme Fiction": "And still the grossest iridescence of ocean / Howls hoo and rises and howls hoo and falls" (*CPP* 331). The crying out of nature (the "mimic motion" of the sea that "Made constant cry, caused constantly a cry, / That was not ours although we understood, / Inhuman of the veritable ocean") in all its plaintive force was a trope to which Stevens returned over and over. The broken corn stalks in the frigid winter scene of "No Possum, No Sop, No Taters" "have trunks // Without legs or, for that, without heads. / They have heads in which a captive cry // Is merely the moving of a tongue" (*CPP* 261). In another severe poem of winter, "The Course of a Particular," the last leaves of bare trees make their own plaintive cries: "The leaves cry. It is not a cry of divine attention, / Nor the smoke-drift of puffed-out heroes, nor human cry. / It is the cry of leaves that do not transcend themselves" (*CPP* 460).

The trope of "body" is developed more complexly throughout the "Key West" poem by its application both to human shape and to ocean and thus creates implicit associations between the two. We learn in line 2, for example, that water never formed to mind or voice "like a body." If that body is "wholly body" [body of water] but with "empty sleeves" [absence of a human body] is the point, then, that body of water and pathetic fallacy are incompatible? But the word that is common to both (body) inevitably makes such a dissociation ironic. (One should note that as late as the seventeenth century the word "sleeve" meant a channel or strait.) Human body is otherwise constantly reinserted into the poem, even without such ironies: body with voice is the woman singing; body with legs is the woman "striding"; body with face is Ramon as "pale," etcetera.

In his *Modern Painters,* Ruskin introduces the question of "what a [classical] Greek's real notion of a God was" (223). In addressing it, he introduces the idea of a "body" of water in which resides a "spirit": "So there may be a power in the water which is not water, but to which the water is as a body;—which can strike with it, move in it, suffer in it, yet not be destroyed with it. This something, this Great Water Spirit, I must not confuse with the waves, which are only its body. *They* may flow hither and thither, increase of diminish. *That* must be indivisible—imperishable—a god" (224). Stevens seems to be making no allusion, at least directly, to Poseidon or Triton, but his question "Whose spirit is this?," following his description of the sea as "merely a place by which she walked to sing," is here notably close to a Ruskin-like "power in water" that possesses its own "spirit."

But similar power is also imputed to the song of the woman. The very music of the speaker's words lulls us into the inherited conventions of romantic interpenetration between song and sea, each somehow copying or echoing the other. By rhyme alone, "she," "we," and "sea" are almost homonyms, each a kind of stand-in for the other two. As John Knight has pointed out, "On the phonetic level . . . the somewhat playful rhyming of 'heard,' 'word,' 'stirred' and 'heard' in the third, fourth, fifth and seventh lines . . . creates the impression of a certain unity between the singer and the sea in the life of the song" (49). It is as if "she" and "sea" are not so much in mutual imitation as in near coalescence. Blank verse, the cadences of the poem itself, is a measuring of the world ("She measured to the hour its solitude"). It, too, is a "striding," and something "portioned out."

But for all these hints at pathetic fallacy and musical harmony between self and world, the sea is also "merely a place by which she walked to sing." And it is a place of turbulence and perhaps even of menace in its plungings and grindings and gaspings. But pathetic fallacy constantly pushes against "merely a place," defiantly including some human agency, even if the sea, where in his youth Stevens found himself "not at home," reemerges here.

About the shifting relations between the sea and its human personifications in the poem, Sara Johnston notes a "replaying that old debate between Coleridge and Wordsworth" in the poem and asks, "Is the human mind really preeminent over the natural world, or does nature possess a strange power of its own, eluding our mental grasp, always hovering somewhere beyond us?" The poem, she believes, suggests both alternatives (75). The romantic and anti-romantic proclivities that jostle back and forth in this part of the poem are the speculations not of the singer but of the speaker, and thus are testimony to *his* own inconclusiveness and weighing of both sides—at least through line 33, the first part of the poem. Mimesis, understood to be the human mimicry of nature, remains qualified and contingent.

For all his indecisiveness, however, the speaker finally—following line 33—arrives at a firm conclusion about the woman's world-as-song:

> And when she sang, the sea,
> Whatever self it had, became the self
> That was her song.

Hesitancy and vacillation now give way to newly found confidence. The speaker's voice is suddenly more dogmatic and less personal as the echoing sounds become choric and hortatory. The chiastic formality of these three lines neatly balances "sang" and "song," "self" and "self," or sea-self and song-self. We have already noted the internal rhyme between "she" and "sea" that pulls the two entities into near coalescence, just as "we" and the first syllable of "beheld," are drawn into the triad ("Then we, / As we beheld. . . .") in the concluding words of that same third line.

One can't help noticing that in these lines the poem tilts away from the poetry of *mimesis* toward that of *incantare,* or incantation, a mode that will become increasingly significant in the remainder of the poem. In his "The Defense of Poetry," Sir Philip Sidney, acknowledging Aristotle, extols *mimesis,* but not in a slavish way: "Only the poet, disdaining to be tied to any such subjection [to nature], lifted up with the vigor of his own invention, doth grow in effect into another nature, in making things either better than Nature bringeth forth, or, quite new, forms such as never were in Nature" (607).

If the singer is maker of her own world through her word song, the speaker presents no overt refutation of such a claim, giving the impression that he is uncritical if not sympathetic to such a creation. (That is indeed the conclusion of many of the poem's critics.) Although he cannot see into her own mind and emotions as he witnesses her song, he thinks he can or imagines doing so. There is an assumed omniscience at this point. Does, then, the speaker conclude, as we are now tempted to conclude, that it is so: we sing our separate worlds as this woman has done, and our world becomes the self that is our song? In an unpublished letter to Robert G. Tucker, written the year before his death, Stevens suggested as much: "['The Idea of Order at Key West'] was designed to show how man gives his own order to the world about him."[10] Is not then the "idea of order" really a vast host of individual and different "ideas of order"— each contingent, momentary, and performative? In a poem that would come later, "Holiday in Reality," Stevens would conclude: "After all, they knew that to be real each had / To find for himself his earth, his sky, his sea" (*CPP* 276).

Although as artificer of her world, the singing woman appears to have created it through a final conjunction between sea, she, and we, I would argue that all the indecisiveness of those preceding lines will not quite permit us to sweep them aside in the face of the speaker's apparently firm conclusion: "And when she sang, the sea, / Whatever self it had, became the self / That was her song." How, we have to ask, can he be so sure? What has happened to all the "and yets" and "althoughs" and "buts"? By his interjections and interruptions of unity between "sea" and "she" hasn't he been insisting that one *cannot* deny the world's autonomy as this singer seems to do ("single artificer of the world / In which she sang")—a world otherwise quite independent of our song makings?

Here the controlling voice of Stevens behind that of the speaker comes more overtly into play. The poet is aware of the overtones of solipsism and inventive fantasy that lie behind the assertion that "there never was a world for her / Except the one she sang and, singing, made." Indeed, the echo of all those preceding qualifying dissociations between "she" and "sea" *cannot* be stoppered. It is as if Stevens were saying through his speaker that only by initially asserting so obstinately the existence of sea apart from she and of she apart from sea that he can then find the confidence to unify them. But the question that is never completely resolved lingers: to what degree does the poet posit a mimesis of reciprocity? Does, in fact, sea mimic song and song mimic sea as a prelude to their merger (sea becoming for her "the self that was her song")? The poem allows that possibility.

Ratio

If we first come to know our worlds and sing them into being, even in isolation, "The Idea of Order at Key West" affirms that such a process begins in *mimesis*—but the poem moves beyond art as mere imitation. It is rather quickly overridden by *ordering* the world into existence, *singing* it into a different form, and enacting it through *social discourse.*

When the speaker, in the company of Ramon Fernandez, turns away from the woman,[11] and the sky becomes "acutest at its vanishing" as darkness falls, he, too, addresses the sea, now in his own voice and as his own harmonizing and poetic singer and maker. The topography of the sea itself changes from the "plungings of water and the wind" to the more tranquil harbor where fishing boats are moored at anchor. He also differs from the singing woman herself in important ways. First, he does not seek to make his world through imitation. Instead of or in addition to mimesis he imposes something like a *ratio,* a configuring of an order of *his* own world. Through his observations of the reflections of the "glassy lights" suspended from the fishing boats in the harbor, he has now created his own response to the sea. It is one that is visual rather than aural; it beholds a body of water more tranquil than the turbulent sea as earlier described, but it, too, is made verbal by the descriptive language that he directly employs. Unlike the words in the woman's song, his words we are permitted to hear, and they, too, become a kind of song. Like a cartographer, he fixes demarcations and distributes zones and poles. As Eleanor Cook has noted, "Zones or lines of longitude are seen on a map of the world, not an actual sea or land" (133). He is "arranging" his world according to his own artificialities.

The speaker orders his world by mastering it, as if it were a force that must first be overcome, a resistance that must be stilled. In his essay "The Sea and the Desert," W. H. Auden describes the same quality of disorder: "The sea or the great waters . . . are the symbol for the primordial undifferentiated flux, the substance which became created nature only by having form imposed upon or wedded to it. The sea, in fact, is that state of barbaric vagueness and disorder out of which civilisation has emerged and into which, unless saved by the effort of gods and men, it is always liable to relapse" (7).

The power to impose order upon a formless world has been identified by some critics as a masculine power of dominance different in kind from the song of the woman as we have seen her earlier in the poem. In the case of the latter, however, the song of the woman is, in fact, even more masterful than the words of the male speaker; she transforms a world of "meaningless plungings" and "grinding water and the gasping wind." This is a powerful claim of the singer's Orphic mastery of her world, one so complete that there is no other world for her outside her song. Far from derogating the power of the woman's song, he hails it as a supreme fiction, a world "she sang and, singing, made." The comparison here with the *poiein* (making) of the poet in general is strongly implied. In both parts of the poem, ordering is not merely arranging but something like appropriating, harnessing, conquering.

Stevens here echoes Nietzsche, especially in his *The Will to Power:* "[Consciousness] has become master. . . . The object is, not 'to know,' but to schematize,—to impose as much regularity and form upon chaos, as our practical needs require" (29). He adds, "A 'thing-in-itself' is just as absurd as . . . a 'meaning-in-itself.' . . . The origin of 'things' is wholly the work of the idealising, thinking, willing, and feeling subject . . . , a simplification, aiming at a definition of the *power* that fixes, invents, and thinks" (64–65).[12]

It is possible that Stevens saw the translation of Julien Benda's "Of the *Idea of Order* and the Idea of God" (italics added) in Eliot's quarterly, *Criterion*, in 1930, three years before writing the poem. In the essay, Benda establishes hierarchies of order with the highest belonging to the perfection of God. For him, our view of order in the phenomenal world is determined by whether we view God as finite in His perfection or infinite; in this essay he assumes an ordering in which God is viewed as finite, though this is clearly not in accordance with his own views. The world itself, having triumphed over a "state of indetermination or non-existence," seeks to "consolidate its victory" by imposing order upon it, whether such ordering be metaphysical or, at a different level, the work of the artist. The world, he argues, "does what any human multitude does which is determined to conquer an enemy: it creates various grades within itself, naturally giving the superior power over the inferior" (87). Where Benda seems closest to Stevens' own view in "The Idea of Order at Key West" is in recognizing the order of the finite world as one that "conquers." Here is Benda on the artist's role: "The act by which the work of art sets up an order within itself implies therefore an idea of a contest to be sustained by that work and a will to conquer: it is, I would venture to say, an essentially *military* act" (90). Making order out of disorder, whether it be the artist conceiving his own world or the finite God creating it, artist-as-conqueror parallels the act of an "*imperial* God" instead of an "*infinite* God" (93).

In place of Benda's "idea of God"—finite or infinite—as a source of order in the world, Stevens seeks an elusive but god-like "spirit."[13] The "blessed rage" to conquer belongs not to the world itself but to the artist set in opposition to the world's power-in-disorder—what, in another context, Stevens calls the "violence from within that protects us from a violence without" (665). What "Mastered the night" for the speaker and for the singing woman in whose "phrases stirred" the grinding and gasping of water and wind is the human synthetic power over the shapeless or ill-shaped phenomenal world. Stevens admired in Van Gogh a similar quality of mastery: "It may be only too true that Van Gogh had fortuitous assistance in the mastery of reality. But he mastered it, no matter how. And that is so often what one wants to do in poetry: to seize the whole mass of everything and squeeze it, and make it one's own" (L 459).

The role of the poet as a maker of order was one that interested Stevens for the rest of his life, but especially in the decade of the 1930s, though not always in a systematic or developmental way. Spurred by his wide and eclectic reading, he teased out nuances related to the ways in which the artist creates and imposes order—and commented further upon them in notebooks and letters.

In one letter to Latimer written shortly after Latimer's publication of *Ideas of Order* Stevens threw out a connection between "The Idea of Order at Key West" and one aspect of Berkeley's idealism. The remarks are brief—one might say "too brief" because of the confusion they have caused: "In THE IDEA OF ORDER AT KEY WEST life has ceased to be a matter of chance. It may be that every man introduces his own order into the life about him and that the idea of order in general is simply what Bishop Berkeley might have called a fortuitous concourse of personal orders. But still there is order" (L 293). One could wish that Stevens had had more to say here about the role of order versus chance in the poem and also that he had consulted his Berkeley more closely. It is not at all clear what Stevens means when he says that life "has ceased to be a matter of chance." But even allowing for that pronouncement, how is one to square it with life as a "*fortuitous* [emphasis added] concourse of personal orders"? Is it that an individual life, such as that of the woman singing along the seashore, involves choosing one's uniquely personal order, while "the idea of order in general" is fortuitous? If so, how does the latter follow from the former? (In a mode of self-defense, Stevens, in the same letter in which he refers to Berkeley, confesses that he no longer thinks "that it is a fixed philosophic proposition that every man introduces his own order as part of a general order. These are tentative ideas for the purposes of poetry" (*L* 293).

As Frank Doggett demonstrated long ago, Stevens has misquoted Berkeley (96). The source is in the second of the "Three Dialogues between Hylas and Philonous." The dialogue addresses only indirectly the issue of choice (selecting one's order) versus chance. It has rather to do with the very foundation of Berkeley's idealism: his attempt to bring it into accord with his Christianity. Philonous posits that "sensible things cannot exist otherwise than in a mind or spirit" and goes on to conclude that "*there must be some other mind wherein they exist*" independently of an individual perceiver. That mind, of course, is God's. Because sensible things have their existence in the mind or spirit of God they have an existence independent of the act of perception—a position that allows Berkeley to escape from his own snares of solipsism. He goes on: "Men commonly believe that all things are known or perceived by God, because they believe the being of a God; whereas I on the other side, immediately and necessarily conclude the being of a God, because all sensible things must be perceived by him" (*Essays, Principles, Dialogues* 276).

Berkeley then goes on to ridicule the folly of atheism: "Those miserable refuges, whether in an eternal succession of unthinking causes and effects, or in a fortuitous concourse of atoms; those wild imaginations of Vanini, Hobbes, and Spinoza: in a word, the whole system of Atheism, is it not entirely overthrown by this single reflexion on the repugnancy included in supposing the whole [world], or any part, . . . to exist without a Mind" (277).

Berkeley's derisive "fortuitous concourse of atoms" as the source of the physical world has become Stevens' "fortuitous concourse of personal orders." The two phrases are not antithetical if one considers, for example, Leibnitz's notion of the lower class of monads as a fortuitous concourse of atoms that constitute for him his own personal order out of what only appears to be disorder. However, for Berkeley the phrase is dismissive— whereas for Stevens it appears to acknowledge an inevitable and universal making of the world. (Whether for Stevens such a "concourse" is "fortuitous" or the more deliberate introduction of one's "own order into the world around him" remains unclear.)

The quotation from Berkeley nonetheless focuses our attention upon an important theme of Stevens' poem. How do we make the orders by which we live our lives? What are such orders? Are some superior to others? In the very selection of the title of the 1935 volume in which "The Idea of Order at Key West" appears, *Ideas of Order,* Stevens implies that such orders are multiple and individually conceived. One could argue that such various conceptions of order themselves, in fact, make up *the* idea of order at Key West. Writing the commentary for the dust jacket of the trade edition of that volume, he states that the poems of the book deal with such ideas of order as "the idea of order created by individual concepts, as of the poet in 'The Idea of Order at Key West'" (*OP* 222–23).

Giving one's own order to the world was much on Stevens' mind. In 1934 he was poring over a book one might find unlikely to attract his interest, *The Divine Order of Christianity Indicated by Its Historical Effects* by Richard S. Storrs. Published in 1884, the book consists of a series of six lectures Storrs had delivered at the Union Theological Seminary in New York and the Lowell Institute in Boston.

It was the third lecture, "The New Conception of Man, Introduced by Christianity," that caught Stevens' attention. Storrs recognizes a deep human yearning for an "affection transcendent" that is directed "toward God." Before the emergence of Christianity, and in what he calls "ethnic religions," the gods did not invite affection (89). Here was a God, through Jesus Christ, who did. Stevens selected only one sentence from the chapter and wrote it out in his commonplace book: "The philosopher could not love the indefinite and impersonal principle of order pervading the universe [typified by the pre-Christian gods], any more than he could love atmospheres and oceans" (89). Whether Stevens' recording of the sentence in his commonplace book precedes the writing of "The Idea of Order at Key West" or occurred shortly after one cannot be sure, though the echo from the poem is unmistakable: "mountainous atmospheres / Of sky and sea," in which the "meaningless plungings of water and wind" (*CPP* 105) echo Storrs' "atmospheres and oceans."

Following the quotation in his commonplace book, Stevens records his own immediate response: "For myself, the indefinite, the impersonal, atmospheres and oceans and, above all, the principle of order are precisely what I love; and I dont [sic] see why, for a philosopher, they should not be the ultimate inamorata. The premise to Storrs is that the universe is explicable only in terms of humanity" (*SPBS* 33). It is not the presence or absence of a human God-Creator that interests Stevens so much as his declaration of "the indefinite, the impersonal, atmospheres and oceans," such as the pre-Christian "ethnic religions" might have found. It is the "principle of order" acting upon an impersonal world that creates for him an "ultimate inamorata," creating what, "above all," he loves. Stevens does not seem to be speaking for everyone in the sense of individually created orders, but for the preferred creation of his own order out of his impersonal world, transforming it into the personal as inamorata.

Of course Stevens' atmospheres and oceans in the Key West poem are *not* entirely indefinite or impersonal, in spite of his stated preference via Storrs: pathetic fallacy, as already noted, is irrepressible, especially as "voice," in his depictions of "dark voice of the sea" and "outer voice of sky." Perhaps more importantly, Storrs had provided for him one more context to affirm his "love" for the creation of individual and personal orders and the application of that to the artist.

In a poem called "The Search for Sound Free from Motion" (*CPP* 240–41) published eight years after the Key West poem, Stevens again sets out the relation between words of sea (and of leaves and a gramophone) and the words of an unnamed "you." In this shorter poem of sixteen lines, the world's words are those of a "hurricane" in "West-Indian weather." The gramophone itself becomes a "gramaphoon" (typhoon). Their language "Parl-parled" (from the French *parler*) through the afternoon as they "all spoke together" noisily. The last quatrain concludes outright that "The world [including the "many-stanzaed sea"] lives as you live, / Speaks as you speak." It speaks the same "speech" of sea, sky, cloud, and air that gives voice in "The Idea of Order at Key West." But also like the Key West poem, the later poem describes a speech uttered by "you" that is more, however, than the speech of the cacophonous world:

> The world lives as you live,
> Speaks as you speak, a creature that
> Repeats its vital words, yet balances
> The syllable of a syllable.

The poem pivots on that final clause because, *unlike* the speech of the hurricane sounds, the human word ("you speak") "balances / The syllable of a syllable." The balancing of syllables within syllables is the act of the poet, the human singer—and not the gramophone/gramaphoon. "Syllable" is here counterpart to "word" in the Key West poem. To balance is to arrange into an order, and only "you," unlike the "world," can weigh such perfection and repeat the world's "vital words" into poems.[14]

"The Search for Sound Free from Motion" is from Stevens' volume of 1942, *Parts of a World*. But *Ideas of Order*, as its title suggests, is the volume in which he repeatedly assesses order-as-value. Other surrounding poems from that volume widen the role of the poet as a maker of order, touching especially upon the impermanence and obsolescence of such orders. In a poem thought to have been written in 1935, "A Room on a Garden," never published by Stevens in his lifetime, he declared, "Behold how order is the end / Of everything" (*CPP* 566). In "Anglais Mort à Florence," the aging subject of the poem now can stand only with the help of church and state ("God's help and the police"). When he was younger, however, and stood alone, he had the consolation of Brahms, his "dark familiar": "He was that music and himself. / They were particles of order, a single majesty" (*CPP* 119–20). The poem stands out among those in *Ideas of Order* because it represents a point of view rarely seen in Stevens, a "spirit" that has grown "uncertain of delight." The "Anglais," dying in Florence, identified with the German composer, identified again in the French title, described by an American poet, is concealed in layers of deliberate disguise. What is undisguised is a *loss* of order, a certain vulnerability and impermanence about created orders, leaving him now tragically "unconsoled." In another poem, "Sad Strains of a Gay Waltz," there is a similar description of forms becoming exhausted and effete, now described through the character of Hoon, reprised from Stevens' earlier poem "Tea at the Palaz of Hoon." In this case, it is something more than the outdated waltz itself that betrays him:

> For whom desire was never that of the waltz,
>
> Who found all form and order in solitude,
> For whom the shapes were never the figures of men.
> Now, for him, the forms have vanished.
>
> There is order in neither sea nor sun.
> The shapes have lost their glistening. (*CPP* 100)

Hoon's "solitude" denies him the very "forms" of sea and sun that are high-lighted in "The Idea of Order at Key West" and "Sea Surface Full of Clouds" respectively. The isolation attributed to the "solitude" of Hoon could, one notes, also be applied to the woman singing in the Key West poem ("As we behold her striding there alone . . ."). The absence of audience in her solitary song lessens the song's efficacy by making for her a world that exists *only* in her song. In "Sad Strains" only a future poet, some "harmonious skeptic," will assume the role of finding societal "figures of men and their shapes," notably not in isolation from such figures; their work will thereby "glisten."

"Polo Ponies Practicing" (*CPP* 563) was not included in *Ideas of Order* but in a periodical in the same year, 1934, that "The Idea of Order at Key West" appeared in *Alcestis*. Once again, the theme of decaying and obsolete orders is introduced: "An order constantly old, / Is itself old and stale." Amid this debil-itated order suddenly appears a new one, "In a freshness of poetry by the sea." Instead of singer and song, however, "flanks of horses" dramatically appear, making a "brilliant air" and offering new "shapes [orders] of the mind."

In the mid-1930s larger and more impersonal orders in the Western world were teetering everywhere under the oppression of economic collapse. Radical social change and the installation of a new macro-order seemed to many to be imminent. To Latimer Stevens wrote in 1935, the year after the publication of the Key West poem, that "the only possible order of life is one in which all order is incessantly changing. Marxism may or may not destroy the existing sentiment of the marvellous; if it does, it will create another." But in the same letter he insists that "poetry introduces order," one that creates an inevitable and necessary peace through art as "illusion" (*L* 291–92, 293). (See the discus-sion of "Mozart, 1935," in the next chapter.)

It is obvious that at the time of the writing of the poems of *Ideas of Order,* Stevens' mind was filled with the necessary emergence of new orders, both personal and social. In "The Idea of Order at Key West," the emphasis is more on the former than the latter, though the "idea of order in general," as Ste-vens states in his reference to Berkeley, seems somehow dependent upon the creation and re-creation of individual orders. I am arguing, however, that the poem insists that private and isolated orders, such as that of the woman and her song, may be satisfying to her but are of little value beyond her own imme-diate gratification. As the poem "Sad Strains of a Gay Waltz" had introduced, other orders, given a social context through the introduction of a listener or the presence of an audience, engender a far greater viability.

Incantare

Because we as readers, like Fernandez, are auditors of the speaker's song and hear its words we witness yet another art form emerge in the poem—different from the modes of *mimesis* and *ratio*. It is the music of *incantare*, "arranging, deepening, enchanting night." Those very present participles move from the "arranging" (or ordering) to become the song of enchantment itself. It is not that a different speaker emerges at this point in the poem but rather that, instead of an interpretation of someone else's song, we now hear his own. When he turns away from the singing woman and, in the company of Fernandez, approaches the town where fishing boats are anchored with their lights reflecting upon the waters of the harbor, he utters his own song.

As early as 1911, when they were still living in New York, Stevens had recalled for his wife a scene he had seen "down by the docks, [where] the lanterns on the masts flickered" (*L* 171), a moment that he perhaps recalled when writing the poem more than two decades later. In the poem, the "Blessed rage for order" is not anger, but the fury of romantic passion, introducing what might otherwise be taken as an emotion antipathetic to making order. This rage is a force of attraction rather than opposition. The lights from the boats are described as "Fixing emblazoned zones and fiery poles," and in this and the surrounding lines the poem becomes most self-consciously musical, an incantation.

Zones and poles, for example, make up a vocalic rhyme, just as the final syllable of "emblazoned" contains and anticipates the following word "zones." "Emblazoned" derives from the Old French word *blason*, meaning "shield." By the seventeenth century, the word "emblazoned" had come to mean "decorated or displayed brilliantly, as a coat of arms or shield," a meaning that it retains today. Of course Stevens' ear hears the word "blaze" within "emblazoned" (as if it were "emblazed"), and three words later in the same line, reinforces the association with the word "fiery." The speaker's zones are dazzling in their splendor, his poles like leaping flames, yet in the sounds of his descriptive words, the music of his song, he composes his own harmony. What Daniel

Schwarz says of Stevens generally seems especially appropriate to this poem: "The ambiguity of the reader's role in responding to Stevens's poems is created by Stevens alternating between traditional narrative and lyric; between representational and what might be called decorative poetry" (18). Although the shift in the Key West poem does not leave the reader in a state of "ambiguity," the movement at this point in the poem from the representational (*mimesis*) toward "lyric" and "decorative poetry" is unmistakable.

The stanza in which these lines appear is addressed to "pale Ramon," and it is in the form of an imperative containing an interrogative: "Tell me, if you know, / Why . . ." The poem does move from a retrospective view directly to the present tense with this address to Fernandez, but then it returns to the retrospective. By the end of the stanza, the imperative/interrogative appears to have been forgotten in the descriptive astonishment of the scene presented. A question, by its very articulation, has been subsumed in exclamation and wonder. The lights of the fishing boats are described through a series of transitive verbs:

> lights . . .   mastered the night
> portioned out the sea
> fixing zones and poles
> arranging, deepening, enchanting night.

The rhythm is determined by all the disyllabic and trisyllabic verbs and participles—all with unstressed feminine endings ("mastered," "portioned," "fixing," "arranging," "deepening," "enchanting")—all enveloping the surrounding monosyllables. When we arrive at that final transitive verb—enchanting—we discover suddenly its simultaneous function as a participial adjective: to enchant the night is to create an enchanting night. The Latin *incantare* itself derives from in + cantare, to be "in song," just as "enchanting" evolves from the same root, *incantare*—to come under the spell of song or chant, but not a song of replication. The speaker himself has become like the woman as a maker of song. The lights are not only singing the night but bewitching it; the night, in all its brilliant configurations, simply *is* enchanting. By the rhythms and rhymes of the speaker's words, his own song addressed to Fernandez, he transcends "sound alone."

The whole of "The Idea of Order at Key West" is a harmonic of musical counterpoints, overtones, and mounting cadences seeking to contain the poem's own verbal song, its own keener sounds. Taken as a whole, the poem possesses a disproportionate number of monosyllabic words, like the following: she, we, me, sea, voice, sing, sang, song, mask, waves, sky, air, sounds, lights, boats, zones, poles, rage, words. The repetition of these words—even out of context— creates a sustained refrain, driving and encapsulating the poem in all its reverberations.

The use of monosyllables typically creates a pattern of regular iambs that set a briskly energetic rhythm—as in the first and last lines of stanza 2, reproduced here. Michael Schmidt has cautioned, however, that Stevens' own reading of the poem on a 1954 recording is not always brisk: "Each line seemed to be endowed (in a quite unmechanical way) not with one but with two caesurae. This broke the apparent tyranny of the driving iamb" ("Arranging, Deepening" 55). Most such pauses, however, are hardly full stops:

> The sea was not a mask. No more was she.
> The song and water were not medleyed sound
> Even if what she sang was what she heard,
> Since what she sang was uttered word by word.
> It may be that in all her phrases stirred
> The grinding water and the gasping wind;
> But it was she and not the sea we heard.

Of the seventy syllables in these lines I count sixty-two monosyllabic words in the stanza and only eight disyllabic words. The intrusion of the latter is forcibly emphasized in the sixth line quoted above. The cadences of each line musically balance within each line: sea/she; water/were not; sang/heard; sang/word by word; phrases/stirred, grinding/gasping, she/sea. There is an implied chiasmus between lines 1 and 7. Four of the seven lines end in a "[vowel]-rd" rhyme. The rhyme is broken in the sixth line of the stanza, and the harmonics of the preceding lines are abruptly muted by the harsh plosives of "grinding" and "gasping"—weighted disyllables that check the lilting rhythm of the preceding monosyllables. For a moment, line 6 seems to overpower the softer melody of the preceding lines. But the reversal of the seventh and final line quickly restores the echoes of song as well as the abandoned rhyme and adds the internal rhyme of "she," "sea," "we": "But it was she and not the sea we heard." (The poem's first line, "She sang beyond the genius of the sea," incorporates the internal rhyme of "she" and "sea," adding the first and unstressed syllable of "*beyond*" and the stressed first syllable of "*genius*." Even the two definite articles impart their own rhyming echo.) The grinding and gasping in stanza 2 are rendered impotent by song—as established in both the meaning and music of the stanza.

The final line of the poem describes the power of our words and origins as they are realized "In ghóstlier demarcátions, kéener sóunds." The eleven-syllable line neatly balances two stresses on each side of the caesura. (The second and third syllables of "ghostlier" can be glided into a single syllable.) The four unstressed syllables that divide the two stresses in "ghóstlier demarcátions" retard the pace of meter in a softer (ghostlier) whisper. But after the caesura, the line reasserts a firm and confident rootedness with stresses on two of the final three syllables: "kéener sóunds." The eight syllables before the caesura and the three after it fall into a satisfying balance and finality.

For all the issues and variations that are introduced into the poem, the reader is never able to stopper the lyrical incantation that informs the body of the poem, most notably in the description of the lights of the fishing boats.

Spectaculum

In addition to *mimesis, ratio,* and *incantare,* there is yet a fourth art form by which "The Idea of Order at Key West" unfolds: art as *spectaculum.* The presence of the speaker addressing Ramon Fernandez and revealing through his interaction with his listener his own lyric response to the scene suggests a dramatic monologue. The action is cast in the present tense, as in all dramatic monologues, but only for the moment in which the speaker addresses Fernandez: "tell me, if you know, / Why. . . ." The speaker who describes the reflections of the lights upon the surface of the harbor differs in a significant way from the singing woman: he is not creating a uniquely personal world solely for himself, but deliberately submits his song to Ramon Fernandez as an auditor and interpreter. For this reason, his song appears to transcend "sound alone," or sound in isolation. As Victoria Shinbrot has pointed out, "The addressee [Fernandez] prevents, in other words, the poet's voice from turning into an empty echo" (265).[15] And, as Daniel Schwarz notes, "Similarly he [the speaker] and Ramon Fernandez as empathetic friends respond to one another, and Fernandez as listener is the essential audience that the process of poetry requires to complete it" (80).

In another way, however, the whole of the poem is laid out as a dramatic performance, a spectacle, to which we as readers are assigned the role as audience, a role we share with Ramon Fernandez. The speaker, especially in the first half of the poem, is a kind of dramatic chorus, just as a voice of the sea becomes a "sunken [choral] water-walled." In the third and fourth lines of the poem, the water is described as costumed, "Like a body wholly body, fluttering / Its empty sleeves." The poem denies that either she or sea is "mask," but thereby implies that each *could* be suspected of theatrically masking the other. The sea is indeed masked as "ever-hooded" (recalling the fluttering sleeves of the sea earlier described) and "tragic-gestured." The ear of the speaker allows for a possible "voice" of sea, sky, cloud, sunken coral, and it hears the "speech" of air. In stanza 4 he sees the larger vista as "Theatrical distances," as if this cosmic phenomenon were a kind of giant stage on which the voices and speech were enacted and sung on "high horizons." In the next stanza, as the speaker looks down upon the woman striding and singing, it is as if an extension of that stage once again were being presented for the benefit of himself and his companions as audience: "Then we, / As we beheld her striding there alone. . . ." Finally, in the last stanza, with its recognition of the universal human "rage to order words," words themselves become "fragrant portals," or passageways, another extension of the poem's stage setting.[16]

Stevens seems to have in mind something like a Greek tragedy in these scattered theatrical hints, but only in a vague and inchoate way. The images of theater, however, take on a cumulative force as they extend over and draw together the whole of the poem. Bart Eeckhout suggests that the "tragic-gestured sea" points toward "the drama that underlies and inspires this poem: a drama resulting from the existential solitude, the darkly inexplicable fate, the vulnerability and mortality of humans in their unsponsored, one-way dependency upon a fundamentally indifferent environment" (*Wallace Stevens and the Limits* 218).

A dramatic poem is not a still life, and Stevens' poem does not summarize consistently a single view of poet and song but an evolving and incremental one that culminates in denouement and a last act, the poem's final stanza. Those critics who have isolated single lines or even single stanzas from the poem without regard to its shifting contexts have done the poem a disservice.

Art as *incantare* is subsumed in the wider view of art-*spectaculum*, just as art as *mimesis* advances in the poem to art-*ratio*. This makes up a highly complex system of discourse in "The Idea of Order at Key West." The poem's search to overcome "sound alone" is inherently dramatic, and Stevens gives the search a stage, a setting, a cast of characters who employ speech, cry, voice, mask, and costume. The poem hints at tragic gesturings, pointing toward the solipsistic song of the singing woman as well as that of the sea. But the poem is not in the end a poem of tragedy. It moves from the indeterminacy of "sound alone" to verbal song as "keener sound" (the poem's final words). It affirms a comedy of survival in an alien world where fixities of order and song prevail over the "meaningless."

The "spirit" at work, at least in this part of the poem, is consequently the human rage to make such conjoinings of ourselves with the obdurate world. The "spirit" is not a transcendent "genius" of the shore (*genius loci*) nor a supernatural "cry" from the natural world. The idea of order at Key West is ultimately a human idea and a human order. The singer sings the world that exists for her, but, as we have seen, only after the poem first so doggedly acknowledges her apartness from it. And, because we never hear the "word[s]" of the singer's song but only the speaker's own song, it is really *his* world that he creates—first through his *interpretation* of the singer's word song and then through *his* own words of synthetic imagination as he goes on to depict the mastery of the night by the water-lights.[17]

There are several listeners in the poem: the speaker, who hears the woman's song, and Ramon Fernandez, who hears the speaker's own words. The reader, like a witness to a theatrical performance of masks and tragic gesturings, makes up a third. No other poem by Stevens is set up in such a layered fashion. Justin Quinn sees the whole poem as "about the attempt to relate a community of listeners in the midst of natural beauty. Working out those communal meanings is the body of the poem" (*Gathered beneath the Storm* 84). Why, we may well ask, has Stevens chosen to establish such a "community of listeners" here? Part of the answer to this question consists of the way in which we recognize the role of Ramon Fernandez, the silent listener and the only named figure in the poem.

As I have already briefly noted, the first part of the poem notably lacks a figure like Fernandez. The singing woman is solitary and apparently unaware of the male speaker and his companion, who have been observing her; she is absorbed in a making that is private and exclusionary, "striding there alone." She is not making a world for the benefit of others but solely for herself. Stevens does not deny the power and appeasement of selves making their own worlds through verbal song, but, as artist, whose words belong to others as much as to herself, this singer is notably isolated, self-absorbed, and incomplete. As the poem "Sad Strains of a Gay Waltz" had introduced, orderings of the world that are socially oriented engender a far greater potency.

It is well known that Stevens himself, responding to queries about the name, first said that it was "arbitrary" and that "I used two every day names. As I might have expected, they turned out to be an actual name" (L 798). Six years later, he modified this disclaimer by adding, "I knew of Ramon Fernandez, the critic, and had read some of his criticisms but I did not have him in mind" (L 798). Then, a few months later, he reiterated, "I simply put together by chance two exceedingly common names in order to make one and I did not have in mind Ramon Fernandez. Afterwards, someone asked me whether I meant the man you have in mind. I had never even given him a conscious thought. The real Fernandez used to write feuilletons in one of the Paris weeklies and it is true that I used to read these. But I did not consciously have him in mind" (L 823). It is difficult to know how seriously to take the poet here who seems to be saying, "Yes, I knew who he was and had read his work, but I pulled the names out of the air for the sake of the poem." The names, of course, are hardly "exceedingly common names," implying, as they do, a Spanish or Latin American persona.

Ramon Fernandez was born in Paris in 1894 and died fifty years later in the same city. He was thus a Frenchman—his father was Mexican and his mother French.[18] He wrote books on Gide, Molière, Proust, Barrès, and Balzac, and he was also a novelist. He was one of the principal pillars of the journal *La Nouvelle Revue Française* (the Paris weekly referred to by Stevens and to which he subscribed) and he wrote book reviews for the French periodical *Marianne*, a source from which Stevens wrote out two quotes (43, 63—not by Fernandez) in his commonplace book, *Sur Plusieurs Beaux Sujects*.

The personal politics of Fernandez shifted through the course of his life with notable zigzags. When an essay by him appeared in the *Partisan Review* in 1934, the editors identified him politically: "Ramon Fernandez is one of the foremost critics on the Continent. Until recently a humanist, his turn to the Left at the time of the February riots in France [1934] illustrates the rapid radicalization of French intellectuals" (See "Editors" of *Partisan Review,* 2). Fernandez, however, would not for long be identified with the left. In his "Open Letter to André Gide" in 1934, he asserted, "But the Communist Party, stocked with the catchwords and formulas of the past, proposes to me a dogmatism which offends in me the defenses I have so carefully erected against the assaults of prejudice" (273). After the German occupation of Paris in 1940 (and after the writing of Stevens' poem), Fernandez became a collaborator, identifying himself with a manifesto supporting Franco at the beginning of the Spanish Civil War and continuing his association with *La Nouvelle Revue Française* after its editorial policy became pro-German. A generation later, Dominique Fernandez, son of Ramon, attempted to come to terms with his father's collaboration in his book *Ramon* (2008). In it he cites numerous essays and speeches after 1936 in which his father expressed his admiration of Goebbels and Hitler, and, according to Alice Kaplan, Ramon, in the company of others, "was the guest of Goebbels on a 1941 junket to Nazi Germany" (32). Fernandez died in 1944, a few days before the liberation of Paris.[19]

Before his years of collaboration, however, and when his essays were innocent of the ostensibly political, Fernandez was praised by T. S. Eliot, who published him regularly in the *Criterion* and translated at least two of his essays for that journal. Of him Eliot once wrote that he was "incidentally, a critic as well qualified to pronounce upon English literature as any English critic living" ("Books of the Quarter" 753). In a letter of 1927, he proudly claimed that "we [*Criterion*] 'found' Fernandez and gave him what reputation he has in England and America" (*Letters of T. S. Eliot* IV, 823).

Having himself served as an unobserved listener to the woman's song in the first lines of the poem, the speaker goes on to introduce Ramon Fernandez now to perform that role. In the absence of a listener, words are monologic, directed interiorly. In a sense, they are as silent as the woman's actual song (otherwise uttered, we are told, "word by word") and as silent as Fernandez's own unreported reply to the "tell me . . . / Why" command. But the speaker himself *does* hear the woman's song, just as Fernandez does hear the melodic euphony of the speaker in describing the lights in the harbor. Moreover, we, too, the readers, are also listeners and interpreters—so many Ramon Fernandezes who want to understand why, if we know, song and lights can possess the power that they do. Fernandez is one with us in illustrating Angus Cleghorn's point that "The reader becomes involved in configuring the poem's compositional world rather than being told about it" (40). The writings of Fernandez, it turns out, are especially helpful in enabling us to understand a hierarchy of values in the poem's various orderings and voices.

The first point I wish to make about Ramon Fernandez, then, is that he is, quite independently of his evolving politics, our own surrogate in the poem and that, as a listener, he is necessary to make it possible for the "rage to order words" to occur. The alternative is to be a "listener" who is "nothing himself" because he has metamorphosed, to cite one example, into a dehumanized snowman, a part of "the nothing that is" (*CPP* 8). Song, without ear (in the words of the Key West poem) is "sound alone": "But it was more than that."

I choose not to separate altogether the silent listener in the poem from the voluble critic of aesthetics and philosophy. Although it may be unlikely that Stevens was consciously setting up the poem as a deliberate absorption of Fernandez's theorizing, I find the similarities sufficiently overt to warrant making some of the connections, if for no other reason than the fact that the poem itself calls his name.

A collection of essays by Fernandez on Balzac, Conrad, Newman, Freud, Stendhal, Maritain, Meredith, Pater, and Eliot appeared in a book called *Messages* in 1926, later translated into English by Montgomery Belgion. Lionel Abel once called the essays "probably the most important book of criticism since Eliot's 'Sacred Wood'" (in Fernandez, "Open Letter," 271). As an introduction to the collection, Fernandez wrote an essay entitled "On Philosophic Criticism," in which he lays out the underlying premises of his own theory of criticism.[20]

"The Idea of Order at Key West," as A. Walton Litz (193–94) and others have observed, progresses from an aesthetic that debates the song of the woman and the plungings of the sea in mutually mimetic representations and then moves on toward a more affective and romantic aesthetic that takes its genesis in "rage for order" and "enchanting night." In this fashion, the poem moves from song as mirror (what I have called *mimesis*) to song as lamp (what

I have called *incantare*). The song of the woman becomes for her the creation of her own world, a solipsistic invention imputed to her by the speaker. But the tension between imitating the world and inventing it remains ineradicably in the background of the poem, each an extreme to which the speaker himself and the poem as a whole refuse to succumb. The pull between the mimetic and the solipsistic forces—and the dangers of each—are in the foreground of Fernandez's "Of Philosophic Criticism."

The essay begins with a criticism of the hazards of perceiving the world purely scientifically, what Fernandez calls in one place "rational analysis" (*Messages* 11), or, in another, "descriptive thought." The latter "tells us of the object as it is revealed by a methodical and normal observation . . . and shows it through the description" (17). Though such description of the object may be necessary for the foundation of the artistic act, it cannot be its end because such an act of impersonal mimesis omits the role of our own psychic responses: "For that is a mediocre art which demands from us an effort of *reflection* in order that we may be in a position to apprehend its images" (8). (He means "reflection" here in the sense of mirroring.) A "masterpiece," he insists, "is not in the least the copy of a thing" (19).

As previously noted, in Stevens' poem the initial response of the observer to the song of the woman is the cry of "mimic motion" and the song is "what she heard" and in whose "phrases stirred / The grinding water and the gasping wind." As readers of Stevens will be aware from other poems, the poet was powerfully driven throughout his career to possess the real as *ding an sich*, as "Part of the res itself and not about it" (*CPP* 404). "The accuracy of accurate letters is an accuracy with respect to the structure of reality" (*CPP* 686). However, in this poem, as we have already seen, the observer is equally eager in the first thirty-three lines of the poem to *dissociate* the song of the singer from the sound of the sea ("But it was she and not the sea we heard"), as if this *imitatio* by the singer must be allowed—if it is allowed at all—tentatively, momentarily, and as a begrudging concession.

If the artist's inclination toward merely copying nature is his first major temptation, the other extreme for Fernandez is equally dangerous and far more insidious. This is the form of art, and, indeed, of perception itself, that is "embalmed in sensibility alone" (48). To illustrate this theme, Fernandez points to the example of Marcel Proust. While admitting that Proust "has established a close reciprocity between intelligence and sensation from which the latter has benefited," nonetheless such "title to glory . . . must not be allowed to mask his inadequacies" (*Messages* 45).

The work of Proust, like that of the other writers referred to in *Messages*, is described by Fernandez in general terms, with few references to individual novels, scenes, or characters. As a result, his reservations are founded upon summary statements and general applications. Proust, he tells us, "instead of seeking to render an account of the object . . . succeeds in *defining* the affective states corresponding to it" (*Messages* 44–45). For him "there is no direct effect of spiritual activity on life, but only one on the memory of life embalmed in sensibility alone. . . . Even as in the philosophy of fact, in the Proustian psychology intelligence, by relation to life, is allowed only a *retrospective* function" (48–49). Elsewhere in the essay, here with no direct reference to Proust, Fernandez states, "I hold that in isolating intelligence from reality, in making of it a sort of receiving-post indifferent to what it registers, intelligence and reality are both put out of gear. . . . Now, what it [such an intelligence] does is to cut up reality into facts and thought into laws, that is to say that it is pretended on principle that it *discovers* what it *conceives*" (30–31). In another essay, Fernandez finds that Walter Pater, too, in his preference for "*life as beauty*" and as "*picture*," failed "*to allow the mind to escape from itself to gain a booty really conquered*" (*Messages* 295).

Fernandez's essay "On Classicism" appeared in 1927, seven years before Stevens' poem. He decries the influence of romanticism that "patterned thought after feeling" (39) when the process should have been reversed. If thought precedes feeling, a "fundamental aim of classicism" is achieved: "the translation into form of a state of full development, of balance, or, as Goethe said, of health" (43). Fernandez gives the final words of his essay to Spinoza: "'Above all, as far as one can at the outset, one must find a way to cure the understanding and to purify it, so that it can get to know things with good result, without error, and as excellently as possible'" (44).

Fernandez's point, so emphatically iterated, is an important one and seems to have a conspicuous relevance to Stevens' poem. If the speaker in the poem moves beyond the mimetic mode in the nature of the woman's song, he seems to arrive at a different mode, one that is given great apparent significance in the poem's song of solipsism:

> She was the single artificer of the world
> In which she sang. And when she sang, the sea,
> Whatever self it had, became the self
> That was her song, for she was the maker. Then we,
> As we beheld her striding there alone,
> Knew that there never was a world for her
> Except the one she sang and, singing, made. (*CPP* 106)

It is the word "never" ("there never was a world for her") that excludes all that is before or after her song as having an existence: the "never" pushes the poem closest to solipsism.

As many commentaries on the poem have observed, such a powerful making seems, on the one hand, to call attention to the Aristotelian notion of *poiein:* to make, to craft, to construct—the artist-poet as the journeyman of the world.[21] However, unlike the speaker, we have not heard this created song, nor do we know the intent of the singer whose words, we are told, create the sea. Fernandez, however, would be immediately suspicious of such a conclusion and so is Stevens.

Stevens struggled with his own leanings toward solipsism. In a poem like "Tea at the Palaz of Hoon" he seems to indulge them: "I was myself the compass of that sea: / / I was the world in which I walked, and what I saw / Or heard or felt came not but from myself" (*CPP* 51). But in "The Pediment of Appearance" he mocks just such "young men" like Hoon who "go crying / The world is myself, life is myself" (*CPP* 314), and in "Notes toward a Supreme Fiction" he insists that one must "Never suppose an inventing mind as source" of the pure "idea" of the sun (*CPP* 329).

The speaker in "The Idea of Order at Key West" is not interpreting or making his world at this point in the poem but reporting the putative nature of the singer's own separate and personal world: *she* was the single artificer of a world in which *she* sang, and there never was a world *for her* except in her song. Once again, in the words of Fernandez she "pretend[s] on principle that [she] *discovers* what [she] *conceives*" (*Messages* 31). Her lyric interlude seems to be the kind described by Donald Davie in *Czeslaw Milosz and the Insufficiency of Lyric:* "The pristine and definitive form of lyric is the song; and the singer of a song is not on oath. The sentiment and opinion expressed in a song . . . are to be understood as true only for as long as the singing lasts. They are true only to that occasion and that mood" (42).

Perplexed, the British poet and admirer of Stevens Charles Tomlinson notes: "[Stevens'] words, like her [the singer's] notes, spilling out over nature or 'reality,' annex it to human needs. Here her music virtually compels it into ordered significance. Yet, curiously, Stevens himself stands apart with 'pale Ramon,' as if he cannot quite believe in the woman's opulent solipsism" ("Wallace Stevens and the Poetry of Scepticism" 404). Stevens' standing apart from the woman's song is vital to the poem because, in the absence of her song's orientation toward the greater world and its listeners, it remains ultimately unsatisfactory, or satisfactory to her alone.

If we may return to Berkeley for a moment, he too is suspicious of a world beyond the knowing of it, as he lays out in these words (quoted by Stevens in "A Collect of Philosophy"): "For, what are the aforementioned objects [houses, mountains, rivers, all sensible objects] but the things we perceive by sense? and what do we perceive besides our own ideas or sensations? and is it not plainly repugnant that any one of these, or any combination of them, should exist unperceived?"[22] Bertrand Russell, for one, thought that Berkeley's idealism "ought, of course, in any case to be solipsism" (292).[23]

The speaker in the Key West poem, as he lays out the processes of associating and then dissociating the unity between "she" and "sea" in the poem's opening lines seems intent on preserving the autonomy of both even as they move toward unity in song. In the light of Fernandez's admonitions on the dangers of "subjectivism," the speaker in the poem never himself succumbs to them. The song of the singing woman, however, does become a song of solipsism—at least in the speaker's interpretation. Of course, one might argue that the singing woman does have a listener, the speaker himself. However, she seems unaware of his presence or at least never gives any evidence that she is aware of him. As we have noted earlier, she seems totally enveloped in the own "striding there alone" in lyric absorption with the world around her. She does not sing to him or for him, intent as she is on making *her world*.

Fernandez returns again and again to the idea that all utterances require an external ear in order to skirt the very danger of subjectivism. To avoid confounding "genuine intuition with the phantoms of the imagination" it is necessary to possess "a public, an *élite* capable of understanding, and especially of feeling, what the critic has felt" (*Messages* 18). And again, "Now, can a personal experience be held valid if it does not enlighten us about others at the same time as ourselves, not in the manner of a dictionary or inventory, that is to say, abstractly, but by an intuition analogous to that which we have of our own being? At least an artistic work which does not rest on this intuition seems destined to a more or less complete failure." Such a "philosophy of life" forces us into "as much repugnance for the solipsism as for the strict methods of science" (35). Stevens' poem proposes *the* idea of order at Key West, not *an* idea or order, not my idea in isolation nor hers. Orders are privately perceived, he implies, but socially validated.

As if he were giving a summary of Stevens' poem, and the song of the woman who sings "word by word," Heidegger exalts the poet as one who "speaks the essential word, the existent is by this naming nominated as what it is. So it becomes known *as* existent. Poetry is the establishment of being by means of the word" (762). But Heidegger also goes on, as Stevens' poem does, to affirm the power of the poet not in isolation but in the society of conversation: "The being of men is founded in language. But this only becomes actual in *conversation.* . . . The ability to speak and the ability to hear are equally fundamental. We are a conversation—and that means: we can hear from one another" (760–61). The language of a poet creates a world, but a world in discourse.

In one other important way, the conclusions of Ramon Fernandez come close to serving as a précis for Stevens' poem. If literalism and solipsism are the twin sirens whose isolated seductions must be circumnavigated, how then can one create a synthetic union between these extremes? In the last lines of the poem the speaker turns to Fernandez in his own dramatic and synthetic intuition. He moves away from the "solitude" that was "measured to the hour" by the singer and turns "Toward the town," moving from isolation into community. His "tell me, if you know, / Why . . . ," addressed to Fernandez, draws the latter into a dialogic relation with the speaker's own act of creation:

> . . . tell why the glassy lights,
> . . . .
> Mastered the night and portioned out the sea,
> Fixing emblazoned zones and fiery poles,
> Arranging, deepened, enchanting night.

He creates his own enchantment of the world, one of color, order, and mastery. Fernandez himself, in his essay on Jacques Maritain, describes such moments of the "luminous spot" for which we all yearn but rarely attain: "We are advancing step by step in a narrow circle of light which is not always displaced to suit us, between the chiaroscuro of the past and the night of the future. Often our ill-timed haste makes us stumble in the blackness . . . ; but the little luminous spot, which moves, which advances when one of us succeeds—after how much effort!—in making flash a clarity, such is intelligence, and our joy" (*Messages* 273).

The speaker in Stevens' poem has discovered his "luminous spot" wherein there is "making flash" a clarity, intelligence, and joy. But, unlike the woman of the song, he has not made his discovery in isolation. If one might say that "there never was a world for him except the one he saw, and, seeing, made," it is not one seen and made "for him" alone.

The basis of his intuition of the world is the world itself, what Fernandez would call "common-sense reality": harbor, sea surface, fishing boats, lights, reflections. The identity of Key West in the title situates us in a real place (a town in Florida) on the map of the world. "The real is only the base. But it is the base" (*CPP* 917), insists Stevens. Fernandez would say that such perceptions of the base, however, are then remade now in balance instead of the distortion of either side: "In spite of our worst extravagances we are moving towards unity: I mean that in us the unity of the dislocated and scattered object is remade, *this time in a purely sentimental form*. . . . Thus are formed in us *psychic equivalents* of things containing within themselves the principle of their elucidation" (*Messages* 43). A similar conclusion results from the fiction of George Meredith ("The Message of Meredith"), whom Fernandez prefers over the fictions of Proust. In Meredith's characters, "the mind escapes from the tyranny of the object, but meets this object in itself and re-creates its essential reality" (*Messages* 162). Earlier, in "Of Philosophic Criticism," Fernandez declares that the "artistic object" can never be swept aside by fancy. Such an object is an "independent complex of which the organic unity and cohesion result from a synthesis ensuring to it a life of its own. . . . In it [the work of art] the mind seizes itself as having accomplished itself in an object" (*Messages* 12). Again, Meredith is the artist's model: "he creates, if one may say so, what he understands, in such a way that his creation incessantly modifies reality without betraying it" (*Messages* 50).

In another essay, "A Note on Intelligence and Intuition," one that was translated by Eliot and appeared in his *New Criterion,* Fernandez implies yet another part in the process: "The poet offers us the concrete side of fact, vision, rhythm, affective emanation, etc., but as we discern through it the abstract side, the *idea* of this reality [emphasis added] attaches itself to the prehension of this reality" (337). That which is concrete, including both "fact" and "affective emanation," leads to the vision of the abstract, or "idea." This observation seems to me to illustrate the final stanza of Stevens' poem: "Oh! Blessed rage for order, pale Ramon, / The maker's rage to order words of the sea." From "affective emanation," in this case artistic "rage," one arrives at "the idea of this reality," or, in the words of the poem, ordering words of the sea in order to arrive at an "idea of order." Stevens modifies this progression in another poem from *Ideas of Order* called "Winter Bells" where "rage for order" becomes "rage against chaos." Here, however, the rage is modulated by "regulations of the spirit" (*CPP* 114), regulations that point to "the spirit that we sought" in "The Idea of Order at Key West."

Ramon Fernandez as critic points to and, I believe, elucidates many of the issues of Stevens' poem, whether Stevens' choice of the name was accidental or not. But his presence in the poem by name and vocative address, I am arguing, is crucial because he establishes the third part of the triangulation that constitutes any work of art: artist, world, and audience. Here Ramon Fernandez as critic and Ramon Fernandez as dramatis persona converge. We do not need his reply to the "tell me . . . / Why" command because, in the very process of being given that command, he authenticates the speaker as his own maker-in-community, his own utterer of "words . . . of ourselves" and not of myself. For *us,* for the speaker, for Fernandez, and for you and me who hear the poem, there never was a world for *us* except the one he sees and sings and, seeing and singing, makes—even as we will go on to make our own synthetic worlds making and singing them in social intercourse. It is only one step further removed to note that Wallace Stevens also speaks to us as his audience through his speaker and through a poem called "The Idea of Order at Key West."

Spiritus

The title "The Idea of Order at Key West" points us toward "*the* idea of order," as if the movement in the poem from "sound alone" to "keener sounds" also transcended the merely aural and led us toward something more Platonic. J. Hillis Miller reminds us that the word "idea" "comes from the Greek *idein*, to see. An idea was a visual image, the image something made on our eyes and therefore on our power of seeing" (286). With the words "fragrant portals" another one of the senses also comes into play. But in this poem sensuous gratification alone is insufficient. The ordering of the various senses is not for the purpose merely of becoming an "artificer of the world," or even of creating enchantment, but, as the speaker has told us in the third stanza, for discovering a version of idea in spirit: "It was the spirit that we sought."

In our present evolutionary history, we remain irremediably divided from our origins in the sea, and our human anguish, never perfectly overcome, derives from that exclusion and fragmentation from the world. But the poem several times hints at the lingering intimations that we still possess of that more perfect union: we do not forget it altogether. It is of this that Stevens speaks most explicitly in "The Idea of Order at Key West" when he refers at the end of the poem to the "words of the sea" as "Words . . . of our origins." Our origins were in the sea and there, in our evolutionary nascence, we enjoyed in some prototypical or primordial way, the unbreached unity between us and sea in what another poem calls a "muddy centre." But we emerged from the sea as complex animal life (now thought to be about 590 million years ago) and evolved into our human identities. We forfeited our original home and, by so doing, found ourselves, but we did so at the cost of losing our unity with the world with which we were once coextensive. As "Notes toward a Supreme Fiction" makes clear, we gained and lost:

> There was a muddy centre before we breathed.
> There was a myth before the myth began,
> Venerable and articulate and complete.
>
> From this the poem springs: that we live in a place
> That is not our own and, much more, not ourselves
> And hard it is in spite of blazoned days. (*CPP* 331–32)

And, we might add, in spite of "blazoned poles." The poem springs from a "myth" that was not only venerable and complete, but also "articulate," a language of perfect unity, a tongue that preceded words and utterance, but to which our present "Words of the fragrant portals" still have passage and purchase.

In a basic sense, the "grand poem" of Stevens, his "whole of *Harmonium*," does spring from the knowledge of lonely separation from a "place" no longer "our own," but once our own—and then from his attempts to find adequate assuagement in "blazoned days" or "emblazoned zones and fiery poles."

Stevens' choice of the word "idea" in his title (both for the poem and the volume in which it appeared) is hardly accidental, and it points toward a later formulation of what he would come to call the "first idea." It is in the "first idea" that "genius" and "spirit" coalesce in a perfection of self and world once enjoyed but now lost. Though we know it now only residually and thus *immaterially* as idea, we can nonetheless draw toward it through our makings of the *material* world through the sensuous matter of words. *Genius loci* (the genius of the place, here "sea") for Stevens is not a realm of tutelary spirits who hover around a designated place but a *genius mundi,* an idea of unity that inhered in conjunction with the physical world and that still unveils its mysterious presence to those who persist in seeking and asking, "Whose spirit is this?"

Such "spirit" assumes a nearly religious significance for Stevens. As Arthur Mizener pointed out many years ago, "Wasn't 'ghost' the Anglo-Saxon word for spirit or soul? Is that why we speak of the Holy Ghost and does Stevens mean that this is his holy ghost" (223)? Stevens' holiness, somewhat ironically, does not look ahead to a bliss following death but rather backward to a primordial one that preceded our birth as fully human. His vision is apocalyptic but not eschatological.

It is perhaps in his nostalgic yearnings for the "first idea" that Stevens draws nearest his Romantic forebears in the poem. James Applewhite in his *Seas and Inland Journeys: Landscape and Consciousness from Wordsworth to Roethke* says of the English Romantic poets that they possess "a consciousness in relation to its point of origin and return" (16). This consciousness makes for an enduring sense of loss and separation from an "ocean of unconsciousness":

On many levels, the separation that brings individuality, clear articulation, consciousness (in and of) time is penalized by loss of community with a ground of being: the One or an ocean of unconsciousness or a

forest or Eden or Edenic landscape that originally sustained the soul
or self in a permanent condition lacking individuality and freedom but
continuous with a whole of things not visibly ending or beginning. . . .
All these versions of consciousness and its origins share a perception
that the first condition of identity with a larger source still exerts a
suasion over our thoughts. (16–17)[24]

Stevens captures this perduring nostalgia in "The Poem That Took the Place
of a Mountain" when he speaks of one who "could lie and, gazing down at the
sea, / Recognize his unique and solitary home" (*CPP* 435).

In Stevens' view, when we were Adam and Eve and commenced to breathe
outside and independently of the sea we found ourselves, in spite of our expulsion, located in an Eden, a "paradise." We had not yet fallen into the Cartesian
chasm of final alienation, or at least we did not yet feel that fall so acutely.
The world beyond the breathing Adam and Eve, described again in "Notes
toward a Supreme Fiction," mirrored a division from the self, but a division
where heaven was, as it were, a mirroring glass, a "second earth" beautifully
varnished green:

> The first idea was not our own. Adam
> In Eden was the father of Descartes
> And Eve made air the mirror of herself,
>
> Of her sons and of her daughters. They found themselves
> In heaven as in a glass: a second earth;
> And in the earth itself they found a green—
>
> The inhabitants of a very varnished green.
> But the first idea was not to shape the clouds
> In imitation. The clouds preceded us. (*CPP* 331)

When we were one with earth and sea and neither was a mirroring reflection of the other ("not to shape the clouds / In imitation"), we did not yet
breathe. Nonetheless, our origins derive from and our unconscious memories
distantly recall that state of the "first idea," that "myth before the myth began."

Now, at Key West, the "spirit that we sought [and seek]" in our postlapsarian division from the world is the spirit of that "first idea," even if it is one that we can never again know perfectly. Because we live in the world of the second idea we now know the world ("the clouds") in imitations and reflections. Our world is *not* perfectly "Venerable and articulate and complete," even though we can articulate it through the "words" that take us closest to that ideal.

Seen in this light, the woman singer in the first part of the poem can be seen as part of the process by which words, song, and sea converge as "She sang beyond the genius of the sea." How would one locate such a "genius" that is "beyond" the physical world? As Daniel Tompsett describes her, "It would be a mistake to read this woman singing as a subjective 'she,' as simply an object of the poem. 'She' is not subjective but cosmological and Stevens seems to consider 'her' 'singing' to be from the 'beyond' of the ontological that lies outside reality, outside of poetry, but to which all things are deemed to be 'connected'" (51).

The restive memory of the "first idea" informs other poems by Stevens (in addition to "Notes toward a Supreme Fiction"), some written before, some after, the Key West poem. It is worth noting them briefly to remind us that this poem is hardly anomalous in its craving for the "spirit" of "first idea." "Anatomy of Monotony," for example, speculates that "If from the earth we came," then it follows that the "earth . . . bore us as a part of all the things" and "Our nature is her nature." But we have become aliens to the earth by the very fact that we came forth from it. We are fated to live in mourning: "this the spirit sees and is aggrieved" (*CPP* 90).

Like "Anatomy of Monotony," "To the One of Fictive Music" predates "The Idea of Order at Key West." (Both poems appeared in *Harmonium*.) The latter poem also remembers that our nature in its origins is one with "wind and sea." We recall "the birth / That separates us from wind and sea, / Yet leaves us in them." Separated "from" wind and sea yet living "in" their memory, we can only see the earth now as "Gross effigy and simulacrum" (*CPP* 70–71).

Toward the end of his life, when Stevens received a postcard from the Cliffs of Moher in western Ireland, he wrote to Barbara Church that the scene was "like a gust of freedom, a return to the spacious, solitary world in which we used to exist" (*L* 760–61). In the poem that followed he identifies "My father's father, his father's father" with the ancient cliffs, "a parent before thought, before speech, / At the head of the past" (*CPP* 427). These fathers, as the poem concludes, live on as one with "earth / And sea and air." Such an ideal union informs "the spirit's base" (*CPP* 427), the same spiritual base that he was seeking many years earlier in "The Idea of Order at Key West."

Does the speaker arrive at the "spirit that we sought" in "The Idea of Order at Key West"? The answer is yes, but only partially so, only as far as "words" ("keener sounds") can take him and only to the degree that he can make his poetic rage socially accessible ("of ourselves"). His demarcations are "ghostlier" because they are distantly recalled, vaguely formed, "dimly-starred." But they are ghostlier in another sense as well. They are not less substantial but more spiritual, closer to the purest idea of order, the first idea.

The poem suggests that our knowing the world in words is our highest power and our deepest gratification. The song of the woman at the seashore in the first part of the poem is "uttered word by word." The speaker imposes his own words upon the lights of the boats in the harbor as "emblazoned zones and fiery poles." Now, at the end, he defines the great passion ("rage") to order words as a kind of revelation, as if they alone can bring us ultimately to the "ghostlier demarcations, keener sounds." A few years after writing the poem, Stevens would write:

> The deepening need for words to express our thoughts and feelings which, we are sure, are all the truth that we shall ever experience, having no illusions, makes us listen to words when we hear them, loving them and feeling them, makes us search the sound of them, for a finality, a perfection, an unalterable vibration, which it is only within the power of the acutest poet to give them. (*CPP* 662–63).

Though its progression is marked more by passion ("rage") than by logic, "The Idea of Order at Key West" traces the movement from "sound alone" to the "keener" sound of order-in-song. "Rage for order" thus leads to "idea of order" and the attempt to articulate it. The poem establishes a making of the world that must be neither merely mimetic nor merely solipsistic, but, in the words of Fernandez, a remaking and ordering of "the scattered and dislocated object." Such makings and orderings must not be merely private and personal to the individual alone but public and shared, a performative art that touches the empirical world and reaches a listening ear. And finally, in making the world, stirred by the passion of rage and employing the power of language and all its incantatory properties, we approach the portals of a "spirit" for which we all hunger, a home in the "first idea," a distant "myth before the myth began, / Venerable and articulate and complete."

3

THE SOCIAL CONTEXT

Poetry And Politics

T he Idea of Order at Key West" is not itself a particularly political poem, though the need to impose order upon an inconstant and intractable world (gasping and plunging) can have political applications. It was notably written during one of the worst years of the Great Depression and at the very time that Roosevelt and Hitler were assuming political power. But even if the Key West poem is not overtly political, Stevens *is* a political poet whose poetic pulse was never far removed from a poem's historical circumstances. In that capacity, and especially for Stevens himself, certain questions immediately arise.

Of what is the politics of Stevens or any other poet made? Who and what are its influences? How does it begin? For this poet his political identity never settled easily into predictable or conventional propositions, but it did become one with his identity as a poet. If we focus for a moment, not on the 1930s, but on the year 1898, when Stevens became nineteen and was enrolled as an undergraduate at Harvard, this was the time when the United States entered upon President McKinley's "Splendid Little War," the Spanish-American War beginning in April of that year. Two months earlier, the American battleship *Maine* had been sunk under mysterious circumstances in Havana harbor resulting in the loss of 260 lives. In the war that followed, Theodore Roosevelt became a national hero by storming the heights of Kettle Hill and San Juan Hill with his Rough Riders, and in May the Spanish Pacific squadron was defeated in the Battle of Manila Bay. The war then ended two months later with decisive naval victories. At the Treaty of Paris in December, the United States found itself in custody of Puerto Rico, Guam, and the Philippines and would soon grant Cuba her independence. In short, America had become a world power.

In Stevens' journals that began in the fall of 1898 there is no mention of the war, though it must have been a constant topic among the young men at Harvard who were of an age for military service. Stevens' father, Garrett, encouraged his second son to resist "the Martial spirit,"[1] even as Stevens' older brother had tried to enlist but was turned down for medical reasons. As Milton Bates reports, "Hundreds of students [at Harvard] began soon after the declaration of hostilities to drill in the gymnasium and participate in practice skirmishes on Soldiers Field. Over four hundred students and graduates eventually enlisted for service in the war, with the Rough Riders drawing more Harvard men than any other command" (*Mythology of Self* 37).[2] Stevens, however, remains curiously silent on his own role or anyone else's in the international crisis.

Already resolved to become a poet and enrolled exclusively in courses in literature, languages, history, and constitutional government, Stevens was performing well as a student. His father, however, was seeking to direct him from what he considered his dreamy poetic ambitions. Writing immediately after the sinking of the *Maine*, Garrett Stevens had nothing then to say about the war fever but recommended what he called the "wild hurly burly activity" of the same business world that he himself had embraced as a lawyer: "For life is either a pastoral dream—the ideal of the tramp, or superannuated village farmer—Or it is the wild hurly burly activity of the fellows who make the world richer and better by their being in it: the fellows whose services make the rest furnish them subsistence and yield them honor, whose services are *always* needed" (*SP* 17–18). Stevens, of course, would never, then or later, surrender his poetic ambitions, though he eventually and, at first, reluctantly, subordinated them to his father's directives as the young poet left Harvard after three years, experimented with journalism in New York, and then followed his father and brothers into the legal profession by enrolling at the New York Law School. With the decision to become an attorney, Stevens set out to resolve a balance between his aesthetic consolations and the course he had set for himself as an American businessman-capitalist. For the rest of his life he would seek to justify and, in his own life, to exemplify an accommodation between art and—eventually—the settlement of surety-bond claims brought against his insurance company. The politics of Wallace Stevens takes its form therefore from a lonely outpost, unable, as we shall see, to feel completely at home either in the more isolated and apolitical world of his aesthetic proclivities or the socioeconomic world that the "office" and the world beyond would come to represent. But he was confident from the beginning that there would have to be a place in his life for both worlds.

At Harvard, three months after the conclusion of the Spanish-American War from which he appears so detached, he worked out for his journal a compromise between the extremes of Walter Pater's aestheticism and "art-for-art's sake," then a popular movement among his generation at Harvard, and the need to be a "part of the system of the world." What is remarkable in these comments is the assurance that he had arrived at some idea of the kind of poetry he wanted to write, even though he was not yet twenty:

> Art for art's sake is both indiscreet and worthless. It opposes the common run of things by simply existing alone and for its own sake. . . . To say that stars were made to guide navigators etc. seems like stretching a point; but the real use of their beauty (which is not their excuse) is that it is a service, a food. Beauty is strength. But art—art all alone, detached, sensuous for the sake of sensuousness, not to perpetuate inspiration or thought, art that is mere art—seems to me to be the most arrant as it is the most inexcuseable rubbish.
>
> Art must fit with other things; it must be part of the system of the world. And if it finds a place in that system it will likewise find a ministry and relation that are its proper adjuncts. (*SP* 38)

Stevens insists that beauty must be a "service," but he defines the word widely. On the one hand, beauty offers a "food," a "strength," something that sustains "inspiration or thought." It acts upon the individual. On the other hand, beauty is also called upon to be "part of the system of the world." How it is to be so is not illustrated, but he implies that beauty can be accommodated to the social and perhaps to the political. Beauty as mere "sensuousness," he insists, is "rubbish!" His mentor at Harvard, George Santayana, had written in *Interpretations of Poetry and Religion,* published in the year that Stevens left Harvard, the following: "If the imagination merely alienates us from reality, without giving us either a model for its correction or a glimpse into its structure, it becomes the refuge of poetical selfishness" (20). Poetical selfishness was exactly the danger that the young Stevens feared.

In the years that followed, Stevens would sometimes emphasize "beauty" as "a service, a food," a suggestion that beauty owes nothing beyond itself and its accessibility to others. At other times, his loyalty was more toward its being "part of the system of the world" as it seeks to "fit with other things." It was a dichotomy that he never completely resolved within himself. The powerful and unnerving intrusions of the events of the larger world upon his consciousness left it for him to discover and to resolve, at least for himself—decade by decade and poem by poem—how to shape the "beauty" of poetry to a proper "fit" with the world. Such an intrusion occurs in the poem "Girl in a Nightgown," first published in *Parts of a World* as America was entering World War II. "Repose" is about to be supplanted by "flames":

> Once it was, the repose of night,
> Was a place, strong place, in which to sleep.
> It is shaken now. It will burst into flames,
> Either now or tomorrow or the day after that. (*CPP* 194)

Ten years after his Harvard deprecation of art for art's sake as "indiscreet and worthless," however, when Stevens was now almost thirty and reading Keats's "Endymion," he acknowledged to his fiancée that "the growth of criticism" had made "poetry for poetry's sake" difficult to justify. Even so, in this instance he was inclined, he confessed, toward the *other* view different from that of the nineteen-year-old student, a position that redefines his idea of "service": "The modern conception of poetry is that it should be in the service of something, as if Beauty was not something quite sufficient when in no other service than its own" (*L* 147). Ten years earlier he himself had resolutely endorsed beauty "in the service of something" beyond its own appeasements.

Not surprisingly, national and international crises had a way of pulling Stevens back to the notion of beauty's "service," as it did at the end of 1939 when World War II had begun. To one correspondent he put himself in the place of the soldier in France: "But if one happened to be playing checkers somewhere under the Maginot Line, subject to a call at any moment to do some job that might be one's last job, one would spend a good deal of time thinking in order to make the situation seem reasonable, inevitable and free from question." He then went on to add, "I suppose that, in the last analysis, my own main objective is to do that kind of thinking" (*L* 346). What, one might ask, would that kind of thinking be for Stevens the poet? To justify politically a soldier's imminent death as "reasonable" and "free from question"? Such an apology Stevens would never attempt. "Man and Bottle" and "Of Modern Poetry," both written shortly after these remarks and discussed below, were, I believe, his attempt to do "that kind of thinking." On this occasion, however, he went on to tell Hi Simons that his most recent poem, "Variations on a Summer Day," had its own "justifications": "to hear and see agreeable things" and from which "anything of that sort [i.e., the circumstance of war] has been excluded" (*L* 346). In each of these separate instances, we see Stevens repositioning himself to reconcile the interior and exterior "services" of art in a time of social rupture, and it is in that very *struggle within himself* that he defines himself as a political poet.

In a career that spans the first half of the twentieth century, however, Stevens lived through a sustained economic depression, two world wars, the Spanish Civil War, the Korean conflict, and some of the most menacing years of the Cold War. National and international politics pressed upon his consciousness with a severity that allowed for little distraction. As a poet, the events of the political order forced him to confront an issue that plagued him for forty years: how, with his own unique sensibility and his own romantic affirmation of the imagination, could he justify writing poetry at all? It was not a whimsical question.

Nor is it an idle question to certain critics who embrace the assumption that a literary text justifies itself to the degree that it furthers progressive political causes and indicts itself if it retreats into timeless aesthetic enchantments. In his essay "Literature as Cultural Studies," for example, Cary Nelson argues that "the search for masterworks has to be replaced with an effort to understand literary texts as part of wider discursive formations. That entails deriving their meaning primarily from an analysis of those relations rather than from an ahistorical and largely immanent formalism or thematics" (65). Writing in 2003, Barbara Johnson is equally emphatic: "In our present moment, the one thing all critics seem to agree about is the danger and political retrogradeness of Art for Art's Sake. . . . While you are parsing a sentence, analyzing a metaphor, or smiling over a meaning entirely produced by the magic of rhyme, you are not paying attention to what is going on in the world" (2–3). To some of his critics, now and earlier, Stevens has seemed just such an irrelevancy. They accuse him of creating a hermetically self-contained poetry that wrapped his work in the "intricate evasions of as" (*CPP* 415). Even Ezra Pound in 1933, on the basis of *Harmonium* poems only, called Stevens "the retiring daisy esthete" (*Pound/Zukofsky* 154) and, in another letter, "Stevens'?????? the amateur ap proach, the gentle decline to take responsibility of being a writer ??? . . . or am I wrong? . . . It is not Stevens [*sic*] ISOLATION, but his damned *laisser aller* at titude RE/ *his writing* that gives me the ache."[3] From Stanley Burnshaw (1935)[4] to Marjorie Perloff (1985)[5] and Frank Lentricchia (1988)[6] he has seemed a poet often insufficiently connected to the social and economic issues that surrounded him in his lifetime. Stevens was of course aware of such accusa tions that issued during his lifetime, always discomfiting him. He responded to Burnshaw by writing "Mr. Burnshaw and the Statue," one of the sections of his longer poem "Owl's Clover." The charge that he was a poet of merely "charming distemper" by a soldier at the front in World War II disturbed him enough to lead to his composition of the poem "Esthétique du Mal."

I want to argue that Stevens as a political poet underwent many incarna tions, that his poetic attachments to the social crises of his lifetime represent varying gradations of engagement with and disengagement from them. It is incorrect to suggest that Stevens' political themes represent a monolithic ideology or even a consistent poetics. James Longenbach has identified one reason for his protean politics: "Stevens had all manner of political opinions, but he did not subscribe to any particular creed" (137).

Stevens never embraced a poetry that saw itself as an arm of a contem porary political agenda; he distrusted political leaders all his life, as I hope to show. But to say that poetry was not a social instrument is not the same as saying that it made nothing happen. Its ministry was, in fact, an indispensable one if it was not "all alone, detached," as he had insisted at the age of nineteen.

War

Unlike the Spanish-American War that had hardly seemed to capture the un dergraduate Stevens' attention, World War II absorbed him. As the war drew closer to America, Stevens noted its increasingly usurping powers over every other consideration. In 1940, he predicted that "what is going on now may be nothing to what will be going on three or four months from now, and that the situation that will then exist may even involve us all, at least in the sense of occupying our thoughts and feelings to the exclusion of anything except the actual and the necessary" (*L* 365). A year later he saw his forebodings intensified: "But when one is trying to think of a whole generation and of a world at war, and trying at the same time to see what is happening to the imagination, particularly if one believes that that is what matters most, the plainest statement of what is happening can easily appear to be an affectation" (*L* 654). At such moments, he continues, events seem simply "beyond our power to tranquillize them in the mind, beyond our power to reduce them and metamorphose them." Instead they "involve the concepts and sanctions that are the order of our lives and may involve our very lives" (*L* 656). At the end of his collection *Parts of a World*, published in the middle of the war, he added a statement at the end of the volume, just after the poem "Examination of the Hero in a Time of War": "In the presence of the violent reality of war, consciousness takes the place of the imagination. And consciousness of an immense war is a consciousness of fact." Nonetheless, he notes the need to transform such facticity: "In war, the desire to move in the direction of fact *as we want it to be* and to move quickly is overwhelming" (*L* 251) (emphasis added).

Even after the war, Stevens continued to absorb its aftershocks. In 1946, for example, he recorded this reaction to the sufferings of the European people: "The misery of Europe, which was greater six months ago than it is now, seems not to have been so real to us then as it is now; and the more real it becomes the more sharply one feels that poetry of this sort [appearing in a Cuban magazine and including his own work] is academic and unreal." Then, rather remarkably, he concedes, "One is inclined, therefore, to sympathize with one's more unsympathetic critics" (*L* 525).

As early as 1940, he was noting, "A few months ago, the universal fear (I use the word fear, because I have no sympathy with communism, instead of expectation) was that the world would go communistic, if in fact it had not already done so without realizing it, except in the matter of putting it into effect. Communism is just a new romanticism" (*L* 350–51). As the Cold War grew more threatening, he explained to his art dealer in Paris that "I regret that the situation is such that I have to think twice about buying pictures, still one could not enjoy books and pictures in a world menaced by poverty and enemies. By enemies I mean the Russians, assuming that they are enemies" (*L* 623). In this case he was suggesting that politics and social conditions preclude the capacity to "enjoy" aesthetically.

I align these various quotations from Stevens' prose and from various periods of his life only to illustrate how relentlessly the events of international politics preyed upon him, compelling him at times to dismiss artistic assuagements as "affectation," even if they were possible at all (events "beyond our power to tranquillize them"). Far from impervious to the national movements that occurred outside his life in Hartford, he anxiously measured their effect upon him and upon society.

In many ways the poem "Contrary Theses (I)" (*CPP* 239) encapsulates the obtrusions of public events—in this case, war—upon the private refuge of the speaker. The poem begins:

> Now grapes are plush upon the vines.
> A soldier walks before my door.
>
> The hives are heavy with the combs.
> Before, before, before my door.

The approaching soldier in the poem abruptly interrupts all the attempts of the poet to elude his presence. The scene is otherwise fixed in a setting of autumnal ripeness or even, somewhat to our surprise, in seraphs and saints, who are themselves art objects. Five times in the poem's twelve lines the soldier's arrival at the door is announced— as disruptive to the poem as it is to the speaker. As a contrary thesis, the soldier cannot be dismissed or forgotten. The word "before" occurs nine times in the short poem, becoming itself a kind of marching reverberation that cannot be silenced. ("Befóre, befóre, befóre my dóor.") And in the final line the soldier who "walks before my door" now "stalks before my door" even more ominously as "Blood smears the oaks."

Typical of Stevens' poems of autumn, a process of stripping away is in progress in this poem: the shadows "lessen" on the walls, a "bareness" returns to the room, and "acid sunlight" casts its glare. Those decreative actions accompany the movement toward the climax marked by the stalking soldier's arrival. In a very real sense, the same soldier stood at the door of every American's residence when the poem appeared in 1942, at a time when casualty rates were soaring and the war seemed to have no predictable end.[7]

At the same time, there is no historical ideology in "Contrary Theses (I)." The setting might just as well be a German household where an American soldier approaches. Rather, war's enveloping powers, sweeping aside everything alien to itself, constitute Stevens' pounding theme. He understood all too well that social anxiety can blot out every consideration extraneous to its own usurping presence. The poem seems at one with Shakespeare's Sonnet 65, "How with this rage shall beauty hold a plea, / Whose action is no stronger than a flower?" (65).

Though the phenomenon of a world war might seem to invalidate or cancel everything beyond its own intrusions, Stevens knew that as a poet he had to respond to them by something more than merely announcing their abrasions. A poem like "Contrary Theses (I)" is an ahistorical response to a particular international crisis: World War II is never directly introduced. In "Martial Cadenza" (*CPP* 217), the war camps of England, France, and Germany are named, but here Stevens apprehends, as he does in few other poems, something approaching transcendence of those circumstances. The actual world, in both war and peace, was often for Stevens both a historical and an epistemological configuration. The soldier before my door was a sure and inescapable "other" that brought with him violence and death, but the more elusive "other" for Stevens, often metonymically defined as sun, sea, star, or a seasonal landscape, is typically known only partially, if at all. In "Martial Cadenza," however, the star above the battlefield assumes an efficacy so powerful that it almost effaces the battlefield.

The poem was written two years before "Contrary Theses (I)" and before America's entry into the war. In spite of the title, the poem begins with no hint of an armed struggle. The poet, on "the street in which I was," glimpses the evening star low on the horizon at the beginning of winter. That glimpse rewards him to a degree that few other poems of similar longings and similar perceptions record. It is "as if" the star on this night finds him "young, still young, / Still walking in a present of our own." It is "like" a time "in a world without time," an instant, in fact, in which time seems to be transcended as the onlooker intuits the pure essence of the star, the night, and the season.

As the poem progresses, the "as if" and "like" are dropped in the direct ap-prehension of the star, "The vivid thing in the air that never changes." In such a triumphant moment even the catastrophe of war is mitigated. That moment is full "Of the silence before the armies, armies without / Either trumpets or drums, the commanders mute, the arms / On the ground, fixed fast in a profound defeat." Weapons and human limbs ("arms") are one on this battlefield of carnage. The star, in fact, hovers indiscriminately "over England, over France / And above the German camps." The poem tells us that the star looked "apart," but, in one of Stevens' favorite recurring puns, it is also truly *a part* of the particular moment. Soldiers and their commanders are dead, but the star's efficacy "shall maintain." He has found "Not the symbol but that for which the symbol stands, / The vivid thing." In death, all soldiers lie in "profound defeat," but for the speaker the moment is one of apotheosis and victory. He enjoys new life: "and I walked and talked / Again, and lived and was again, and breathed again / And moved again and flashed again, time flashed again."

In "Martial Cadenza" Stevens has, in fact, eluded the insistent soldier at the door—or, more precisely, he is able, in this revelatory moment, to see above him in a moment of transcendence, however fleeting, however gratuitous. Stevens' historical and epistemological worlds have, in this poem, come together in such a way for the speaker that the pleasures of the latter are made into a brief transfiguration that is made to compensate for the horrors of the former.

Such moments when the real—here depicted as a star— seems totally possessed were all too rare for Stevens, and not just within the context of war poems. More typically, they are attained by forfeiting one's own humanity and becoming the snowman, this no man, in order to possess perfectly "the mind of winter" as a kind of faux man. In "Martial Cadenza" no such suppression occurs. If "Contrary Theses (I)" represented the triumph of the public over the private, in "Martial Cadenza" the private supersedes the public. In the presence of the star's pure substance, war is a tragic accident, but an accident nonetheless.

But *like* "Contrary Theses (I)," the poem stubbornly refuses to take a clear political "side," a recalcitrance that can leave its readers dissatisfied in the wake of all that was historically at stake at the moment of its composition.[8] It is too "isolationist," they claim, from the world it evokes. I would put it somewhat differently: the poet subordinates the political to what for him is a higher metaphysical end, not because he is indifferent to political "sides" but because he wants the star's sympathy to be shared indiscriminately as a universal appeasement. "What had this star to do with the world it lit?" the poem asks. And the answer seems to be that the star's "constant fire" is universally accessible. Stevens reiterated the point a year later in his essay "The Noble Rider and the Sound of Words": "I am thinking of life in a state of violence, not physically violent, as yet, for us in America, but physically violent for millions of our friends and for still more millions of our enemies and spiritually violent, it may be said, for everyone alive" (*CPP* 659).

Seamus Heaney's address at Oxford University in 1989, "The Redress of Poetry," imagines an example of an English poet at the front during World War I and speaks of the "pressure" upon the poet to "contribute to the war effort, preferably by dehumanizing the face of the enemy." If, however, the poet sees the German soldier "as a friend and secret sharer," he is adding "a complication where the general desire is for a simplification." But such a complication it itself a redress, a "countervailing": "In the activity of poetry too, there is a tendency to place a counter-reality in the scales—a reality which may be only imagined but which nevertheless has weight because it is imagined within the gravitational pull of the actual and can therefore hold its own and balance out against the historical situation" (*Finders Keepers* 282, 283). Stevens' refusal to choose his "side" in "Martial Cadenza" is not unlike what E. E. Cummings, hardly an isolationist, said about the Germans in World War I. Questioned by the French authorities about his loyalty in fighting with the Allies at a time before America's entry into the war, he was asked if he hated the Germans. He replied, "No, I like the French very much" (in Kennedy 148).

Stevens' political poetry is more typically represented by a stance quite different from both "Contrary Theses (I)" and "Martial Cadenza," opposing extremes as they are. In the letter to his Cuban friend José Rodríguez Feo in which he designated the poetry of 1946, written in the setting of postwar European suffering, as "academic and unreal," he went on define his own apology for art in general and his own poetry in particular in such times of crisis. "Yet to live exclusively in reality is as intolerable as it is incomprehensible" (*L* 525). In short, poetry must exert its countervailing pressure or redress ("violence from within") against its minatory "violence without." In doing so, it has "something to do with our self-preservation; and that, no doubt, is why the expression of it, the sound of its words, helps us to live our lives" (*L* 665).

Such a defense of poetry acknowledges the value of escapism, but it is not an evasion of the realities of war and suffering by ignoring them or even distracting us briefly from them. The social pain generated by war or by economic deprivation needs no jolt to the consciousness; it is ineluctably there. But translating that pain into the imagination, making it also recognizable there, and then relieving it through cathartic expression was the role he came to adopt. When he read Stephen Spender's essay "The Creative Imagination in the World Today," in his copy of *Folios of New Writing*, he found these words, "Moreover we are constantly being disturbed by shattering material events, such as wars and revolutions." Stevens then underlined the sentence that follows and added a vertical line in the margin beside it: "The problem is to understand the nature of these events and transform them into a lucid language of the imagination, where they exist in their own right, coherent visions independent of reality, but nevertheless reflecting the truth of reality" (148). Stevens, too, aspired to visions transliterated into the "lucid language of the imagination"—independent of reality and yet reflecting its truth. He had written in the previous year, at the time of writing "Martial Cadenza," "My own way out toward the future involves a confidence in the spiritual role of the poet, who will somehow have to assist the painter, etc. (any artist, to tell the truth) in restoring to the imagination what it is losing at such a catastrophic pace, and in supporting what it has gained" (*L* 340).

When Stevens told Hi Simons late in 1939 that his own "main objective" was to do "that kind of thinking" represented by the soldier at the Maginot Line, "subject to a call at any moment to do some job that might be one's last job" (*L* 346), he did not mean that such thinking in poetry for him could be reduced to a *political* justification, a position that could all too easily succumb to shades of jingoism, propaganda, or cant. In the light of two poems he wrote shortly after these remarks, "Man and Bottle" and "Of Modern Poetry," such thinking becomes a form of social consciousness, an absorption of the war into one's identity and self-awareness. The poet teaches us how to live mentally in the climate of war. Such thinking, at least in these poems, is not cathartic or socially corrective but an awakening and probing into a new consciousness. Part of that thinking is destructive thinking, an elimination of the old shibboleths, what he calls "romantic tenements / Of rose and ice" in "Man and Bottle" (*CPP* 218). Like the soldier at the Maginot Line, the "mind" that is "the great poem of winter" must *content the reason concerning war* (emphasis added):

> It has to persuade that war is part of itself,
> A manner of thinking, a mode
> Of destroying, as the mind destroys,
>
> An aversion, as the world is averted
> From an old delusion.

Such destroying and averting are hardly soothing; they sharpen the edge of the poem as it "lashes more fiercely than the wind."

"Of Modern Poetry" (*CPP* 218–19), originally published simultaneously with "Man and Bottle" in 1940, also proposes the "poem of the mind." It, too, must completely absorb its surroundings and attain a level of sufficiency in a time of urgent need:

> It has to face the men of the time and to meet
> The women of the time. It has to think about war
> And it has to find what will suffice.

In describing "Mr. Burnshaw and the Statue" to Latimer in 1935, Stevens reminded his publisher that even in that poem his "principal concern" remained "not so much with the ideas as with the poetry of the thing," all those elements that made a poem different from a tract. He was serving notice that the poem that would become a part of "Owl's Clover" could not be reduced simply or merely to an "idea." He then recounted an "amusing incident" that had recently occurred, his reading a poem by Sir James Frazer, "the GOLDEN BOUGH man." The purpose of Frazer's poem was "to express the very general condemnation of Mussolini." But Frazer was "not enough of a poet to make a go of it." And even if he had made a go of it "he would have been a typical poet of ideas." His disapproval of the primacy of "idea" over the "poetry of the thing" in a poem then leads him into a reluctant double-negative: "I cannot say that I do not think such a poet [of ideas only] should be the chief figure among poets" (*L* 289). Even so, he implies, *he* would never be the "chief figure" on such terms.

When Stevens relaxes his guard and attempts to write a poem about the tyranny of Stalin, for example, as in "Mountains Covered with Cats," he invariably comes up short. Tony Sharpe rebukes him for his "bad-tempered outburst" (*Literary Life* 174) in "Memorandum": "Say this to Pravda, tell the damned rag / That the peaches are slowly ripening. / Say that the American moon comes up / Cleansed clean of lousy Byzantium" (*CPP* 597). When Stevens succumbs to the merely topical—doing so in this case, in the petulance of Cold War politics—the poem itself buckles under its own rhetoric.

In a different mode Stevens wrote "Burghers of Petty Death" (*CPP* 314–15) (1946) in the aftermath of Hiroshima and Nagasaki. The poem more skillfully focuses on the graves of a man and woman, perhaps two of his ancestors among those whom he had begun to seek out and whose graves in Pennsylvania he had begun to visit. Theirs is a "slight part of death," and they are "small townsmen of death." They remain "like two leaves / That keep clinging to a tree, / Before winter freezes and grows black." Their personal winter of blackness is simply juxtaposed in the poem without comment beside the larger nuclear winter so powerfully made real in the previous year:

> But there is a total death,
> A devastation, a death of great height
> And depth, covering all surfaces,
> Filling the mind.

"Burghers of Petty Death" is a slight poem that calmly evokes the horrors of the largest cataclysm of Stevens' time.

In 1954, nine years after the atomic blasts in Japan, Stevens reflected in a letter to a correspondent that President Eisenhower, whom the poet had favored over Adlai Stevenson in the election two years earlier, had recently predicted that the geopolitical state of the world was likely to maintain its status quo for another forty years. Stevens himself found such "adaptation" impossible to imagine while living in the Atomic Age: "I cannot say that there is any way to adapt myself to the idea that I am living in the Atomic Age and I think it a lot of nonsense to try to adapt oneself to such a thing" (*L* 839). The Communist menace in the context of the Cold War, harshened by the reality of nuclear weapons on both sides, was constantly on his mind.

Two years after Hiroshima and Nagasaki he was writing his longer poem "The Auroras of Autumn." In that poem, the spectacular display of luminous streamers in the northern evening sky, known as the aurora borealis, becomes the central trope of the poem. That display has many associations in the poem, but Charles Berger, in his *Forms of Farewell: The Late Poetry of Wallace Stevens*, first proposed that the "apocalyptic drama" of that poem "might be connected to war, and that the auroras themselves might be seen as a figuration of the atomic bomb" (xii). Berger points to the "gusts of great enkindlings" (*CPP* 356) in Canto II as "capturing the aerial terrors of the recent past as well as prefiguring a greater fire next time" (47). A similar foreboding is registered in the sixth canto when the "single man" "opens the door of his house / On flames. The scholar of one candle sees / An Arctic effulgence flaring on the frame / Of everything he is. And he feels afraid" (*CPP* 359). Something of a future nuclear winter is suggested in the ninth canto:

> Shall we be found hanging in the trees next spring?
> Of what disaster in ["is"] this the imminence:
> Bare limbs, bare trees and a wind as sharp as salt?
>
> The stars are putting on their glittering belts.
> They throw around their shoulders cloaks that flash
> Like a great shadow's last embellishment. (*CPP* 362)

Here is Berger's assessment of the shifting emphases in Stevens' use of the auroras: "It still might seem odd to readers that Stevens should invoke the auroras at a historical moment when they are bound to appear natural analogues for human destructiveness, to describe them in ways that only further the resemblance, and then declare the auroras to be a part of natural 'holiness.' His point in making the comparison and then trying to break it may be to insist that there is still a version of natural power uncontaminated by man" (67). To this I would add that the auroras, described vividly but not without ambiguity and not without competing symbolic applications, are a far more evocative and disturbing conjuration of the great cataclysm of the twentieth century than the more literal description of the bomb in "Burghers of Petty Death."

Jahan Ramazani makes a valid contrast between Stevens' war poems and those of Wilfred Owen, the British poet-soldier who died in battle at the end of World War I: "Whereas Owen writes 'elegies . . . in no sense consolatory' in the hope that he may 'warn,' Stevens, in war elegies less historically responsive than Owen's, seeks to console and not to warn, despite the ambiguity over *whom* he would console—himself, an élite, soldiers, contemporary mourners, or future generations" (*Poetry of Mourning* 106). Ramazani does not deprecate Stevens' poetry to a lesser status than Owen's because he fails to warn; rather he acknowledges a different purpose. Owen evokes the blood "gargling from the froth-corrupted lungs" of the dying soldier ("Dulce et Decorum Est" [140]), while Stevens transforms the same blood into the "rose that is the soldier's wound" (*CPP* 281). The first seeks to repel the reader by shock; the second to draw the reader close through empathy. Owen recoils and wishes his reader to do the same; Stevens requites, a peacemaking he invites his reader to share.

Seen in the context of his total oeuvre, Stevens' political poetry is not inherently different. Certainly such poems possess a context of urgency, and Stevens' more usual pastoral world is conditioned in these poems by the threats to that world. Asked by *Partisan Review* in 1939 about the responsibilities of the writer in a time of war, Stevens insisted that a "military state of affairs" was different from the "literary." There was no difference in kind imposed upon the poet in a time of war, only one of degree—the propagandists notwithstanding: "A war is a military state of affairs, not a literary one. Conceding that the propagandists don't agree, does it matter that they don't agree? The role of the writer in war remains the fundamental role of the writer intensified and concentrated" (*CPP* 805). He seems to affirm such intensification in "Gigantomachia" (1943), even as he seems impatient with "complacent trifles" and "seductions." This is the second stanza of the three-stanza poem:

> But to strip off the complacent trifles,
> To expel the ever-present seductions,
> To reject the script for its lack-tragic,
> To confront with plainest eye the changes,
> That was to look on what war magnified.
> It was increased, enlarged, made simple,
> Made single, made one. This was not denial. (*CPP* 258)

War both "magnified" its realities, but it also "made simple," just as the "role of the writer in war" is both "intensified and concentrated."

What Stevens' war poetry shares is a quality different from that of other contemporary poets of his own time. Stevens is primarily interested in war as a general condition. For those engaged in it and those who survive it, war is a profound defeat. There are no victors, only tragic casualties. There is no nationalistic boasting, only a uniting of all sides into a transnational demise. The only ideology is one of resigned but wrenching regret. It is a psychology of war rather than its realism that absorbs him. How, he asks, do soldiers and civilians alike live under the relentless consciousness of war? And then, how does poetry itself address the psychology of universal defeat and universal loss? May not the poem itself validly become a peaceful shelter in the maelstrom and malaise of radical personal and social upheaval? The poem as a contradiction of war's ruthless realism will always seem to some as evasive and irrelevant, but for Stevens it is refuge and a means of recovery.

In a large number of his poems (usually associated with the seasons of autumn and winter) Stevens suppresses his metaphors and other subjective impositions upon the world in order to draw closer to the world's independent and autonomous selfhood—like the star in "Martial Cadenza": "Not the symbol but that for which the symbol stands." But such an interior chastening, as Geoffrey Hartman has reminded us, has its own valuable social and political implications, even though Stevens himself never made such explicit claims. Hartman argues that social shibboleths and political doctrines need, from time to time, to undergo their own purgings. He speaks here of "The Snow Man," but his words apply more generally to Stevens' program of radical self-purgation:

> To see winter, one must have a mind of winter; to see the sun one must have a sunny mind. But if we pollute our environment by 'meanings,' by pathetic fictions, we see merely ourselves in nature when our real desire is to see nature. Stevens asks us, therefore, to reverse ourselves and become what we see instead of seeing what we are. Since we have remade nature in our image—and behold, it is not good—now the link between us and the earth should no longer be balanced in our favor, even imaginatively. Unless we stop occupying nature with our

ideas and anxieties we shall be in the dilemma recently expressed by Theodor Adorno. 'I cannot look at nature,' said Adorno, 'I cannot look at the shadow of trees without the shadow of Buchenwald interposing.' The woods of Arcady are dead indeed. What man has made of man and what man has made of nature are intimately joined, yet through the politics of poetry we may still open a chink in this claustrophobic mind and see 'Nothing that is not there and the nothing that is.' (*Beyond Formalism* 257)

Hartman's rather novel "politics of poetry" seems to suggest that poets like Stevens can rescue us from our pollution of nature: we have corrupted it by seeing "merely ourselves in nature when our real desire is to see nature." We have "remade nature in our image" to catastrophic ends. Stevens, particularly in his poems of autumn and winter, proposes a rigorous adherence to the ever-changing and ever-reconfiguring reality (whether viewed as political or epistemological); it must be seen as scrupulously discerned, independent of ourselves, and in opposition to a preconceived and personally biased program, where "our ideas and anxieties," in the words of Hartman, obtrude.

For a man who makes it clear over and over in his correspondence and essays how much he abhors fascism, Nazism, and communism, he nonetheless removed himself from those passions when he came to write his war poems. In reading an address by E. M. Forster delivered in 1935, Stevens was moved to record Forster's words in his commonplace book, "I am worried by thoughts of a war oftener than by thoughts of my own death, yet the line to be adopted over both these nuisances is the same. One must behave as if one is immortal, and as if civilization is eternal. Both statements are false . . . ; both of them must be assumed to be true if we are to go on eating and working and travelling, and keep open a few breathing holes for the human spirit." Forster adds, "If a writer is courageous and sensitive he has to my mind fulfilled his public calling. He has helped to rally humanity in the presence of catastrophe" (in *SPBS*, 41–43). Rallying humanity in the circumstance of war was for Stevens a summons to look boldly into its horrors, but not to shock. It was left to the poet to refocus that reality into whatever compensation language with all its resources and resonances could generate.

The Fallen Soldier

No political issue imposed a greater pressure upon Stevens than that of war. For him, war almost always meant the soldier in the front lines, often the casualty of combat. As we have now seen, Stevens had little interest in displaying the soldier by his nationality, his ideology, or the horrific realism of his life under conditions of battle. Rarely is he personalized—with a couple of exceptions, never named. His physical attributes go unrecorded. He is typically the soldier as every-soldier or everyman.

Stevens' birth as a modernist poet coincides almost directly with the beginning of World War I. Almost thirty-five years old at its outbreak, he had spent the preceding decade caught up in a foundering and uncertain career as an attorney in New York. But by early 1914, he had been named a resident vice president for the New York branch of the Equitable Surety Company, and, in a somewhat tentative way, he began to experiment with the writing of poetry, a practice he had all but abandoned since the end of his undergraduate days almost fifteen years earlier.

One of these early experiments consisted of a sequence of eleven short war poems vaguely titled "Phases." He sent the suite to Harriet Monroe of *Poetry: A Magazine of Verse* for inclusion in a special war number of that publication. She accepted four of the eleven, and the group appeared late in 1914.[9] "Phases" does not mark a breakthrough in Stevens' evolution as a modernist: it was in some ways a false start. But it represents his first sustained effort to address a political theme in his poetry. Here is the second of the four poems published by Monroe:

> This was the salty taste of glory,
> That it was not
> Like Agamemnon's story.
> Only, an eyeball in the mud,
> And Hopkins,
> Flat and pale and gory! (*CPP* 526)

Stevens' unfortunate choice of rhymes forces him into the stagey contrast between "glory" and "gory." The otherwise unidentified Hopkins is shockingly reduced to "an eyeball in the mud," an attempt to startle the reader with jarring realism. Such a depiction of war's brutality was for him, however, unnatural and extreme; he never employed such imagery in his war poetry again.

The fourth and final poem from the sequence in *Poetry*, beginning "Death's nobility again," reappeared three years later in Harriet Monroe and Alice Corbin Henderson's anthology *The New Poetry*, but with the title "In Battle." Instead of an eyeball in the mud, Stevens gives us "Death's nobility," a foretaste of the poems of the fallen soldier that would follow a few years later. Here is the first stanza in which the casualty of war is "Beautified," remade by "nobility" and the "pride" of Agamemnon:

> Death's nobility again
> Beautified the simplest men.
> Fallen Winkle felt the pride
> Of Agamemnon
> When he died. (*CPP* 527)

In the immediate years just after the "Phases" poems, the war itself was striking down a whole generation of men throughout Europe, America itself drawn into its vortex in April 1917. Stevens' own letters during these war years, limited in number as they are, say little about the war, but its all-consuming presence did not elude him. Exactly one year after he published the "Phases" poems, Monroe published "Sunday Morning," and no reader of the time could hear the poem's refrain, "Death is the mother of beauty," without thinking of the war. In another group of his war poems published in the same magazine in May of 1918, Stevens would have read a review of Edward Thomas's poems by Alice Corbin Henderson, *Poetry*'s associate editor: "Edward Thomas . . . was killed at Arras on Easter Monday, 1917. Although the war is barely mentioned in these poems, one is conscious of it perpetually as a part of the background, as we fancy the author was" (102). Henderson was suggesting the difficulties of reading any kind of poetry without an awareness of the international cataclysm, even as the war itself was claiming English poets like Thomas.

After an evening in 1918 with Harriet Monroe and her family in Chicago, Stevens wrote to apologize about "my gossip about death, at your house." Even so, he confessed, "The subject absorbs me, but that is no excuse: there are too many people in the world, vitally involved, to whom it is infinitely more than a thing to think of. One forgets this" (*L* 206). Stevens' own sister Catharine, serving with the Red Cross in France just after the war, was stricken with meningitis and died there just after her thirtieth birthday. On the occasion, Stevens wrote to his wife, "I am completely done up by the news of Catharine's death. . . . How horrible it is to think of the poor child fatally ill in a military hospital in an out-of-the-way place in a foreign country, probably perfectly aware of her helplessness and isolation!" (*L* 212).

Sometime in 1917, three years after writing the "Phases" sequence but before the war's end, Stevens came across an unlikely book that turned out to have a major and enduring influence upon the way he would depict the soldier in future poems. I believe the book's importance for Stevens, though noted, has been underestimated. The collection offered Stevens a stance by which the artist, fully sharing and absorbing all the shocks of war, could adopt a mode to transcend them through his art. Written by a casualty of World War I, the book by Eugène Emmanuel Lemercier was called *Lettres d'un Soldat*, a reproduction of letters written to his mother between August 1914 and his disappearance at the front eight months later. Reminiscent in many ways of Wilfred Owen's letters to his own mother in the same war, Lemercier, an unmarried twenty-eight-year-old painter, courageously resigns himself to certain doom, as Owen also did, as he moves with his regiment through the trenches and battlegrounds of his native France. His one consolation to which he clings tenaciously in the letters is the seasonal beauty of the countryside, even as the ferocities of war wage all about him:

> You [his mother] must call on your imagination a little and see purples in most astonishing stripes, and limitless stretches of sky and earth to the left and right. This [daybreak] is what I have seen several times of late. But for the moment, a soft sky is in harmony with the orchards where we are at work on trenches. The little post which I am filling exempts me from handling the pickaxe, at least for the time being. Such are the pleasures which at a distance appear to be calamities. (75)

Lemercier himself became Stevens' model. Surrounded on every side by the grisly carnage of trench warfare, the French soldier repeatedly found sustenance from nature's tranquility and unquenchable beauty. By such recourse in the face of adversity, he must have emerged at once as Stevens' own alter ego. Lemercier's book had appeared in 1916, and Stevens, discovering it under unknown circumstances, read it in the original French.

Selecting seventeen quotations (OP [Morsc] xix) from the book, Stevens made them into epigraphs for a suite of poems that he again sent to Harriet Monroe for publication in *Poetry: A Magazine of Verse*.[10] Morse indicates that "Stevens sent Miss Monroe thirteen poems" (xix). Dispatched on September 1, 1917, the poems were enclosed with his personal copy of *Lettres d'un Soldat*—along with the suggestion that, if she wished to publish the poems, "you might like to refer to the translation, even to extract my citations in a note, although I assume that most of your readers know French sufficiently not to need a translation" (*L* 202).

Six months after submitting the suite to Monroe, Stevens was in Chicago on business and called on Monroe. He described the visit in a letter to his wife: "Late this afternoon I went up to *Poetry*'s office and saw Miss Monroe about my war-poems. We went over them together and weeded out the bad ones. They will be published bye and bye" (*L* 205). They had selected nine from the thirteen originally submitted. These were finally published in *Poetry* in the issue of May 1918, the same edition in which Henderson's review of Edward Thomas' poetry appeared. From these nine, only three were ultimately reproduced by Stevens: "The Surprises of the Superhuman," "Negation," and the poem that would later be entitled "The Death of a Soldier" were added to the 1931 edition of *Harmonium*. *Lunar Paraphrase* was not among the nine selected by Monroe but was added to *Harmonium*. In so doing, he then elected to omit the epigraphs, although for the nine poems that appeared in *Poetry* the epigraphs had been included.

The epigraphs make up an invaluable source in tracing the importance of Lemercier's book.[11] In one of the poems, untitled but numbered by Monroe as "VI," Stevens cites a vocative from Lemercier to his mother (and I quote from the English translation that Stevens had recommended to Monroe): "As regards thy heart, I have such confidence in thy courage that it is a great source of comfort to me. I know this mother of mine has attained the freedom of soul which makes it possible for one to contemplate the universal drama" (81). Stevens' poem that follows the epigraph is not about the mother of the French soldier, however, but rather "another mother whom I love," one who, the soldier in the poem affirms, "Is mother to the two of us" (*CPP* 542). This other mother does not appear in Lemercier's remarks but is Stevens' own invention. She is, the speaker insists, "Not France!" She is beyond the specific nationalities, adversaries, and contexts of this war, a "mightier mother" who will be defined by her cry, whether it be a cry of resignation or outrage or perhaps even a "will or wish" for peace. Here are the poem's final lines:

> There will be voluble hymns
> Come swelling, when, regardless of my end,
> The mightier mother raises up her cry;
> And little will or wish, that day, for tears. (*CPP* 542)

Apparently intended as a sonnet without regular rhymes, the poem is not completely successful. But it is important as perhaps Stevens' first attempt to remove the poem of war from the immediacy of history and endow it with a larger significance, what the epigraph looks to as that "which makes it possible for one to contemplate the universal drama" in the universal benevolence of the earth even behind battle lines.

A similar mother appears in one of the four poems from the sequence that Stevens included in the 1931 *Harmonium*, "Lunar Paraphrase" (*CPP* 542). Not exactly a formal epigraph, the first line of the poem (repeated as the final line) is "The moon is the mother of pathos and pity." Above the line is the epigraph taken from Lemercier as Litz surmises: "I have supplied as an epigraph the passage from *Lettres d'un Soldat* which Stevens must have had in mind" (316).

> Such were some of the beauties of yesterday. What can I tell thee of the preceding evenings when the moon reflected on the roads the embroidery made by the bare branches of the trees, the pathetic outlines of the calvaries, and the shadows of houses which we know to be only heaps of ruins but which the obscurity of the night presents as if peace had built them up again? (*A Soldier of France* 72)

The moon from the apparent epigraph becomes for Stevens the "mother of pathos and pity." The poem reconstitutes the scene of battle as a pastoral haven where the bodies of soldiers have been replaced with that of Jesus and the shrinking figure of His mother. Apparently outdoor shrines,[12] the "calvaries" from the poem are made to include Jesus and Mary: "the body of Jesus hangs in a pallor, / Humanly near, and the figure of Mary, / Touched on by hoar-frost, shrinks in a shelter / Made by the leaves." Jesus' death and the leaves of November ("rotted and fallen") are the only specific casualties of the scene, itself a "golden illusion," perhaps referring to the moon itself. The moon "Brings back an earlier season of quiet / And quieting dreams in the sleepers in darkness." (These lines refer to Lemercier's preceding letter that calls attention to "the contrast between the consequences of these military activities and the peace accustomed to reign in this spot" [70].) The "sleepers" in "Lunar Paraphrase" are, of course, the soldiers who find their own peace, "the quieting dreams in the sleepers," in this evocation of beauty and calmness delicately enveloped in "pathos and pity." Stevens has found in the prose of Lemercier a context and tone of an all-enveloping empathy and pity in the immediate crossfire of warfare, one that would have a strong and permanent appeal for the poet.

The poem that would later contain the title "The Death of a Soldier" (*CPP* 81 & 544) when published in *Harmonium* (1931) was Poem no. XI in Monroe's assemblage. The poem itself is otherwise identical in both versions, though the epigraph was dropped in *Harmonium*. Harold Bloom calls the poem "the emergence of the poet's most characteristic voice" (*The Poems of Our Climate* 48). Like "Lunar Paraphrase," it evokes pathos and pity. For its epigraph, Stevens chose a single sentence from Lemercier: "*La mort du soldat est près des choses naturelles*"; it is a summary of an earlier quotation by the French soldier:

> How harmonious death is in the ground, and how much more genial it is to see the body returning to mother earth than to see it the victim of the human paltriness of our conventional funeral ceremonies. But yesterday I would have felt that those poor abandoned dead were wronged, yet now, after attending a few hours ago, the formal burial of an officer, I am convinced that nature has a more tender pity for her children than has man. Yes, indeed, the death of a soldier is almost a natural thing. . . . Many times recently I have passed near dead bodies in uniform that were slowly sinking away into a natural grave and this new life of theirs with earth was less repulsive to me than the cold and unalterable sight of the city tombs. (*Soldier of France* 146–47)

Perhaps like no other, this remark by Lemercier shaped the sensibility and tone for Stevens' future direction as a poet of war and its victims.

The evocation of pity, named in the epigraph in "Lunar Paraphrase," is again employed "The Death of a Soldier." The poem begins:

> Life contracts and death is expected,
> As in a season of autumn.
> The soldier falls.

Merely to say that death is "expected" joins the soldier to all humanity for whom death is viewed, not as convulsion, but as a *chose naturelle*." The soldier in "Lunar Paraphrase" evokes the suffering of Jesus on the cross, "Humanly near." In this poem the soldier is contrasted to the crucified Jesus to make the point that "He does not become a three-days personage," awaiting a supernatural resurrection on the third day or an absorption into the life of a three-personed God. In many of his future poems of the fallen soldier Stevens, as he does here, will resist the rituals of religious affirmation and consolation. Lemercier too finds the rituals of religion wanting ("paltriness of our conventional funeral ceremonies"). For Stevens, there are no memorials for the fallen soldier. Death is, in fact, "without memorial" except for the commemorations of nature herself: "When the wind stops, // When the wind stops, and, over the heavens, / The clouds go, nevertheless, / In their direction." The contrast between "stops" and "go" is obvious: the soldier "falls" in the season of fall; the life of the soldier "contracts" as the lines in each stanza contract in length. At the same time, as the wind "stops," the clouds "go, nevertheless, / In their direction." The mortal soldier, like all humans, has found his inevitable "direction"; his burial, without "pomp," reunites him with the rhythms of the earth itself. As Lemercier wrote elsewhere in the collection: "To-day overhead we have the sky filled with cold flying clouds such as the Dutch landscapists like to paint" (29). In a letter written a few days later he marveled, as Stevens' poem does, at the durability and continuity of nature in the midst of human destruction: "How noble the country looks and how good nature is. She tells all those who will hear her that nothing will be lost" (*Soldier of France* 33).

The twelve thin lines of "The Death of a Soldier" take on a kind of monumentality. A soldier falls; death is expected. The circumstances of the falling are left to our own imaginations, and the "pomp" of religion is adamantly withheld. Boldly and cleanly decreed, the absoluteness of death transcends war calmly in order to embrace all living things, human and nonhuman. Autumnal wind, heavens, and clouds go and stop, but with a stark and incluctable "direction." With the supple economy of restraint, the poem declares death in a world that is as fleeting as the seasons, nature's stopping and going, and, yes, also the madness of war.

From the Lemercier letters was born the Stevens war poem as epitaph, an appeal to pathos and, in places, pathetic fallacy. The topographies of nature, omnipresent and aloof from human folly, even when surrounded by violent carnage, offer the final balm. Here was a mode in which poems could be "part of the system of the world," as Stevens had demanded in 1899, while at the same time "a service, a food" (SP 38).

Even as the German juggernaut of the next great war was beginning its sweep across Europe in 1938, Stevens' "Dry Loaf" (CPP 183–84) took note of "living in a tragic land" and "in a tragic time." (It was now twenty-one years since Stevens had first read the Lemercier letters.) The scene laid out in the poem is not that of battlefield corpses but one of rocks, river, and birds all engaged in a flowing and spreading motion. The birds, "Flying from burning countries," cover the sky and disperse "as waves spread flat on the shore." Lemercier had noted a similar phenomenon: "The little wood near our guardhouse has been taken possession of by a flock of green birds with white-bordered wings, the males having black heads with a white spot. What a whiz they made in the surrounding tranquility. Here we have another example of gentleness in the midst of these warring folk" (37–38). At its conclusion, "Dry Loaf," in similar fashion, unites the birds with the warring folk as marching soldiers:

> It was soldiers went marching over the rocks
> And still the birds came, came in watery flocks,
> Because it was spring, and the birds had to come.
> No doubt that soldiers had to be marching
> And that drums had to be rolling, rolling, rolling.

Again and again, Stevens returns to the image of the fallen soldier in the context of World War II as it unfolded. We have already seen a hint of this in the poem "Martial Cadenza" where the stars hover over the "armies without / Either trumpets or drums, the commanders mute, the arms / On the ground, fixed fast in a profound defeat" (*CPP* 217). In such poems as these, there is an exaltation of the fallen soldier as the cleansed hero, the figure now restored to a brotherhood at one with the earth itself. A victim of history, he now transcends it; a party to violence, now he reposes in peace. Even though the soldier is viewed with the intensity of pathos, he is coolly distanced from the historical circumstance of his demise. His death in battle is seen not as a catastrophe but as a "good," and the serenity that warfare denied him is now reclaimed. The view of the soldier is romanticized by making him into a symbol, another representation of "Death is the mother of beauty" from "Sunday Morning."

For those who would see in such a romantic view of the fallen soldier an ingenuous retreat from the reality and brutality of war, their criticism will stand. For Stevens, however, such a view is an exaltation and apotheosis of the fallen victim, an attempt to create a poetic ritual by which war's casualties, and those left behind to mourn their horrible deaths, may find solace in a new "meaning" of personal sacrifice. For Stevens, the soldier is not viewed as friend or enemy, victor or defeated, but as a native of the earth itself to which he peacefully returns.

"Esthétique du Mal" (*CPP* 277–87) was written in the wake of an anonymous attack that had appeared in the *Kenyon Review* near the end of World War II: "The commandos of contemporary literature are having little to do with Eliot and even poets of charming distemper like Wallace Stevens (for whom we all developed considerable passion). . . . I find the poetry in *Kenyon Review* lamentable in many ways because it is cut off from pain" (in Ransom, "Artists, Soldiers, Positivist," 276). As the title implies, Stevens' poem is an attempt to justify an "aesthetic" in a time of "mal"—be it the mal of war or of pain in general. The poem's seventh canto (*CPP* 281) reintroduces the fallen soldier:

> How red the rose that is the soldier's wound,
> The wounds of many soldiers, the wounds of all
> The soldiers that have fallen, red in blood,
> The soldier of time grown deathless in great size.

It is clear from the opening lines that Stevens views the soldier as a Lemercie-
rian emblem of all soldiers—his death in company with a symbolic brotherhood, "deathless in great size." As in "The Death of a Soldier," written twenty-six years earlier, in which the dead soldier is surrounded by clouds and
wind, this soldier lies beside a mountain and beneath the motions of the wind.
In this case, however, he is not alone but surrounded by his "fellows" who
stand in the calmness of a summer night, the setting of a similar ritual. The
night and the season bestow the source of consolation, "fragrance," "somno-
lence," and "summer sleep," not unlike the "quietening dreams in the sleepers
in darkness" in "Lunar Paraphrase." The canto concludes with these benisons
for "the soldier of time":

> In which his wound is good because life was.
> No part of him was ever part of death.
> A woman smoothes her forehead with her hand
> And the soldier of time lies calm beneath that stroke.

Fredric Jameson, without reference to this particular poem or any of Stevens' war poems, concludes "that Stevens' *only* content, from the earliest
masterpieces of *Harmonium* all the way to the posthumous *Rock,* is landscape
. . . , nothing but a given, a ready-made occasion for speech—birds, wind,
mountains, the sun, always ready to hand whenever poetic speech needs
some kind of objective content for its own production (11). For Jameson,
that "speech" is "an impoverishment or hollowness of content," even though
stated in "an astonishing linguistic richness" (11). For social critics like
Jameson, the use of landscape such as Stevens employs in "Esthétique du
Mal"—landscape as a source of solace, renewal, and momentary peace—is
insufficient as merely "symbolic or poetic, as fictional, such that the poetry
will now come to turn on itself and in all of its rotations continue to desig-
nate nothing but itself" (19). But surely in this poem Stevens' remoteness
from the immediate circumstances of military engagement and historical
ideology does not distance him from his readers of 1944 who were living in
the general condition of the war's immediate and cooptive field of force. Because history had become overpowering, the poet sought the assuagements
that might create a possible mode of survival. The poem could not end the

war but it could contribute a momentary surcease from its all-absorbing envelopment. Such a poem cannot be dismissed as "hollowness of content"—however much one might question the use of pools of blood from stricken soldiers assuming the attar of roses.

This section of "Esthétique du Mal" seems to owe something to Stephen Crane's poem "God lay dead in heaven" where God's death is marked by "blood / That fell upon the earth."[13] Pathetic fallacy accompanies the event in Crane's poem: "Purple winds went moaning." "Monsters" appear in war-like guise: "They fought, / Wrangled over the world." The poem then concludes with an image of the fallen soldier and anticipates Stevens' pathos: "But of all sadness this was most sad,— / A woman's arms tried to shield / The head of a sleeping man / From the jaws of the final beast" (41). Here is Stevens' echo: "A woman smoothes her forehead with her hand / And the soldier of time lies calm beneath that stroke." Pathos is imposed in both poems but Stevens' is the more consoling. Once again, "Death is the mother of beauty" (CPP 55) because she is the guarantor of summer's return and prodigality of nature and all of life. One with "summer sleep" Stevens' soldier is not really dead at all (he is called "deathless" three times in the canto) but immortal ("No part of him was ever part of death"). His life force, one with the earth, transcends his body as casualty. One soldier's death enacts the death of all soldiers; his "wound" becomes "The wounds of many soldiers, the wounds of all / The soldiers that have fallen, red in blood." This poem and the others like it summon the poet to a task that belongs to a long tradition: the reconfiguring of unthinkable horrors into the conventions of various modes of pastoral elegy.

Written a few months before the end of World War II, "Flyer's Fall" (CPP 295) compresses a whole post-theological cosmology into six short lines:

> This man escaped the dirty fates,
> Knowing that he did nobly, as he died.
>
> Darkness, nothingness of human after-death,
> Receive and keep him in the deepnesses of space—
>
> Profundum, physical thunder, dimension in which
> We believe without belief, beyond belief.

The man who has died "nobly" and who "escaped the dirty fates" is identified as a soldier only by the word "flyer" in the poem's title and its date of
publication, 1945. It recalls Yeats's fallen flyer from World War I, Major Robert Gregory, who is remembered in "An Irish Airman Foresees His Death."
Stevens' flyer "escaped the dirty fates," but Yeats's knows "that I shall meet
my fate." There is no nobility in the death of the latter, however, only Gregory's "lonely impulse of delight / [that] Drove to this tumult in the clouds"
(*Poems* 135). Stevens directly addresses not the soldier but, more generally,
"nothingness" itself in the invocation to "Darkness, nothingness of human
after-death"—perhaps the most desolate line in all of Stevens. "Nothingness"
must, the poem implores, "Receive and keep him in the deepnesses of space."
Such a consignment is clearly a poetic and symbolic one—not a metaphysical
or literal one: a "Profundum" (connecting with "deepnesses") and "physical
thunder" (connecting with "space"). The poem then ends with this "dimension" in which "We believe without belief, beyond belief." Belief, as such,
appears to be resignation to the demise of all humans, but also to a higher
symbolically liminal state that is not quite transcendent: "Receive and keep
him in the deepnesses of space." This poem, like "The Death of a Soldier,"
sees the fallen casualty without the consolation of religious faith. But in this
poem, nature—depicted in "The Death of a Soldier" as clouds, wind, heav-
en—offers little of Lemercier's own recourse ("How noble the country looks
and how good nature is. She tells all those who will hear her that nothing will
be lost" [33]). Stevens' "nothingness" is his destiny of total loss as the soldier
is assigned to a distant beyond, now made one, not with the earth, but with
the vastness of the universe. Such an absorption into the distant cosmos is the
soldier's ironic "fall." Only in the absence of a supernatural object of belief,
Stevens suggests, can we stoically affirm that in which "We believe."

"Flyer's Fall" pushes the soldier beyond all historical circumstance and setting, even beyond the rhythms of the changing but beautiful earth. He seems
suspended between the implicit violence of war that has claimed his life ("the
dirty fates") and his place in the ultimate "nothingness," a "Profundum" as
a liturgical-like benediction. What lingers from the other poems of the fall-
en soldier is the tragedy of Lemercier's "pathos and pity" borne by those he
leaves behind and the fact that he died, not futilely, but "nobly." In death, he
is presented by Stevens with typical tenderness and commiseration. As in all

these poems, the field of battle is redolent of death's cruel intrusion but here "escaped" and enshrined in empathic nobility.

Stevens assigns a powerful role to the poet, who, priest-like, utters the words that exorcise the soldier from the agony of his death and transmits him into a sublimity larger than life. In "Asides on the Oboe," he speaks of the need of a "final belief" that "Must be in a fiction" (*CPP* 226). In that poem he professes a "central good" that can be made out of a "central evil" (*CPP* 227). One can't help feeling at times that Stevens' "solution" comes across as too pat, too mechanical, too idealized: "Profundum, physical thunder, dimension in which / We believe without belief, beyond belief." In the end, our only "belief" is that which comes from the priest-poet's words, and the power of those words to elevate us through his empathy, sympathy and yearning and thereby to create an aura of solace, a magnitude of peace, if only momentarily. That solution defines a fundamental element of Stevens' political poetry and runs unremittingly through his poems of World War I and World War II and the aftermath of both.

"I did have the Spanish Republicans in mind" (*L* 798), says Stevens of "The Men That Are Falling" (*CPP* 173–74), here not a flyer's fall but that of earthbound soldiers. From Stevens' remark, it would appear that his dying soldier has some kind of identity with the legally elected government of the Republicans in Spain, supported by Soviet communists, who had been attacked by the rebellious Nationalists led by General Franco—himself supported by the Catholic Church and the rising fascists of Italy and Germany. But Stevens' siding with the Republicans (if having them "in mind" is a "siding") is ambiguous: the soldier is "Thick-lipped from riot and rebellious cries," which might seem to suggest a Nationalist rebel soldier, and the "demagogues" addressed at the end of the poem seem to be fascists such as Franco. As we have noted, it would be highly unusual for Stevens to ally himself with a "side" in a particular conflict, especially war, and he doesn't really do so here. In any case, William Carlos Williams found the poem "the most passionate and altogether the best work in this selection [volume]—one of the best poems of the day" (50).

The poem's fifteen couplets again present a recent casualty of war, nowhere defined as the Spanish Civil War, though the poem was first published in 1936. The image of the fallen, prostrate soldier occurs, as it does in so many of Stevens' war poems: "He lies down and the night wind blows upon him here."

This offering of his life is his singular gift with the "Taste of the blood upon his martyred lips." His martyrdom is his canonization, but not dispatched to "deepnesses of space," as in "Flyer's Fall," but to the earth itself. Whatever he utters is spoken "only by doing what he did":

> The head of one of the men that are falling, placed
> Upon the pillow to repose and speak,
>
> Speak and say the immaculate syllables
> That he spoke only by doing what he did.

"What he did" was to sacrifice his life. Why and how exactly did he do this? The poem begins with the surprising first line, "God and all angels sing the world to sleep." Such a sleep, however, is a kind of anesthesia which is in contrast to the awakened "desire" of the soldier. The word appears six times in the poem.[14] Such passionate "desire" contrasts with the world sung to sleep, and, to draw out the contrast, the poem concludes, "This man loved earth, not heaven, enough to die." The deceased soldier of the Spanish Civil War gives over his life out of his love for the earth and its beauty. His end, while it is of course tragic ("Taste of the blood" is on his lips), is also heroic, an embrace of the mortal world ("earth, not heaven") as part of his ritualistic martyrdom. As abstractly wispy as such a pronouncement may appear, Stevens seems still to be embracing the paradigm of Lemercier: the soldier dies for the earth, not the earth of war, but of nature's soothing beauty: "Now that the moon is rising in the heat // And crickets are loud again in the grass. The moon / Burns in the mind on lost remembrances." Lemercier calls his own such appreciation a dominating and conciliating of "all this discord": "This fearful human turbulence has not succeeded in disturbing the majestic serenity of nature. It is true that at times man seems to surpass all imaginable restraints, but a penetrating soul distinguishes rapidly the harmony which dominates and conciliates all this discord" (52).

In his poem on this same war, "Spain," W. H. Auden seems almost to be echoing Stevens' consolation by rejecting the dramatic "fall of the curtain" on the dying "hero" of yesterday in favor of the poet's "whispers" today among the pines and waterfall as part of his proper "struggle":

> Yesterday the belief in the absolute value of Greek,
> The fall of the curtain upon the death of a hero;
>> Yesterday the prayer to the sunset
>> And the adoration of madmen. But to-day the struggle.

> As the poet whispers, startled among the pines,
> Or where the loose waterfall sings compact, or upright
>> On the crag by the leaning tower. (52)

The fallen soldier appears repeatedly in Stevens' poems written during World War II and reproduced in *Parts of a World* and *Transport to Summer*. Some of the others include "Thunder by the Musician," Section III of "Asides on the Oboe," Section VIII of "Extracts from Addresses to the Academy of Fine Ideas," "Dutch Graves in Bucks County," "A Woman Sings a Song for a Soldier Come Home." In varying degrees, they all coalesce around the Lemercier theme: a wounded or dead soldier whose wound or death is elevated into those of all soldiers, creating a kind of community of the fallen into which the individual soldier is absorbed. The instant of his death becomes the enlargement of his life, an amplification of his humanity. It defines and gives meaning to his life, but only as he surrenders it. His death is a scrupulous abjuration of religious immortality (different from Lemercier); a pastoral union in death with the earth in all the rhythms of its seasons as a "*chose naturelle*"; a consolation in the rituals that enact and inscribe elegy and epitaph. In the words of "Gigantomachia": "to look on what war magnified. / It was increased, enlarged, made simple, / Made single, made one. This was not denial. // Each man himself became a giant" (*CPP* 258).

In all these hymns to the fallen soldier, Stevens rejects politics for elegy. He adopts a macro-view over a micro one, namely, that "his [the soldier's] wound is good because life was." Death in war as *chose naturelle* remained for Stevens his abiding consolation. It is as if the poet is saying, "I am fully cognizant of what the soldier's lying in the pool of his own blood means in terms of evil and loss; I do not disguise it. But I choose to transcribe that scene onto the restorative pastoralism of the Grecian urn and the soldier into the timeless gladiator who peacefully sleeps in the rhythms of the earth." By mythologizing the scene of carnage and disentangling it from the immediacy of history that has otherwise consumed its victim, he offers catharsis and his own form of healing. No poet ever made a greater claim upon the power of "esthétique" to challenge "mal." Through the soldier's stoic death, violence for a moment is tamed, suffering finds ease, and the horrific is reshaped into a silent, somewhat eerie beauty. All the literal reality of war remains unchanged except for the poet's only recourse: to relieve its unspeakable pain by giving, even if momentarily, some visionary alternative. Stevens' fallen soldier is his most romantic proposition and projection, and his poetic attempts to metamorphose war's casualties can never succeed absolutely. But neither are they empty or futile gestures.

The Great Depression

In 1936, Stevens surveyed the present rise of Nazism in the wake of World War I: "The pressure of the contemporaneous from the time of the beginning of World War to the present time has been constant and extreme. No one can have lived apart in a happy oblivion. . . . We are preoccupied with events, even when we do not observe them closely. We have a sense of upheaval. We feel threatened. We look from an uncertain present toward a more uncertain future" (*CPP* 788). Coterminous with that decade leading up to World War II was the Great Depression, and Stevens stated outright in a letter in 1936, "From the point of view of social revolution, IDEAS OF ORDER is a book of the most otiose prettiness; and it is probably quite inadequate from any social point of view. However, I am not a propagandist" (*L* 309). Those same misgivings had already been expressed in the first stanza of "A Fading of the Sun" (1933):

> Who can think of the sun costuming clouds
> When all people are shaken
> Or of night endazzled, proud,
> When people awaken
> And cry and cry for help? (*CPP* 112–13)

In this poem Stevens finds that any restoration of "joy" will depend, not upon the "book," but by looking "Within" in order to find the "pillars of the sun, / Supports of night." The poem, however, decrees its solution rather than persuading us of its efficacy. As Longenbach suggests, the poem "concludes too easily" (131)—or too glibly—in posing introspection and inner strength as a solution to circumstances where "the people die" as they "cry and cry for help." "Joy," the poem ends, "lies . . . Within" as unconsecrated bread and wine:

> . . . Within as pillars of the sun,
> Supports of night. The tea,
> The wine is good. The bread,
> The meat is sweet.
> And they will not die.

Perhaps aware of the poem's thinness, Stevens explained it to Latimer in these words: "In A FADING OF THE SUN the point is that, instead of crying for help to God or to one of the gods, we should look to ourselves for help. The exaltation of human nature should take the place of its abasement. Perhaps I ought to say, the sense of its exaltation of human nature should take the place of its abasement. This sounds like a lot of fiddle-dee-dee, and it may be. But if it is, that is probably more true of the way I express it than of the thought itself" (*L* 295–96). Note Stevens' uneasiness ("This sounds like a lot of fiddle-dee-dee") in putting forth these propositions. Resort to such human "exaltation," however inadequately it convinces us here, was the resource that Stevens returned to repeatedly and more successfully in other poems.

In "A Fading of the Sun," the costuming and endazzlings of art seem impotent in the face of such distress. In the first of the sections for Stevens' longest poem, "Owl's Clover" (1935), he presented the victim of economic oppression as an old woman: "She was that tortured one, / So destitute that nothing but herself / Remained and nothing of herself except / A fear too naked for her shadow's shape" (*CPP* 568).

At the bottom of Stevens' social aesthetic is never final defeat but even a kind of unassailable optimism. No defeat is too absolute that it cannot find a palliative in the poet's incantation, whatever the waste that surrounds him. The second part of the poem "Mr. Burnshaw and the Statue" was first published in 1936 in *The New Caravan* and in the Alcestis Press edition of the poem. It was later shortened for inclusion in *The Man with the Blue Guitar and*

Other Poems and retitled "The Statue at the World's End." The social conditions of the mid-1930s are graphically described as part of the "waste":

> There buzzards pile their sticks among the bones
> Of buzzards and eat the bellies of the rich,
> Fat with a thousand butters, and the crows
> Sip the wild honey of the poor man's life. (*CPP* 572)

The poem then defines two kinds of such surrounding "waste":

> And there are the white-maned horses' heads, beyond
> The help of any wind or any sky:
> Parts of the immense detritus of a world
> That is completely waste, that moves from waste
> To waste, out of the hopeless waste of the past
> Into a hopeful waste to come. There even
> The colorless light in which this wreckage lies
> Has faint, portentous lustres, shades and shapes
> Of rose, or what will once more rise to rose. (*CPP* 573)

Asked about these lines in a letter, Stevens explained: "One assumes further that the evolution of what ought to be is not now in its final stages (as all the world supposes), and that the future of the mass is not an end of the future, but that change is incessant. It is a process of passing from hopeless waste to hopeful waste. This is not pessimism. The world is completely waste, but it is a waste always full of portentous lustres" (*L* 367).   It is perhaps in moments when beauty is most remote, most improbable, that it becomes "portentous." Lemercier seems to have had a similar reaction: "A soft sky is in harmony with the orchards where we are at work on trenches [of battle]" (75).

The reference to the present as "waste" inevitably invites a comparison with Eliot's "The Waste Land." Some read that poem as an enactment of hopeless waste and failing to pass beyond it, in spite of Eliot's invocation of the words of the thunder, his collocation of eastern and western asceticism, and his question, "Shall I at least set my lands in order?" These of course would not be Stevens' conduits to a hopeful waste and, upon reading

"The Waste Land" for the first time in 1922, he called it "the supreme cry of despair" that was "Eliot's and not his generation's. Personally, I think it's a bore" (*CPP* 940).

Stevens turned to the poet, the artist, to create the "portentous lustres" that rescued one from hopeless waste and despair. Of course "portentous lustres" and "otiose prettiness" do nothing to relieve unemployment lines, social unrest, and empty bellies, but Stevens never makes that claim. In his comments upon receiving an honorary degree at Bard College in 1951, he concluded, "An awareness of poetic acts may change our sense of the texture of life, but it does not falsify the texture of life" (*CPP* 837). It "does not" because it cannot. At the same time, he holds fast to the ideal that the order imposed by art is its own countermand to general disorder. Seamus Heaney, addressing the political conflict of Northern Ireland in "Frontiers of Writing," speaks of a certain poetic "equivalency" that the artist holds out: "If our given experience is a labyrinth, then its impassability is countered by the poet's imagining some equivalent of the labyrinth and bringing himself and the reader through it" ("Frontiers of Writing" 191). Stevens puts it somewhat differently in one of his "Adagia": "Poetry is a purging of the world's poverty and change and evil and death. It is a present perfecting, a satisfaction in the irremediable poverty of life" (*CPP* 906). Poetry purges poverty as a "satisfaction," but only for the moment: the conditions of poverty remain unrelieved. If Heaney speaks for poetic equivalence, Joseph Riddel has spoken of the originating role of the imagination: "But Stevens is consistent, knowing as he does that poetry dies in the service of politics or morals—knowing, that is, that the role of imagination precedes either and is fundamentally the origin of both" (114).

As the title indicates, "Mozart, 1935" (107–8) is another poem that points to the economic collapse in America, although the Great Depression is never named as such in the poem. (It was first published in the magazine called *Alcestis* in its Spring 1935 issue; "The Idea of Order at Key West" had appeared in the same magazine the previous year.) The poem records outbursts of "angry fear" and "besieging pain." The streets outside are "full of cries." Some even "throw stones upon the roof" because a mysterious "body in rags" is carried down the stairs.[15] In another poem from the same volume (*Ideas of Order*) in which this poem appears, "Farewell to Florida," Stevens bids farewell to the Florida of Key West as he sails to "My north" where a similar scene of social unrest is presented. A "slime of men in crowds" awaits him there, a "return to the violent mind / That is their mind, these men" (*CPP* 98). As Patrick Reddy has noted, "So often in his poems of the mid-1930s, Stevens represents politics as an unwelcome disturbance to the peace, an interruption to the normal flow of creative private life" (272). Also in *Ideas of Order*, the poem "Sad Strains of a Gay Waltz" presents "these sudden mobs of men, // These sudden clouds of faces and arms, / An immense suppression, freed" (*CPP* 100). What can the artist possibly do in such disturbingly nightmarish circumstances?

In a series of commands, "Mozart, 1935" addresses the poet-musician, directing him to take his place at once at the piano. His music must address the urgent social and political conditions that surround him. His injunction is to "Play the present." In the first stanza Stevens lays out the sounds of the present in what appear to be nonsense noises, notably unmusical. Here are the first four lines of the poem:

> Poet, be seated at the piano.
> Play the present, its hoo-hoo-hoo,
> Its shoo-shoo-shoo, its ric-a-nic,
> Its envious cachinnation.

The "ric-a-nic" could be the sounds of the stones hitting the roof, and the "hoo" and "shoo" sounds appear vaguely daunting, perhaps desperate. Stefan Holander identifies the sounds as "sirens, hooting horns, or creaking machinery" (50). In any case, they are pre-verbal sounds and pre-musical sounds that must be absorbed into the transformative art of the poet-musician.

These sounds are important to the poem because the command to "Play the present" is also Stevens' command to himself as a poet-artist. Whatever service or relief a poet like Stevens can offer in 1935 depends upon his ability, not to evade, but to capture the reality of the social circumstances in which he finds himself. "Mozart, 1935" thereby creates its own social stereophony.

In February 1935 Stevens was on a business trip to Florida, a trip he made annually during the late 1920s and 1930s, and each year he met in Florida with Judge Arthur Powell, described by Peter Brazeau as "one of those rare individuals with whom Stevens was comfortable as both poet and businessman" (103). Brazeau reproduces this surviving note from Powell:

In February, 1935, we were at Key West again; and his poem 'Mozart [1935]' . . . was forming in his mind. In the second and third lines, for sound effect, he uses the phrases, 'hoo-hoo-hoo,' 'shoo-shoo-shoo,' and 'ric-a-nic.' I now have in my possession a scrap of brown paper, a piece of a heavy envelope, with this written on it in his handwriting:

'ses hurlements,
ses chucuotments, ses ricaments.
its hoo-hoo-hoo,
Its shoo-shoo-shoo, its ric-a-nic.' [sic] (104)

Stevens' longhand can be difficult to decipher at times or the words may be misspelled, but "*hurlements*" is French for howling or bellowing, and "*ricaments*" is apparently intended as *ricanements*, meaning sneers or sniggers—also, giggles. "*Chucuotments*" is apparently *chuchotement*[s]—or whispers.[16] Though Stevens omitted these three French words from the poem itself, they are part of his original design for an aural representation of the circumstances of 1935. The "*hurlements*" of "howling" is a word picked up later in the poem by "the great wind howling," and the whispers and sniggers also suggest unrest and anger, perhaps even madness. The "envious cachinnation" of line 4 is not referred to in Powell's preserved note, but "cachinnation" of "envious cachinnation" is a Latinate word meaning loud laughter and recalls the word "*ricaments*" (*ricanements*) indicating sneers, giggles, etcetera. When we learn at the end of the poem that "the streets are full of cries," we have already heard them in the phonetics of the poem's earlier lines. The metrically emphatic and prolonged vowels of "oo" ("hoo-hoo-hoo" and "shoo-shoo-shoo") suggest a vaguely childlike, Halloween-like evocation of the ominous, while the plosive consonants of "ric-a-nic" and "cachinnation" make a more noisy clatter, like "stones upon the roof."

Later in the poem Stevens will move dramatically away from these harsh and threatening sounds. Beginning in the fourth stanza, he transforms "you" to "thou" ("Be thou the voice . . ."). The poet-musician's ability to release sorrow is then captured in the softer and more liquid sounds of "By which sorrow is released, / Dismissed, absolved / In a starry placating." And in the music of Mozart.[17]

In his instructions to the poet-musician, the speaker introduces the question that becomes paramount to the poem: what can Mozart's music of the eighteenth century do to help us address the depredations of America in 1935? In answer to this question, I want to propose two contradictory roles that the poem seems to be assigning to Mozart and his music.

The very title of the poem invites a Mozartian relevance to the conditions of 1935 without apparent irony. The poem itself addresses Mozart's work most directly in stanza 3 where two forms frequently adopted by him, the *divertimento* and the *concerto,* are introduced. No specific *divertimento* or *concerto,* however, is named, but the former is identified in the poem as a "lucid souvenir of the past," while the *concerto* is called an "airy dream of the future" and "unclouded."

Mozart's divertimenti are typically set to jaunty and exuberant expression, sometimes incorporating folk tunes and popular dance melodies. Often composed for a special occasion such as a birthday or wedding, they are a tuneful entertainment. They do not typically convey the darker moods of Mozart's other works. They may have as few as two or three movements or as many as thirteen or fourteen, but all are short in duration. They are performed by a chamber ensemble or small orchestra, sometimes using only two or three instruments. Maynard Solomon, a recent biographer of Mozart, has this to say about the importance of this mode in Mozart's development: "Mozart initially established his creative individuality in the great variety of serenades, *serenade-divertimentos,* and related works that he composed to order for his Salzburg patrons and friends. . . . His serenades . . . convey simple moods of tranquillity, contentment, cheerfulness, and grace" (126). If there is a slight tone of derogation in Stevens' speaker's describing the divertimento as a "souvenir" ("That lucid souvenir of the past"), the musical form itself carries with it a certain ephemerality, a work composed for the moment, the souvenir of a holiday.

Mozart's concertos, on the other hand, while they may appear like an "airy dream" or "unclouded," nonetheless are a considerably more complex form than the divertimento. Writing to his father at the age of twenty-six, Mozart described a recently composed triptych: "These concertos[18] are a happy medium between what is too easy and too difficult; they are very brilliant, pleasing to the ear, and natural, without being vapid" (1242). But it is difficult to see in the piano concertos a quality that is in all cases sunny and "unclouded," especially when one considers works with the "Concerto in C Minor" (K491) or the "Concerto in D Minor" (K466), both of which Stevens owned on 78 rpms.[19]

Mozart's own life was often cloudy, even dark. His short life of thirty-five years personally knew great suffering. All his biographers speak of the dominating control of his father, Leopold, who not only nurtured the precociousness of his son's musical genius almost from birth, but, beginning when Mozart was only six, traveled throughout Europe with his prodigy son to exhibit his brilliance and exploit the financial opportunities. Leopold was himself the assistant conductor of the orchestra in Salzburg (deputy *Kapellmeister*); he fought to maintain an iron control over his son's life, blaming, for example, his son for his mother's (and Leopold's wife's) death after she had accompanied her twenty-one-year-old son to Paris, where she unexpectedly died. Leopold protested vehemently and threateningly Mozart's later decision to leave the father's home in Salzburg for Vienna. The rupture with his father and older sister led to their refusal to attend his wedding and a more or less permanent estrangement. Thereafter, Mozart and his wife had six children but suffered the loss of four of them at early ages. For all his musical achievements, he struggled throughout his life to earn a sufficient income to support his sometimes extravagant style of living. He was never able to land a permanent professional sinecure that would provide stability and predictable income for him and his family. In the last years of his life he found himself increasingly burdened by debt and an inability to complete certain of his compositions, occasioning bouts of severe depression. There were periods when his popularity subsided and opportunities for performance all but disappeared. For whatever reasons, after his death he was buried in a pauper's grave, unmarked, in Vienna. He struggled throughout his life with bouts of rheumatic fever and quite possibly died of it. In short, the life of Mozart was frequently plagued with family, financial, health, and creative difficulties. This side of Mozart, which figures dramatically in much of his work, is unacknowledged in "Mozart, 1935," but, one could argue, it is surely implied in the very reference to Mozart's name and all that it evokes. Stevens' poem even sets up implicit parallels between the economic and social conditions of 1935 and the life of Mozart in the eighteenth century. For both eras it was a time of "besieging pain." In addition, Solomon reports that, at the time of Mozart's death in the month of snowy December, "People gathered in a vigil outside the house, weeping and wailing, and fluttering their handkerchiefs to express their grief and condolence" (494), a detail perhaps carried over into the disturbances of

1935: "The snow is falling / And the streets are full of cries." There is no known event in which stones were thrown upon Mozart's roof, but at the time of his death his was "a body in rags,"—being "sewn into a linen sack" (Solomon 495) for common burial without a coffin.

Turning to the music itself, Solomon notes this progression in Mozart's "most characteristic adagios and andantes": "a calm, contemplative, or ecstatic condition gives way to a troubled state—is penetrated by hints of storm, dissonance, anguish, anxiety, danger—and this in turn is succeeded by a restoration of the status quo ante, now suffused with and transformed by the memory of the turbulent interlude" (187). Works like the A-Minor Piano Sonata are especially illustrative of this pattern. One can assume that Stevens was aware of this complex background in the life and work of Mozart and saw in his work a model for how poetry and music can address human suffering and create a surcease from it. Mozart survives in 1935 ("He was young, and we, we are old") precisely because and not in spite of these powers. The final stanza begins with the line "We may return to Mozart," as if, in fact, we *should* return to Mozart.

These connections to Mozart in the conditions of 1935 notwithstanding, the fact remains that Stevens' poem at no point explicitly identifies the dark side of Mozart's life and work. Stevens' reaction to Mozart's "lucid souvenir of the past," "airy dream of the future," and "unclouded concerto" reminds us of the way Schubert remembered him: "As from afar the magic notes of Mozart's music still gently haunt me. . . . They show us in the darkness of this life a bright, clear, lovely distance, for which we hope with confidence. O Mozart, immortal Mozart, how many, oh how endlessly many such comforting perceptions of a brighter and better life hast thou brought to our souls" (60). In a biography of the composer by Marcia Davenport that first appeared in 1932, just before the writing of Stevens' poem and perhaps read by the poet at the time, she makes a similar commentary:

> The familiar conception of temperament—the torn hair, the blazing eye, the groaning, the throwing of manuscript into the fire—is totally inapplicable to him. This quietness of spirit has led some critics to interpret his gentleness as weakness and to characterize his music as superficial. Much of the world's education in music has come from the

romantics, in whose eyes rebellion burned bright and who hurled their private lives into their scores. Mozart lived before they did, in a much more objective age. Neither in his life nor in his music was he intent upon proving anything. Pleasure is the first, most obvious reaction to his work. He intended it to be so, for he believed that music should delight. (80–81)

Heretofore, I have been suggesting how the life and work of Mozart accommodates the poet-musician of Stevens' poem, why Mozart's music must be played and heard in the America of 1935. It is this very quality of pleasure and delight that Stevens' characterization of Mozart seems to be noting, but from which—and I now want to suggest a different reading of the poem—he wishes to distance himself. Instead of the consolation of Mozart one can argue that his music represents an irrelevancy. In short, the year 1935 and the name of Mozart are in tension, if not opposition.

In his one commentary from his letters, Stevens says rather surprisingly: "Mozart is out. It is curious that I have never been able to go for Mozart. He makes me as nervous as a French poodle. I realize that every now and then he gets away from himself, but most of the time he seems to me merely a mechanical toy. Beethoven is my meat" (L 604). The music of Mozart as mechanical or not, we know that Stevens possessed thirty-nine recordings of Mozart's music, including nine of the concertos and almost all of the operas. (Stegman 90–91). Why, I think we may ask, would the poet who finds Mozart a "mechanical toy" and sees him as unable for the most part to get away from himself—as if he were self-contained and fixed upon his own mechanical technique—be recommending him in this poem, particularly under such disturbing social circumstances?

If we note that the speaker of Stevens' poem commands the poet-musician to "Play the present," the works of Mozart are identified in stanza 3 as not of the present: "souvenir of the past" and "airy dream of the future." In this light, Mozart's compositions are not here being directly presented as models for the musician of the 1930s in the United States—quite the contrary. The harsh "ric-a-nic" and triple "hoo" and "shoo," the "envious cachinnation" of the present are incompatible with such dreaminess and airiness.

The poem, however, sets us up to expect that Mozart's music will provide "the voice of this besieging pain" of the present. The title has brought the composer into juxtaposition with the present (though they are separated, perhaps significantly, by a comma), and the first line, "Poet, be seated at the piano," lures us into thinking of a Mozart piano concerto about to be performed on command. The poet-musician practices Mozartian "arpeggios" in the second stanza. It is not until the third stanza that the dissociation between Mozart and the present begins to be suggested.

Even the beginning of the final stanza, "We may return to Mozart," can be taken as an invitation to seek him out. It is possible to read "may return," however, not so much as "We have permission to return to Mozart" or "must return to Mozart" as "We may be *tempted* to return to Mozart" and thereby lose our way. The following line, "He was young, and we, we are old," points perhaps to Mozart's early death at the age of thirty-five or to his personality, often given to childish behavior and a willful innocence of the responsibilities of adulthood. "We," however, those living in 1935, are "old." The present circumstances are hardly innocent or childish; it is as if life itself in this time of calamitous turmoil has become burdensome, leaving us bent and stooped in age.

If, as I am suggesting here, Stevens rejects the works of Mozart in the poem that bears his name, then Stevens is insisting that art in the time of social cataclysm must not divert itself in divertimenti, must not succumb to "airy dream" or "unclouded concerto." It must contain "the voice of angry fear." It must be a part of the "system" of the world as it is. In this case, the voices outside must be subsumed in the music of the artist, not shunned. Only by doing so can the afflicted of the present find a release from their infirmity:

> Be thou the voice,
> Not you. Be thou, be thou
> The voice of angry fear,
> The voice of this besieging pain.
>
> Be thou that wintry sound
> As of the great wind howling,
> By which sorrow is released,
> Dismissed, absolved
> In a starry placing.[20]

The poet-musician cannot correct the circumstances of social upheaval. He does not declaim a programmatic poetry of social reform. Instead, he is commanding that the social ruptures and traumas must be experienced in the music itself. Such "placating" of sorrow may be only momentary, but the need for its consolation is so great that the artist must immediately "be seated" (a command heard three times in the poem, including the first and final lines).

Stevens himself said of the poem that it was a "very slight suggestion" of what he hoped to set out in its stanzas, "the status of the poet in a disturbed society," and this was a matter he held "very much at heart" (L 292). Whether the music of Mozart is being commended or condemned (and I am presenting the case for both readings), the important fact is that the poet-musician must connect his "arpeggios" to the "piercing chord" of the economic conditions that surround him in the twentieth century; only by being such a musical "voice" can he expect to release sorrow or dismiss it or absolve it. Stevens would go on to write many versions on this theme of the inextricable relation between art and anguish even if it could otherwise be taken as a pallidly insufficient response. And, as we have seen, there were moments when even he was inclined "to sympathize with one's more unsympathetic critics" when confronted with the overpowering actuality of the world. At the same time, he saw no other role for the poet in such moments except to offer his readers "the piercing chord" of poetry itself, resistant to propaganda and unencumbered with external ideology.

The Politician

If the solution to social upheaval lay in politics, and politics lay in the hands of politicians, why, one might ask, did Stevens seem so indifferent to such recourse? Stevens followed closely the course of politics in his lifetime and was a faithful voter in elections from the year 1900, when he had just turned twenty-one and voted for Bryan over McKinley. He certainly entertained political opinions, sometimes aligned with the left, sometimes the right. In 1935, he hoped, "I am headed left," though not the "ghastly left" (L 286) associated with the radicals who were identified with the New Masses journal. In 1940 he professed that "I believe in doing everything practically possible to improve the condition of the workers," and "I regret that we have not experimented a little more extensively in public ownership of public utilities" (L 351). Eight years later, however, he resented the assessments of the income tax, whatever its social applications. President Truman, for example, is "one of those politicians who keep themselves in office by taxing a small class for the benefit of a large class. If I had been able to save during recent years what I have been obliged to pay in taxes, I should be much more secure and so would my family" (L 623).

Politicians and poets had separate roles. In a note written for the *Yale Literary Magazine* in 1946, Stevens noted that the poet "absorbs the general life: the public life. The politician is absorbed by it. The poet is individual. The politician is general." The politician is bound to a political network while the poet remains "individual": "As individual he must remain free. The politician expects everyone to be absorbed as he himself is absorbed. This expectation is part of the sabotage of the individual. The second phase of the poet's problem, then, is to maintain his freedom, the only condition in which he can hope to produce significant poetry" (CPP 814).

Stevens' distrust of politicians dates to his teen years. In the jottings of his journal when he was nineteen, he contemplated his own future, wanting more than anything else a literary life. Instead, he rebuked himself by writing that he "*must* make concessions to others"; he must come down to the level of "a bustling merchant, a money-making lawyer, a soldier, a politician," and in doing so he might have to be "if unavoidable a pseudo-villain in the drama," but he would preserve himself "a decent person in private life" (SP 53). Stevens, of course, elected the course of the "money-making lawyer," even as he accommodated the "politician" as an equally necessary compromise.

Distrust of political leaders, nonetheless, spills over into Stevens' poetry. "Anecdote of Canna" (CPP 44) was a poem written during the First World War after Stevens "was walking around the terraces of the Capitol in Washington" (L 464). In the canna blooming in those terraces he imagines the dreams "of / X, the mighty thought, the mighty man," presumably President Wilson himself or some such surrogate. The point of the poem seems to be that Wilson and politicians of his ilk go about in a trance, in "thought that wakes / In sleep" and "may never meet another thought / Or thing." The speaker's commander-in-chief in wartime is an idle dreamer.

In "The Glass of Water" Stevens presents himself playfully as "fat Jocundus," but he is a worrying Jocundus as he "continue[s] to contend with one's ideas." His mental fidgets probe a physical world in stanza 1, a metaphorical one in stanza 2, a poetic one in stanza 3, and, finally, a political one in the last stanza, and I want to point only to the last stanza here. America is still, in the words of the poem, "a village of the indigenes." It still defines itself as "dogs and dung." Not even poetry is an antidote for such a setting. Instead, we have only "the politicians / Playing cards" among the indigenes, almost certainly a glancing allusion to Franklin Roosevelt, who was famous for his poker games (*CPP* 182).[21] The mere juxtaposition of the politicians and the indigenes mandates a satirical dismissal of the former. Roosevelt is also vaguely satirized as the "President" who "ordains the bee to be / Immortal" in "Notes toward a Supreme Fiction."[22] By ordaining permanence in that part of the poem entitled "It Must Change," he immediately draws suspicion. The canto concludes as spring "vanishes the scraps of winter," creating a "beginning, not resuming." The president seems an obsolete and rather silly creature in comparison with the "lovers at last accomplishing / Their love" with the arrival of the "new-come bee" (*CPP* 337–38) in spring.

The pseudo-politician is also satirized in "The Man with the Blue Guitar" in Canto X ("A pagan in a varnished car" [*CPP* 139]). Though the poem was written during the Roosevelt administration, Stevens later explained the canto with a reference to Harry Truman. Instead of the ideal "major man" figure we have the president who had just left office at the time Stevens wrote his letter: "He would not be the typical hero taking part in parades, (columns red with red-fire, bells tolling, tin cans, confetti) in whom actually no one believes as a truly great man, but in whom everybody pretends to believe, someone completely outside of the intimacies of profound faith, a politician, a soldier, Harry Truman as god. *This second-rate creature is the adversary.* I address him but with hostility, hoo-ing the slick trombones" (*L* 789).

In the light of these suspicions and aspersions, how, we might ask, could the Stevens who was consistently suspicious of American political leaders identify himself as "pro-Mussolini personally" (*L* 289) in a letter to Latimer dated October 31, 1935? Stevens himself does not provide a detailed answer. It is worth taking a moment, I think, to locate that response in the 1930s. Although Mussolini and his Blackshirts had consolidated his absolute power by eliminating democracy in Italy and withdrawing many freedoms from the

Italian people, he enjoyed immense popularity and the favor of King Victor Emmanuel III, who had named him prime minister. During the years of economic depression, Mussolini had made "the trains run on time" by increasing grain production, reducing unemployment, and successfully converting marshlands into farmlands and new towns. In 1934, he had forced Hitler to back down on his plan to seize Austria after Nazi gunmen had assassinated the Austrian chancellor. As Richard B. Lyttle states, "Mussolini, emerging as a hero in the world press, won praise from England and grudging admiration from France" (106).[23] When Stevens declared his sympathies for Mussolini in 1935, the Italian dictator had not yet declared his alliance with Franco at the beginning of the Spanish Civil War the next year. Mussolini's alliance with Hitler unofficially began only after his visit to Germany in 1937.

Just days before Stevens' pro-Mussolini sentence to Latimer, however, the fascist government had initiated its invasion of present-day Ethiopia, then called Abyssinia. The conquest was completed seven months later. Latimer, Stevens' correspondent, must have challenged his endorsement of Mussolini in the light of such expansionist demonstrations; two weeks later Stevens felt compelled to explain. "While it is true that I have spoken sympathetically of Mussolini, all my sympathies are the other way." The "other way," in this case, is defined in Stevens' baldly racist rhetoric, "with the coons and boa-constrictors" of Ethiopia. With considerable prescience, however, he goes on to foresee the menace of Mussolini's expanding power: "A man would have to be very thick-skinned not to be conscious of the pathos of Ethiopia or China, or one of these days, if we are not careful, of this country. But that Mussolini is right, practically, has certainly a great deal to be said for it" (L 295). Three and a half years later, when the very threat of Mussolini that he had foreseen had become manifest, he wrote to another correspondent of the relentless pressure of "Hitler and Mussolini so drastically on one's nerves constantly" (L 337). Whatever Stevens meant by saying to Latimer that he was "pro-Mussolini personally," he was quick to qualify that claim two weeks later, and, not long afterward, to disavow it altogether. The history of Stevens' response to Mussolini follows a pattern similar to that of Yeats's own response to the fascist leader—idealization, disenchantment, and then disavowal. In Stevens' case, he must have found his inveterate distrust of politicians in general reinforced in the wake of that disenchantment.

Because of his disillusion and distrust of politicians, Stevens turned away from the world of contemporary politics and created his own solution, an ideal "hero" who would be imaged as a composite political leader-soldier-poet. Northrop Frye, without specific reference to Stevens, has defined such arrogation of god-like powers to human avatars: "The god, whether traditional deity, glorified hero, or apotheosized poet, is the central image that poetry uses in trying to convey the sense of unlimited power in a humanized form" (120). Over and over, Stevens returned in his poetry to the hero *extraordinaire*, "major man," a figure who would possess nothing of "humanism nor Nietzschean shadows" (*L* 485), and be "beyond / Reality" but "composed thereof" (*CPP* 294). As Stevens explained in 1953, looking back to "The Man with the Blue Guitar," published sixteen years earlier, he could not in that poem affirm a "truly great man" as a political leader. He added, "The cheap glory of the false hero, not a true man of the imagination, made me sick at heart" (*L* 789). He seems to be suggesting that only the inventions of the imagination might devise a believable hero.

Not a politician but a poet, the hero would write the "supreme fiction" on which we could securely base our lives and live in community. He would be "fictive man created out of men" (*CPP* 294). In another poem he is called the "impossible possible philosophers' man" (*CPP* 226). This eschatological figure of an indefinite future was of course an ideal whom Stevens could only inscribe "notes toward." To some social critics, such imaginary projections and idealized yearnings will seem fraught with problems. Such an epitome-man or composite of the ideal is the invention of a dreamer who chooses to bypass immediate political urgencies as he looks toward an impossible poet-savior. Besides, the figure himself may share something of "the common man" but will possess masculine extravagances and patriarchal stereotypes. Here is part of his depiction in "Examination of the Hero in a Time of War":

> If the hero is not a person, the emblem
> Of him, even if Xenophon, seems
> To stand taller than a person stands, has
> A wider brow, large and less human
> Eyes and bruted ears: the man-like body
> Of a primitive. (*CPP* 247)

Perhaps aware of the reductiveness of such a description, Stevens says in the same poem: "It is not an image. It is a feeling. / There is no image of the hero" (*CPP* 248). But in another place in the poem he invites us to join in his projection by making just such an image: "Unless we believe in the hero, what is there / To believe. . . . / Devise. Make him of mud, / For every day. In a civiler manner, / Devise, devise. . . ." (*CPP* 246). Whatever his incarnation, the hero will think for us or summarize our thought; he will write the poems on which we can base our lives; he will contain by some kind of shared inclusion all of our humanity—even if he remained vaguely penciled upon tomorrow's horizon. Yet, he was one to whom Stevens returned in many poems from "The Man with the Blue Guitar" in 1937 to "An Ordinary Evening in New Haven" in 1949, the very years in which his disenchantment with the politicians on the American and world stage was most acute. He was surely aware that his variously outlined projections of the hero were tentative gropings, insufficient at best, another "fiction" we are asked to "believe," and, at worst, impossible to render creditably.

When Stevens was once asked in a questionnaire, "*Do you take your stand with any political or politico-economic party or creed?*" he responded tersely, "I am afraid that I don't" (*CPP* 771). Against the politician and his political creed Stevens posed the poem itself, its own instrument of order and peace. In one letter he summarizes a personal politics of poetry: "If poetry introduces order, and every competent poem introduces order, and if order means peace, even though that particular peace is an illusion, is it any less an illusion than a good many other things that everyone high and low now-a-days concedes to be no longer of any account? Isn't a freshening of life a thing of consequence?" (*L* 293). In the midst of war, for example, the poet can induce an authentic peace.

Suggesting that poetry introduces an order that is also an illusion, Stevens also asks if it is "any less an illusion than a good many other things," including ideologies themselves, one might presume. Louis Althusser makes this very point: "However, while admitting that they [ideologies] do not correspond to reality, i.e. that they constitute an illusion, we admit that they do make allusion to reality, and that they need only be 'interpreted' to discover the reality of the world behind their imaginary representation of that world (ideology = *illusion/allusion*)" (241).

Whether Stevens' social poetry "balances out," in the words of Heaney, with his own historical situation is a question that no doubt will remain disputed. Put beside poets like Wilfred Owen; or the early Auden; or the poets of the Harlem Renaissance like Claude McKay and their successors like Gwendolyn Brooks; or Robert Lowell or Adrienne Rich, Stevens can be made to appear reticent and refractory.

But three points about Stevens must be assayed in making these judgments and have not adequately been weighed in the past. First, he was never an apolitical poet; he never saw his poetry as indifferent to the great social struggles of the first half of the century. To be apolitical was to write "rubbish," as he knew at the age of nineteen.

Second, political leaders, political parties, and political ideologies were too fractured, convulsive, or compromised to merit the blind endorsement of the poem, which is not to say that they could not merit the criticism and support of the poet.

And finally, for the purposes of the poem itself, individual survival in a time of cataclysm depends on inner resources of the spirit as much as public proposals socially broadcast. Of Marianne Moore's "romanticism," he once wrote, "It means in a time like our own of violent feelings, equally violent feelings and the most skilful expression of the genuine" (*CPP* 778). If Stevens' poetry is one of escapism, it is not an escapism of evasion but one of recompense. He participates in the suffering of those around him, whether it be the death of a soldier or the hunger of an unemployed laborer. But the voice is not directed toward redressing the system of oppression but reducing the spiritual poverty of all such victims and all who mourn them. Yeats once wrote, "The mind of man has two kinds of shepherds: the poets who rouse and trouble, the poets who hush and console" ("A Scholar Poet" 102). Stevens clearly belongs with the latter.

Such poets, Stevens believed, could remain a public voice without compromising their independence as poets. In response to a question posed in 1946 about the greatest problem facing the young writer in America at the time, he contrasted the poet with the politician. As stated earlier, the poet "absorbs the general life: the public life," but, unlike the politician, he is not "absorbed by it." "This does not mean," Stevens went on to say, "that [the poet] is a private figure. . . . He must remain individual. . . . The poet's problem, then, is to maintain his freedom, the only condition in which he can hope to produce significant poetry" (L 526).

Beauty's freshenings for Stevens had their own autonomies and owed no subservience to anything beyond their own gratifications. There was an urge within him, therefore, to shelter and enshrine beauty from the disruptions surrounding it. But Stevens learned at an early age to redirect such isolations away from what Santayana had called "poetic selfishness." Far from a disinterested aesthete, he saw his task as a "morality": "The morality of the poet's radiant and productive atmosphere is the morality of the right sensation" (CPP 679). Knowing when by right sensation to embrace the true and reject the false—or, in another mode, to embrace the falsity of the imagination as the "power of the mind over the possibilities of things" (CPP 726)—was his poetic morality. But there was also the social extension of such an ethos. As I have noted earlier, when he asks himself in "The Noble Rider and the Sound of Words" what is the "social, that is to say sociological or political, obligation" of the poet, he responds, "He has none" (CPP 659). But the poet has another obligation that is no less urgent: "I think that his function is to make his imagination theirs and that he fulfills himself only as he sees his imagination become the light in the minds of others. His role, in short, is to help people to live their lives" (CPP 660–61). This is a powerful and consequential vocation, not to be brushed aside as socially irrelevant. The poet, he concludes, "fulfills himself," not in the poem that is aloof from history, but by making his private apprehensions socially accessible in the moment of historical calamity. As he said in a lecture in 1936, "The poet cannot profess the irrational as the priest professes the unknown. The poet's role is broader, because he must be possessed, along with everything else, by the earth and by men in their earthy implications" (CPP 792). Six years before his death, in a lecture delivered at Yale, "Effects of Analogy," he pointed to the dangers of the "ivory tower": "The ivory tower was offensive if the man who lived in it wrote, there, of himself for himself." But it was not offensive, he added, if his concentration as a poet "happened to be the community and other people, and nothing else. It may be that the poet's congenital subject is precisely the community and other people" (CPP 718). These quotations echo the words he recorded in his undergraduate journal: "Art must fit with other things; it must be part of the system of the world" (SP 38).

One might call this an appropriate place to end this essay as a summary of Stevens' social poetics. Yet he found himself never entirely at ease with the final manifestations of his poetics in his poems. To the steady march of catastrophic events that seemed never to subside during the first half of the century and when he was writing, he made his responses according to his own terms, even if not always consistently.

As he was preparing the poems that would appear in *Ideas of Order* at the time of the Great Depression, he addressed his ambivalences to his editor. In the letter, he moves back and forth on the issue of poetic relevancy and then, having given voice to each side, declares for himself an ultimate harmony and balance between life and literature. But it is Stevens' lingering uncertainty about such harmony that is registered here: "But we live in a different time [from the poems of *Harmonium*], and life means a good deal more to us now-a-days than literature does. In the period of which I have just spoken, I thought literature meant most. Moreover, I am not so sure that I don't think exactly the same thing now, but, unquestionably, I think at the same time that life is the essential part of literature" (*L* 288).

As late as 1952 he remained troubled by some lingering sense of inadequacy. To Barbara Church he wrote:

> There is going to be a *Selected Poems* published in London shortly. I returned the proofs yesterday. The book seemed rather slight and small to me—and unbelievably irrelevant to our actual world. It may be that all poetry has seemed like that at all times and always will. The close approach to reality has always been the supreme difficulty of any art: the communication of actuality, as [poetics?], has been not only impossible, but has never appeared to be worth while because it loses identity as the event passes. Nothing in the world is deader than yesterday's political (or realistic) poetry. Nevertheless the desire to combine the two things, poetry and reality, is a constant desire. (*L* 760)

How to make that combination bedeviled Stevens. He never completely escaped the fear and frustration of being "irrelevant to our actual world," even as the mere "communication of [political] actuality" was a temptation to which he would not succumb. As a result, in writing the poetry he did, he knew the risks he was taking and the exposure to censure.

Stevens seems never to have resolved to his complete satisfaction the ambivalence we have noted in his journal entry written at the age of nineteen: how to write a poetry that justified itself as a "service, a food . . . to perpetuate inspiration" and a poetry that also "must be part of the system of the world." To attain such a balance became for him an evolving apology for the purposes of poetry generally. The Northern Irish poet Michael Longley has spoken of the ultimate obligation of the poet to his contemporary society in these terms, terms which summarize succinctly Stevens' poetic profile:

> I would insist that poetry is a normal human activity, its proper concern all of the things that happen to people. Though the poet's first duty must be to imagination, he has other obligations—and not just as a citizen. He would be inhuman if he did not respond to tragic events in his own community, and a poor artist if he did not seek to endorse that response imaginatively. (In O'Driscoll 96)

Stevens knew that the stakes were high for his own poetry and for art itself. As we have been noting in poems and in prose, he consistently disdained, at one extreme, a poetry that was merely "sensuous for the sake of sensuousness," even as he refused to subordinate his work to immediate and overt political diagnoses at the other extreme. Resisting both of these polarities, his poetry of an aesthetic middle ground retains its unsettled inconclusiveness but also makes him nuanced and *sui generis* among the poets of his generation. What I think has not been sufficiently recognized is the degree to which Stevens contended with these ambivalences for over forty years and in poem after poem; in that sense, no poet of his time was more political.

4

THE MUSIC OF THE POEM

Style and Prosody

When Wallace Stevens was fifteen and vacationing with his two brothers, he sent home an account of his older brother's wooing in a letter to his mother: "At present he is on the top of the house with his Rosalie . . . and while they together bask[,] Buck's kaleidescopic [*sic*] feelings have inspired the keen, splattering, tink-a-tink-tink-tink-tink-a-a-a that are gamboling off the hackneyed strings of his quivering mandolin" (*L* 6). Those tinks of his brother's mandolin are here replayed in the younger sibling's arch and bemused commentary. Fourteen years later, when Stevens was doing some courting himself, he sent off to his future wife another account of his own delight in oral expressiveness:

> Bechtel told me a good story to-night. It was about a Pennsylvania Dutchman that went to the World's Fair. When he had been there a day he wrote a post-card to his wife; and this is what he said:
>
> > Dear Maria:-I-yi-yi-yi-yi! I-yi-yi-yi-yi!
> > I-yi-yi-yi-yi!   Sam.
>
> That's the best story I've heard for a long time. (*L* 784)

Both of these accounts occur years before Stevens began writing his modernist poetry, but they anticipate the later poet's irrepressible pleasure in the music of words and the role of those sounds in the style that he made uniquely his own.

In a certain sense, when we turn from a consideration of the poetry of

Stevens as embodying the social and political contexts that gave rise to many of his poems to a focus upon the coalescing quality of sounds and music within the poems themselves we might be said to be moving in an entirely different direction. But of course for Stevens there was never such a divergence. No poem for him consisted solely in its paraphrased content apart from its unique expressiveness.

Pleasure in prosody, indulged so openly by Stevens in these early letters, has sometimes escaped the notice of his readers. Seamus Heaney has spoken of the "magical incantation" of poetry, its "power of sound to bind our minds' and bodies' apprehensions within an acoustic complex" ("Sounding Auden" 109). Our reading of poetry is sometimes reluctant to acknowledge the power of spoken language to create just such a binding: we are quick to call it subversive, an insulation from the greater issues of our immediate history, even to dismiss it as decadent. Yet, speaking of such basic pleasure in reading poetry, Stevens once exclaimed, "People ought to like poetry the way a child likes snow" (L 349). And poets ought to write poetry, he suggests in "The Irrational Element in Poetry," with an equal spontaneity: "You can compose poetry in whatever form you like. If it seems a seventeenth-century habit to begin lines with capital letters, you can go in for the liquid transitions of greater simplicity; and so on. It is not that nobody cares. It matters immensely. The slightest sound matters. The most momentary rhythm matters. You can do as you please, yet everything matters. . . . You have somehow to know the sound that is the exact sound; and you do in fact know, without knowing how" (CPP 789–90).

The reader of Stevens comes to recognize certain traits of speech, sound, and rhythm that, by the frequency of their occurrence, become notably "Stevensian." Here are a few among those that I have noted:

1. *elements of apposition* in which the elements (words, phrases, clauses) move outward and centrifugally, at times ironically, to represent the "rapidity of thought" (L 319)

2. *compressed parataxis within one or two lines:*
   "'The House Was Quiet and the World Was Calm'" (CPP 311)
   "Nothing that is not there and the nothing that is." (8)

"The world is ugly, / And the people are sad." (69)
"'God Is Good. It Is a Beautiful Night'" (255)
"The rock cannot be broken. It is the truth." (324)

3. play on *puns*, especially words such as: apart, lie, sense, nothing, eye, mere, cry, etc.

4. *titles of comic and reductive surprise* by elements of internal opposition or usurpation:
    "The Emperor of Ice-Cream." (*CPP* 50)
    "Hymn from a Watermelon Pavilion" (71)
    "Saint John and the Back-Ache" (375)
    "Lytton Strachey, Also, Enters into Heaven" (564)
    "Bad Money At The Six O'Clock Mass," (#243, "From Pieces of Paper,"
        Lensing, *A Poet's Growth* [180])
    "Naked And Playing The Harp," (# 41, "From Pieces of Paper," Lensing, *A
        Poet's Growth* [168])

5. frequency of *titles beginning with "of" and "on"* that sometimes make for genitive constructions that introduce certain ambiguities:
    "Of the Surface of Things" (*CPP* 45)
    "Of the Manner of Addressing Clouds" (44)
    "Of Hartford in a Purple Light" (208)
    "On an Old Horn" (210)
    "Of Modern Poetry" (218)
    "On the Adequacy of Landscape" (221)
    "Of Bright & Blue Birds & the Gala Sun" (224)
    "Of Mere Being" (476)

6. *nonsense words and sounds*
    "Ti-lill-o!" (*CPP* 9)
    "ai-yi-yi . . . ai-yi-yi" (146)
    "Such tink and tank and tunk-a-tunk-tunk" (47)
    "Ha-eé-me . . . Ha-eé-me . . . Ha eé-me . . . tip-tap-tap . . . Ha-eé-me" (295)
    "da da doo" (215)

7. *full rhymes, part rhymes, repetition rhymes, stress rhymes* irregularly distributed but strategically situated:

> *End words of tercets* (Stevens' preferred stanzaic form) that modify or
> displace terza rima: from "Poesie Abrutie": field, fields, hell // are,
> Februar, Februar // cloaked, snow, go // green, itself, sheen (*CPP* 268)

> Prominence of *internal rhymes, part rhymes, and homonyms* within a
> stanza and at times within a single line:

> "But it was she and not the sea we heard." ("The Idea of Order at Key
> West," 105).

> "The President ordains the bee to be." ("Notes toward a Supreme Fic-
> tion, 337).

> "Her green mind made the world around her green. / The queen is an
> example . . . This green queen." ("Description without Place," 296)

8. *Repetition of words,* especially in a poem's conclusion:

> "While the domes resound with chant involving chant." ("Ghosts as
> Cocoons," *CPP* 99)

> "Completed in a completed scene, speaking / Their parts as in a youthful
> happiness" ("Credences of Summer,"326)

> "Nothing that is not there and the nothing that is." ("The Snow Man," 8)

> "And the giant ever changing, living in change." ("A Primitive Like an
> Orb," 380)

> "The river motion, the drowsy motion of the river R." ("An Old Man
> Asleep," 427)

9. *repetition of single words from line to line* and thereby propelling the whole of the poem:

> "Autumn Refrain" (*CPP* 129)
> gone
> gone, sorrows
> sorrows, gone, moon, moon
> moon
> measureless measures, bird
> name, bird, name, nameless
> never, never

stillness, gone, still
still, resides
residuum
never, never, hear, bird
stillness, key
stillness, key.

"The House Was Quiet and the World Was Calm" (*CPP* 311)
house, quiet, world, calm
reader, book, summer night
book
house, quiet, world, calm
book
reader, leaned, page
Wanted, lean, wanted
book, true
summer night, perfection
house, quiet
part, meaning, part
perfection,
world, calm, truth, calm, world
meaning.
calm, summer, night
reader, leaning, reading.

10. The *constant reconfigurations of metaphor*—affirming its seemingly infinite adaptability so that even when for Stevens metaphor must be dismantled (as in many of the poems of winter) it remains irrepressible.

11. grammatical function of an *unreferenced or vaguely referenced "it"* metrically unstressed and followed by a verb-copula:
   "If it was only the dark voice of the sea. . . ." (*CPP* 105)
   "It is the tower of all the world." (323)
   "It is desire at the end of winter, when // It observes the effortless weather turning blue. . . ." (330)

"It is posed and it is posed." (182)

"It might and might have been." (346)

"It is a kind of total grandeur at the end." (434)

12. *Rhetorical strategies of desire:* "it may be," "the longed for," "the more than," "as if," "if only."

13. *Multiple perspectives:* seeing at an angle: thirteen ways, variations, notes-toward, prologues, versions, extracts, landscapes, contrary theses, repetitions, this as including that, etc.

As John Serio has said, "Rhetorical gestures constitute the transformative magic of his poetry" (xviii). These characteristics, and of course others, make for a style that is both jocund and monitory; nimble and full of caprice and wit; supple in the mode of unstructured thought—and singing! Stevens' poems consistently sing, but variously.

Rhythm and diction, separated out in the two parts of this essay, are always complementary for Stevens as aspects of verbal soundings. Once he began to move on from his earliest experiments, he quickly moved to adapt or violate "rules" for the sake of the poem's stylistic effect—never subordinating the latter to the former.

> The truth is that there comes a time
> When we can mourn no more over music
> That is so much motionless sound.
>
> There comes a time when the waltz
> Is no longer a mode of desire, a mode
> Of revealing desire and is empty of shadows.

Stevens was acutely aware, as these lines from "Sad Strains of a Gay Waltz" (*CPP* 100–101) suggest, that he was writing at a time in which the music of poetry was being transformed. "No longer a mode of desire," the waltz has become a cliché, but the need for a new mode of revealing desire is urgently pressed. Somewhat surprisingly, it was to Eliot that Stevens turned to illustrate his new "music." Quoting several lines from "Rhapsody on a Windy Night" ("'A washed-out smallpox cracks her face, / Her hand twists a paper rose, / That smells of dust and old Cologne, / She is alone / With all the old nocturnal smells / That cross and cross across her brain.'") Stevens commends the rhymes at "irregular intervals" and irregular rhythms "intensely cadenced":

> This is a specimen of what is meant by music today. It contains rhymes at irregular intervals and it is intensely cadenced. But yesterday, or the day before, the time from which the use of the word 'music' in relation to poetry has come down to us, music meant something else. It meant metrical poetry with regular rhyme schemes repeated stanza after stanza. All of the stanzas were alike in form. As a result of this, what with the repetitions of the beats of the lines, and the constant and recurring harmonious sounds, there actually was a music. But with the disappearance of all this, the use of the word 'music' in relation to poetry is as I said a moment ago a bit old hat: anachronistic. Yet the passage from Eliot was musical. It is simply that there has been a change in the nature of what we mean by music. (*CPP* 719–20)

"Sad Strains of a Gay Waltz," first published in 1935, followed a long period of gestation, of trial and error, in which Stevens moved slowly but steadily toward his own new mode. Starting with a series of sonnets that were written and published while he was a student at Harvard, he began under the tutelage of Keats, Wordsworth, Sidney, and Rossetti. Other exercises by Stevens, not sonnets, betrayed the imitation of Herrick, the poet of the *Rubáiyát*, and others. Later, Stevens remembered, "When I was here at Harvard, a long time ago, it was a commonplace to say that all the poetry had been written and all the paintings painted" (*CPP* 783).

Only in his poem "Ballade of the Pink Parasol," published just before leaving Cambridge, does the twenty-year-old Stevens break out of his inherited conventions. Here is the second stanza:

> Where in the pack is the dark spadille
> With scent of lavender sweet,
> That never was held in the mad quadrille,

And where are the slippered feet?
Ah! we'd have given a pound to meet
The card that wrought our fall,
The card none other of all could beat—
But where is the pink parasol? (*CPP* 496)

The poem's inventive brio lies not in its meter, a swaying back and forth between tetrameters and trimeters, nor in its sometimes awkward syntax ("card none other of all could beat"), nor in its simplistic rhymes. Rather, the young Stevens has discovered that colors (lavender, yellow, tan, pink) can be applied as thickly as paint on a canvas, and words can be selected for their sounds (spadille, quadrille, calash, sedan, etc.) and infuse the poem with a bold audacity that marks the poem out from all his other apprentice work. The "dark spadille," for example, derives from the Spanish *espada* (sword) and refers to the highest trump card in a given card game; the pink parasol would be such a trump. The "mad quadrille" also derives from a Spanish word, *caudrilla*, referring to a single knight in a group of four engaged in a tournament, or to a square dance, or to a carousel. The card game is likened to such a tournament. But, because of the misplaced parasol, the spadille "never was held" in the quadrille—in spite of the rhyme that otherwise draws them together.

What were Stevens' successors to "Ballade of the Pink Parasol"? They would not come until poems like "Peter Parasol" and "The Ordinary Women"—but still two decades away. Following his three years at Harvard Stevens elected to undergo a long hiatus as a poet—thirteen years or so during which he was in New York as a reporter, law student, and unsettled practicing attorney. Writing poems took a second place in his life, though not in his interest and reading.

During the middle of those years, he wrote in his journal: "Sonnets have their place, without mentioning names; but they can also be found tremendously out of place: in real life where things are quick, unaccountable, responsive" (*SP* 80). When writing a series of short lyrics for his fiancée's birthday in 1908 and 1909, he shunned the sonnet but seemed no less aware of the limitation of his latest efforts. To Elsie Moll, his fiancée, he wrote: "I read, and then I said, 'I'll write poetry. Young men in attics always write poetry on snowy nights, so—I'll write poetry.' I wrote, 'Only to name again / The leafy rose—' To-to-tetum, la-la-la. I couldn't do another line—I looked at my ceiling, frowned at the floor, chewed the top of my pen, closed my eyes, looked into myself and found everything covered up" (CS 127). The young poet mocks himself in these lines but ironically proceeds to compose the very poem about a "leafy rose" in the predictable rhythm of "To-to-te-tum." In so doing, he succumbs to the conventions he otherwise scorns but for which he has not, as yet, seen his way beyond:

> Only to name again
> The leafy rose—
> So to forget the fading,
> The purple shading,
> Ere it goes. (CPP 512)

Stevens was a few months from his thirtieth birthday when he composed these lines; his development as a poet during the ten years from "Ballade of the Pink Parasol" (1899) to "Only to name again" (1909) remained, almost without exception, stillborn.

Altogether different specimens began to appear in the ensuing decade— partly anticipating and partly influenced by the imagists, as well as the Fauves and Cubists (whose work Stevens probably saw at the Armory Show in 1913), Verlaine and other French symbolists, and the work of friends such as William Carlos Williams, Walter Arensberg, Donald Evans. Absorbing these influences and perhaps, most importantly, trusting the instincts that made him suspicious of the sonnet and self-mocking about the "leafy rose" poem, he at last emerged a new poet.

Almost simultaneously, Stevens developed two different prosodic voices that I have elsewhere defined as the "ironic mode" and the "prophetic mode" (A Poet's Growth 109–10). The poems of the former tend toward a highly self-conscious tone of playfulness and even flippancy, in which impressions are quick, pared, and spontaneous. The poet's exhortations are submerged in inventive sounds, highly irregular meters, and witty opacity. The prophetic mode, on the other hand, is a remaking of the tone of the undergraduate sonnets in a voice that remains formal and sonorous but resists the earlier preciosity and mannerism. Its diction is largely Latinate and the measure is a highly pliable blank verse. As Eleanor Cook has said, "the play of rhetoric and dialectic against each other . . . is word-play that is essential, not ornamental, for Stevens' poetry" (xi).

The two modes, one the "beauty" of wordplay, wit, and inflection; the other the "beauty" of whistling reverberation and echo, both attract the poet. In the fifth way of listening to his blackbird, Stevens savors both equally:

> I do not know which to prefer,
> The beauty of inflections
> Or the beauty of innuendoes,
> The blackbird whistling
> Or just after. (*CPP* 75)

His high and low rhetoric, lyric and ludic, had its own registers and recalibrations. Later the two voice modes tended to merge into one more dominantly prophetic and elegant, but never silencing altogether the devices of irony and mockery.

"Depression before Spring" appeared in the *Little Review* in 1918 and five years later in *Harmonium*, Stevens' first volume. The poem is a *tour de force*, an exercise by a poet who has finally and satisfactorily found an idiom within the ironic mode that commends his confidence:

> The cóck cróws
> But nó quéen ríses.
>
> The háir of my blónde
> Is dázzling,
> As the spíttle of cóws
> Thréading the wínd.
>
> Hó! Hó!
>
> But kí-kí-rí-kí
> Brings nó rou-cóu,
> Nó rou-cóu-cóu.
>
> But nó quéen cómes
> In slípper gréen. (*CPP* 50)

One notes at once the contrast between the sounds of the present cock and the absent dove; the latter is, of course, royally feminine ("queen"), while the cock is rudely and sexually masculine. "My blonde," whose hair is "the spittle of cows" will later yield to the favored queen, just as the "paltry nude" will give way to the "goldener nude" (*CPP* 4–5) in another spring poem, "The Paltry Nude Starts on a Spring Voyage," written a year later. In "Depression before Spring," the last vestige of winter is already yielding to the softer pleasure of spring—even as "Depression" gives way to enjoyment and self-mockery, or the nudge in the ribs of an inside joke ("Ho! Ho!"). But the debate is preeminently aural: a contrast between the velar plosives of the cock ("ki-ki-ri-ki") and the elongated vowels of the doves ("rou-cou-cou": from the French *roucouler:* to coo).[1] The cock's sound (k) is captured in his name and the sound he makes, "cock crows," while the same k-sound of "queen" yields at once to the glide of the softer w-sound (kween). At the end, the poem softly echoes "queen" with "green" in the final couplet—the poem's only full rhyme. Though literally absent from the scene ("no queen comes"), the dove is installed in the poem by the very cooing that the speaker both yearns for and, and so doing, verbally interjects. The cooing triumph of the queen-dove over the staccato of the rude cock is complete. In a similar mode, Stevens would go on to write of the Oklahoma dance of "Bonnie and Josie" in "Life Is Motion," and their celebratory cry: "'Ohoyaho, / Ohoo'" (*CPP* 65), with the play of meter and sounds upon the state's name. There would be many other poems hooing their nonsense sounds for noticeably prosodic purposes.

"Depression before Spring" pushes back and against soothing iambs. A notable exception occurs from the staccato "But ki-ki-ri-ki" to the iambs of the next line, "Brings no rou-cou." Trochees and spondees otherwise dominate. (The iambic and anapestic rhythms of the second stanza lure us into the expectation of dove-like beauty and solace with the feminine image of "my blonde." But the blonde's hair described as cows' spittle is followed by the poet's own reductive spondee, "Ho! Ho!" checking abruptly the lull of such deceptive rhythms.) To read "Depression before Spring" without attention to its self-conscious prosody is, of course, to miss the poem entirely. This kind of poem by Stevens could be profitably taught and grasped by a primary-grades English class.

In the remarkable poem "The Creations of Sound," Stevens examines how "syllables" precede "speech" or "words / Better without an author, without a poet." Speech "is not dirty silence / Clarified. It is silence made still dirtier." A poem in its essential characteristics is not clarification or a making of the poet "too exactly himself." Rather, it rises from the particles of sound, something pre-verbal and preceding the process of meaning ("A chorister whose c preceded the choir" [CPP 452]), and these particles surround us everywhere. "We say ourselves," he concludes in "The Creations of Sound," "in syllables that rise / From the floor, rising in speech we do not speak" (CPP 274–75). As we have seen, the sounds of the sea in "The Idea of Order at Key West" are first "dark voice of sea," "outer voice of sky," and "heaving speech of air"—they are "sound alone"—before they can become "more than that" (CPP 105). In "Of Mere Being," it is only in the branches of "The palm at the end of the mind" that is "beyond the last thought"—like the instant of death itself—that the "gold-feathered bird" (CPP 476–77) sings without human meaning, without human feeling, but with all the power of mere [merus: pure, unadulterated] being.

From its first lines, "Sunday Morning" (CPP 53–56), another early poem published three years before "Depression before Spring," identifies itself as written in the prophetic mode rather than the ironic. Here is the voice of exhortation and rumination cast in the more traditional rhythms of blank verse. In a sonnet composed during his undergraduate years, Stevens had begun, "If we are leaves that fall upon the ground . . . / Then let a tremor through our briefness run" (CPP 484–85). In "Sunday Morning" (CPP 53–56), too, we are leaves. If death, in fact, "strews the leaves / Of sure obliteration on our paths," then life remains to be savored with heightened intensity. Death causes, not a "tremor," but a "shiver": "She [death] makes the willow shiver in the sun." "Sunday Morning," however, demonstrates a voice altogether superior to that of a decade and a half earlier. One cause of that advance is the poet's greater musical versatility with the same iambic pentameter rhythm as the undergraduate sonnets. The "measures" of poetry itself, as the poem declares in Stanza II, are—like "All pleasures and all pains . . . destined for her soul." The men who chant their biblical devotion to the sun in Stanza VII

> . . . shall know well the heavenly fellowship
> Of men that perish and of summer morn.
> And whence they came and whither they shall go
> The dew upon their feet shall manifest.

Stevens has taken the Psalms or, in a purer mode, *The Song of Songs,* and re-written them into his own secular scripture of the changing earth. But even in "Sunday Morning" there is room for mockery. Unlike the contesting sounds of dove and cock in "Depression before Spring," here is an extended succession of alliterative "m's," as Stevens mocks the motherless Jove, the first and totally inhuman god: "No mother suckled him, no sweet land gave / Large-mannered motions to his mythy mind. / He moved among us, as a muttering king, / Magnificent, would move among his hinds."

The most subtle modulation of rhythm and sound in the poem, however, occurs in the poem's conclusion:

> Déer wálk upón our móuntains, and the quáil
> Whístle abóut us their spontáneous críes;
> Swéet bérries rípen in the wílderness;
> Ánd, in the ísolátion of the ský,
> At évening, cásual flócks of pígeons máke
> Ambíguous úndulátions as they sínk,
> Dównward to dárkness, on exténded wíngs.

These familiar lines are full of action and motion (walk, whistle, ripen, make, sink), which, as we might expect, are captured in the poem's pattern of stress-es. Counterpoint replays the lines of blank verse. The sequence is steadily marked by trochees and spondees: Déer wálk; quáil / Whístle; Swéet bérries rípen; úndulátions; Dównward to dárkness. The rhythm is in the fall of the trochee rather than the rise of the iamb, another kind of sinking downward.[2] Though action is vigorous, the pace is decelerated, appropriate to the poem's final diminuendo approaching cessation. The motion downward toward final-ity is complemented by the images themselves: autumnal berries, isolation of the sky, and evening yielding to a terminus both of poem and perhaps of life itself. Deer, quail, berries, and pigeons are caught up in their own unique actions and motions, but we are drawn into those actions because deer hover about and upon "*our* mountains"; the quail whistle their sounds "about *us*" (emphasis added). Indeed, "walk," "Whistle," "cries," and "Sweet" are all ap-propriate to human action and sensation. In the magnitude and plenty of life is the "Ambiguous" presence of imminent death toward which all life is destined, as the poem has earlier made clear. Except for the poem's last three words, its ending would attain a climactic somberness. "On exténded wíngs" returns us ever so briefly, however, to the rise of the iamb, just as the vowel sounds of the stressed syllables rise in pitch in opposition to the emphatic lowering in pitch of "Downward" and "darkness." The extended wings are themselves ballasted, if only momentarily, against the sinking downward of the birds' flight, mitigating the poem's inexorable finale in a brief gratuitous respite.

After *Harmonium*, twelve years would elapse before the publication of the next volume, as the poet turned his attention to business and family. The poet Donald Justice has noted of Stevens' metrical evolution that it seems to have grown directly out of his own experiments with the blank-verse line: "Pound, early in his career, working from the common iambic toward looser rhythms, took his descent in part from Browning . . . , and Eliot from the minor Elizabethan and Jacobean dramatists, as he himself suggested; but the later Stevens, following along the same path of loosening the common iambic, seems to descend from no one so much as from the younger Stevens himself" (27). As early as 1921, two years before *Harmonium*, Stevens in a letter to Ferdinand Reyher set forth an account of his prosodic goals that demonstrates the importance he placed on aesthetic theory:

> The fact is that notwithstanding the large amount of poetry that is written over here at the moment there is practically no aesthetic theory back of it. Why do you scorn free verse? Isn't it the only kind of verse now being written which has any aesthetic impulse back of it? Of course, there are miles and miles of it that do not come off. People don't understand the emotional purpose of rhythm any more than they understand the emotional purpose of measure. I am not exclusively for free verse. But I am for it. ("Letters to Ferdinand Reyher" 390)

Stevens' differentiation here between the purposes of measure and those of rhythm is one that Mutlu Blasing has laid out in her *Lyric Poetry: The Pain and Pleasure of Words*: "Rhythm entails interpretation, both in its production and its reception. It is a subjective, mental echo or interpretation of the [more mechanical] metrical measure" (58).

By free verse, Stevens may have been thinking of a poem like "Depression before Spring" and justifying his own right to abandon regular meter. I think it is equally likely, however, that he had begun to discover the range of new freedoms *within* traditional forms but *away from* the metronome. It was the "emotional purpose of rhythm" that was more important than counting stresses. Neither was he "exclusively" for free verse. Paramount for him was the "aesthetic impulse back of it." In 1921, however, he was only beginning to see how his own poetry might fully embrace such pliability without confining himself to free verse and imagism. ("Not all objects are equal. The vice of imagism was that it did not recognize this" [*CPP* 918]).

Stevens' own growth as a poet would require more than the reductions of the dimeter or trimeter line. The conduits between self and world, of imagination and reality, required a wider field of play. At the same time that he was writing poems like "The Snow Man," "The Paltry Nude Starts on a Spring Voyage," "Anecdote of the Jar," "Infanta Marina," and dozens of others (including "Depression before Spring") Stevens also saw that other poems could be rewritten in a mode different from the minimal compression of image and form. To make such forms, of course, is precisely what he set out to do. The versatility of the heroic line became increasingly apparent in such poems as "Autumn Refrain" (1932), "The Idea of Order at Key West" (1934), and "Evening without Angels" (1934). The later "Owl's Clover" (beginning in 1935) suffers from the prolonged weightiness of the thrumming line (a problem perhaps more of diction and syntax than meter),[3] but after that poem Stevens deliberately turned to a loose tetrameter in the thirty-three cantos of "The Man with the Blue Guitar." Preparing the parts that would make up that poem, Stevens wrote: "Apparently, only the ones over which I take a great deal of trouble come through finally. This is contrary to my usual experience, which is to allow a thing to fill me up and then express it in the most slap-dash way" (*L* 316). Two years earlier he had exclaimed, "[A recent poem] is a carefully worked thing, about which I am in some doubt for that very reason. I like the slap-dash and the fortuitous."[4] As early as "Le Monocle de Mon Oncle," he was setting out his purpose to proceed "In verses wild with motion, full of din, / Loudened by cries, by clashes, quick and sure" (*CPP* 13). As he composed the title poem for his third commercial collection, *The Man with the Blue Guitar,* confidence in the more spontaneous "slap-dash way" continued:

Róll a drúm upón the blúe guitár
Léan from the stéeple. Crý alóud,

"Hére am Ī, my ádversáry, that
Confrónt you, hóo-ing the slíck trombónes,

Yét with a pétty mísery
At héart, a pétty mísery. (*CPP* 139)

Deviating from the regular tetrameters of the poem, Stevens employs a pentameter in the first line (appropriate to the drum roll), followed by two tetrameters, and then trimeters in the last two. In four of the six lines, trochees push aside and contest (like an adversary) the regular iambs. We *hear* the drum and slick trombones but then a *decrescendo* into the repetition of "petty misery" as trochees concede to the iambs of the final line. Taken as a whole, the "slap-dash," the irregular and unpredictable beats and sounds of the canto, defy mere measure in favor of a more plucky and rollicking rhythm. That contrast is played out also in the sounds of the words themselves. As Iván Fónagy notes in a commentary on the work of a Hungarian poet, the phonemes l, m, and n "are definitely more frequent in tender-toned poems," whereas the phonemes k, t, and r "predominate in those with aggressive tone" (195). We hear the latter tone in "Roll and drum," "adversary," and "slick trombones," while we hear the softer m-sound and gliding y-sound in "misery" (repeated in successive lines).

After "The Man with the Blue Guitar," the prophetic mode predominated, and Stevens turned with renewed confidence to the blank-verse line. Poetry, he increasingly discovered, could eavesdrop on thought—not as stream of consciousness or dreamlike surrealism—but as self-conscious interior discourse put to a rhythm successfully freed of set stresses and fixed syllables per line. At the same time, the roomy lassitude that the blank-verse lines of "Sunday Morning" and "The Comedian as the Letter C" had provided now became the paradigm on which such freedom could evolve.

The rhythm of Stevens' later verse is everywhere and typically influenced by his pattern of appositional elaboration. Ideas unfold in a fluidity like the waves of the sea, each like its predecessor but subtly different. Stevens, in fact, used this very trope in a letter to his future wife in 1909: "From one of many possible figures—regard the mind as a motionless sea, as it is so often. Let one round wave surge through it mystically—one mystical mental scene— one image. Then see it in abundant undulation, incessant motion—unbroken succession of scenes, say. —I indulge in heavenly psychology—I lie back and drown in the deluge. The mind rolls as the sea rolls" (*L* 118–19). The syntax and rhythm of his poems contract and expand, decelerate and hasten, drift and steer at a pace that only seems without direction. The unfolding of the appositional elements themselves in a poem by Stevens may *mimic* a logical rigor, but that implication is in many instances deceptive because his items in apposition invariably nudge the thought in subtly centrifugal directions—apposition even becoming, in some cases, opposition.

These lines from "Credences of Summer" (*CPP* 323) show the direction of that evolution:

It is the nátural tówer of áll the wórld,	31
The póint of súrvey, gréen's gréen ápogee,	32
But a tówer more précious than the víew beyónd,	33
A póint of súrvey squátting like a thróne,	34
Áxis of éverything, gréen's ápogee. . . .	35

In these lines, apposition itself is reinforced by repetition, and this, of course, is not uncommon in Stevens. How, one might pose, is the *It* (line 31 above) defined within these five lines? To what the "It" is referring from the previous stanza is unclear, but in Stanza III, "It" is united by copula with *tower*, the principal noun source of the sequence. Tower, in turn, becomes *point, apogee, tower* (repeated), *point* (repeated), *axis, apogee* (repeated), and, by simile, *like a throne.*

The first line (line 31) might take a stress on the first syllable ("It"), but I have interpreted it as Stevens reads the line in the Caedmon recording ("It is the nátural . . ."). In the second line, iambs more boldly assert themselves, but the line concludes with the rare molossos (' ' ') of "gréen's gréen ápogee." Both lines 32 and 34 begin with "point of survey," followed by "Green's green apogee" and "squatting like a throne" respectively, each line also staked out by a caesura. Three lines later, the line is rewritten (continuing as apposition) where "survey" (line 34) evolves subtly into the sound of "every" (line 35), and "green's apogee" is repeated from line 32—again following a caesura. Line 34 above recalls the cadence to five stresses with regular iambs, but the sequence pulls toward tetrameter, as I have indicated in the scansion. The fifth line, however, is set to the steadily falling rhythm of dactyls ("Áxis of éverything, gréen's ápogee") with strong internal rhyming.

What is noteworthy is the great range of versatility with which Stevens has here adopted an accentual verse rooted in the heroic line and set to the fluidity of appositional discourse. The iambic pentameter is merely a point of departure, and the iamb itself as a defining pattern is all but lost. As Justice says, "From about the midpoint of Stevens' career on, practically any trisyllabic substitution [for the metrical foot] imaginable can be found," (31) and Stevens' fondness for the substitution of the anapest for the iamb, says Justice, "in the history of versification . . . is probably unprecedented" (29). Here, even a quadruple foot ("It is the nátural. . . .") occurs.

More than any other critic of Stevens' prosody, Natalie Gerber has summarized the pliability of Stevens' adaptations of the blank-verse line. She concludes that "his late blank verse can be described as loosened and modernized through a greater sense of the phrasal unit at the expense of the more artificial metrical foot. As such, it approaches free verse in interesting ways" (211).

It was only by thoroughly mastering the iambic pentameter line that Stevens found its hidden resources for a poetry that sought to reproduce the "rapidity of thought" (L 319) in all its freedom. At the end of his life Stevens told Edwin Honig, "Now I never worried about the line. I've always been interested in the whole thing, the whole poem" (Honig 12). By then, I think that Stevens meant he had no need to count syllables or stresses. The cadenced rhythm had become as natural to him as thought itself. It is well known that many poems were written as he walked the two-mile route in Hartford between his home on Westerly Terrace and the office. "Walking helps me to concentrate," he told a correspondent, "and I suppose that, somehow or other, my own movement gets into the movement of the poems" (L 844).

Randall Jarrell once remarked on the dominant influence upon American poets of Stevens' "scannable" rhythms over the more experimental and modernist rhythms of Pound and Eliot.[5] Harvey Gross, Donald Justice, and Dennis

Taylor are correct when they note Stevens' unique contribution to the prosody of modernism by extending the heroic line toward accentual verse, and perhaps even free verse.[6] But Stevens never went as far as Whitman or H.D. The difference lies in Stevens' retention of the framework of blank verse, however skeletal the remnant: "My line is a pentameter line," he said in 1942, "but it runs over and under now and then" (*L* 407). For a mind and temperament that liked the extension of ideas, the elasticity of thought, the modes of repetition (nuances, thirteen ways, decorations, variations, extracts, two versions, two illustrations, prologues, etc.), relaxed, irregular and pliable cadences inevitably prevailed.

"One is always writing about two things at the same time in poetry and it is this that produces the tension characteristic of poetry. One is the true subject and the other is the poetry of the subject. The difficulty of sticking to the true subject, when it is the poetry of the subject that is paramount in one's mind, need only be mentioned to be understood" (*CPP* 785). The "poetry of the subject" and its subversive influence upon the poet's "true subject" engages to some extent the hand of every poet. For Stevens such rewritings in prosody were especially "paramount." He put the issue this way in one of his "Adagia": "There are two opposites: the poetry of rhetoric and the poetry of experience" (*CPP* 902). In the poems of *Harmonium*, he told Ronald Lane Latimer, a kind of "pure poetry" had made a strong claim upon him: "I liked the idea of images and images alone, or images and the music of verse together. I then believed in *pure poetry*, as it was called" (*L* 288). Four years later, in another letter, he revealed that he had not abandoned that preference: "I am, in the long run, interested in pure poetry. No doubt from the Marxian point of view this sort of thing is incredible, but pure poetry is rather older and tougher than Marx and will remain so" (*L* 340). In spite of these acknowledgments, Stevens never practiced *la poésie pure* in its absolute sense, even in *Harmonium*, but his pleasure in the sounds of language, what he called the "sensuous reality" of poetry (in Lensing, "Wallace Stevens and Stevens T. Mason," 35), never took a secondary importance. Stevens preferred, among his own poems, "The Emperor of Ice-Cream" because of its "essential gaudiness" (*L* 263). Parts of "Gubbinal," he told another correspondent, were "purely stylistic" (*L* 287). He described "The Curtains in the House of the

Metaphysician" as "a poem of long open sounds" (*L* 463). The "sole purpose" of "Domination of Black" was "to fill the mind with the images & sounds that it contains" (*L* 251). Bernard Heringman remembers Stevens' remark that in writing "Peter Quince at the Clavier" "*he was thinking in terms of musical movements—sort of libretto*" (200). "The Comedian as the Letter C," Stevens later explained, consisted of the "sounds of the letter C" and "all related or derivative sounds" that accompany Crispin as he "moves through the poem . . . . The sounds of the letter C include all related or derivative sounds. For instance, X, TS and Z. To illustrate: In 'Bubbling felicity in Cantilene' the soft C with the change to the hard C, once you notice it, ought to make that line a little different from what it was before" (*L* 351–52). Stevens' penchant for the sounds of the letter C remained a dominant part of his musical sterophony: "The Bird with the Coppery, Keen Claws" (*CPP* 65), "That scrawny cry—it was / A chorister whose c preceded the choir" (*CPP* 452), "and bid him whip / In kitchen cups concupiscent curds" (*CPP* 50), "Cock–robin's at Caracas" (*CPP* 239), "Chieftain Iffucan of Azcan in caftan" (*CPP* 60), etcetera. Of all American poets, Stevens most savors the sensuousness of words—aural, tactile, and what Beverly Maeder calls the "visual materiality of words, not just from their denotation and connotation" ("Stevens and Linguistic Structure" 152). In a special sense, we do not just analyze Stevens' language but are absorbed by it, awash in it—even in poems of winter where his perceptions are ostensibly chastened.

Rhyme itself is a mode of repetition, but Stevens' rhymes are only occasionally full rhymes. More typical are part rhymes, repetition rhymes, stress rhymes, internal rhymes. (One wants to add to the list "accidental rhymes" because of their placements in irregular patterns.) Unlike Yeats or Eliot or Frost, Stevens was not drawn to traditional stanzaic forms set to regular rhymes. (The couplet and tercet were otherwise particularly amenable.) The dominant rhyming pattern for Stevens is the pattern of given words repeated within lines and from one line to the next—even becoming the driving progression and structure of poems like "Metaphors of a Magnifico," "Domination of Black," "Autumn Refrain," "The House Was Quiet and the World Was Calm," and "The World as Meditation," to name a few. It should be noted that word repetitions and partial rhymes constitute for Stevens two of his principal modes of lyric echo and song.

Stevens is perhaps most romantic and most symbolist when he extols the power of the poem's persuasion apart from its "meaning": "When we find in poetry that which gives us a momentary existence on an exquisite plane, is it necessary to ask the meaning of the poem? If the poem had a meaning and if its explanation destroyed the illusion, should we have gained or lost?" (*CPP* 786). As Valéry reminds us, the poem does not exist apart from its utterance but only "*sur quelque bouche humaine, et cette bouche est ce qu'elle est*" ("through some human mouth, and this mouth is what a poem is") (II 1255).[7] In an interview at the end of his life, Stevens summarized his work: "Communication is more a showing of the pleasure which the poet felt when he wrote his line than an understanding of the sense he was intending" (in Culbertson 11–12).

Robert Frost spoke more than once of the need to train the ear in poetry to the sentence-sounds of speech, recommending that "the best place to get the abstract sound of sense is from voices behind a door that cuts off the words" (*Letters* 122). In a poem like "Depression before Spring," the competition in sounds between the cock's "ki-ki-ri-ki" and the absent dove's "rou-cou-cou" is just such an exposition of hearing "behind a door," while, in a different way, the drop and rise in pitch in the vowels at the end of "Sunday Morning" replay another competition between descent to death and ascent to life. Roland Barthes refers to the sensuous reality of all texts: "Due allowance being made for the sounds of the language, *writing aloud* is not phonological but phonetic; its aim is not the clarity of messages, the theater of emotions; what it searches for (in a perspective of bliss) are the pulsional incidents, the language lined with flesh, a text where we can hear the grain of the throat, the patina of consonants, the voluptuousness of vowels, a whole carnal stereophony: the articulation of the body, of the tongue, not that of meaning, of language" (66–67).

The range of Stevens' lexicon, from rabbinical formality to colloquial patois, from Latinate abstraction to native (Germanic) idioms and clichés, creates a surface tone in his poetry where diction constantly highlights itself.

The poet is also an utterer without final words, but for whom there is nothing else: "It is a world of words to the end of it, / In which nothing solid is its solid self" (*CPP* 301). The effusion of language within a poem is a relentless quest of a fluxional Heraclitean world: "We say / This changes and that changes. Thus the constant // Violets, doves, girls, bees and hyacinths / Are inconstant objects of inconstant cause / In a universe of inconstancy" (*CPP*

337). On the one hand, "Poetry / Exceeding music must take the place / Of empty heaven and its hymns," but so lofty an aim ("Exceeding music") may be realized in very quotidian terms: "Even in the chattering of your guitar" (*CPP* 136–37). The poet "mumbles" (*CPP* 380), even as he speaks "the poets' hum" (*CPP* 170). At times, he is more successful, but modestly so: "A few words of what is real or may be // Or of glistening reference to what is real" (*CPP* 273). In other instances the language can take on a more assertive finality: "the characters [both poets and their alphabets of language] speak because they want / To speak, the fat, the roseate characters, / Free, for a moment, from malice and sudden cry, / Completed in a completed scene" (*CPP* 326). Stevens' diction contains French and German words, employs modified coinages, and always prizes the unexpected; it gives every impression of being an improvisatory assault upon the real, every articulation at once obsolete and in need of immediate restatement. The world itself passes before us in a kind of appositional succession. Even when most successful, the poet's utterance is only "for a moment."

In the fourteenth of his twenty "Variations on a Summer Day," Stevens plays with the connection between "words" and the "senses" as he describes the area around Christmas Cove in Maine where the poet vacationed with his family in the summer of 1939:

> Words add to the senses. The words for the dazzle
> Of mica, the dithering of grass,
> That Arachne integument of dead trees,
> Are the eye grown larger, more intense. (*CPP* 214)

"Dazzle," "dithering," and "Arachne integument" are just such words that add to the senses. ("Arachne" of Greek mythology is the woman made into spider, here applied to a webbed weaving of dead branches.) These words enlarge and intensify the eye as it beholds "mica," "grass," and "dead trees" respectively. The result is that such words enable one's eye to see uniquely and dramatically. In "Description without Place," he proposes that the descriptive power of words creates the world. As a result, for him the "buzzing world and lisping firmament / . . . is a world of words to the end of it" (*CPP* 301). (The near homonym of word and world reinforces the same point.) Again, in the third part of "Certain Phenomena of Sound," he plays off the name of the speaker, "Semiramide, dark syllabled," with that of Eulalia, "Gold-shined by sun,"— concluding, "There is no life except in the word of it" (*CPP* 256–57). In "An Ordinary Evening in New Haven," "said words of the world are the life of the world" (*CPP* 404).

As Mervyn Nicholson has noted, "One of the functions of poetry is to stimulate this heightened consciousness. The first form of the poem is a certain kind of 'sound'; that is, it is a sensation that awakens attention; for example, the sound of a cat running on ice—'Moving,' as Stevens says, 'so that the foot-falls are slight and almost nothing' [*CPP* 295]—or 'the catbird's gobble in the morning half-awake—'[*CPP* 276]. The sound marks a shift from unconscious—routinized—existence to a different kind of consciousness" (69). Stevens became the noisiest of the modernists. He seemed instinctively to have understood, as he says in "Pieces," that "There is a sense in sounds beyond their meaning" (*CPP* 307).

The same principle of apposition that I have associated with Stevens' development of the heroic line applies to his choice of diction. The succession of words and phrases in lengthened apposition often accompanies a heightening intensity building toward a climactic stop:

> Desiring the exhilarations of changes:
> The motive for metaphor, shrinking from
> The weight of primary noon,
> The A B C of being,
>
> The ruddy temper, the hammer
> Of red and blue, the hard sound—
> Steel against intimation, the sharp flash,
> The vital, arrogant, fatal, dominant X. (*CPP* 257)

The "weight of primary noon" is the finality of pure being from which metaphor shrinks in these concluding lines to "The Motive for Metaphor." And yet, as Beverly Maeder has pointed out, there is in this poem both "a tendency toward and a retreat from" (*Experimental Language* 70) metaphor. "Primary noon" is *itself* a metaphor describing the near absence of metaphor—or the emaciated metaphor—and it is recast in a succession of appositive metaphors whereby the "shrinking from" subtly becomes a moving toward: "ABC of being," "ruddy temper," "hammer," "hard sound," "sharp flash," and, finally, "X." Each of these designations is a word of Germanic origin (or, with "X," a letter of the alphabet). The contrast in English between native Germanic words and the later, borrowed Latinate ones comes conspicuously into play in the poem. In this instance, Stevens constructs the poem upon the contrast and conflict between these two lexical sources. The starkness of "primary noon" is redefined by apposition in the hard sounds of Anglo-Saxon nominals. The sound-drama is played out self-consciously in the poem as it moves from "hard sound" to its "exhilarations of changes," and such sound is itself identified as "Steel against intimation": the Latinate "intimation" is literally resisted by the Anglo-Saxon *stele*. Only in the final line is the "X" itself identified by a succession of four Latinate adjectives: "vital, arrogant, fatal, dominant," as if, in the end, the metaphoric "noon" of being *cannot* be denied or shrunk from but submitted to as a powerful, commanding presence, both living ("vital") and deadly ("fatal"). As Maeder says of a different poem, "The power of metaphorical description invites us to look both *through* the words to the allegory of art suggested by the poem and *at* the words to the working of this art" (*Experimental Language* 67). Working throughout this poem is the irony that being itself ("primary noon"), from which metaphor is said to shrink in order to *motivate* metaphor ("The Motive for Metaphor"), is itself and in its appositives presented as a succession of just such metaphors themselves. Shrinking from being itself ("X") is only a defining embrace of it through one metaphor after another—a truth that Stevens' breathless crowding of words and phrases in apposition almost camouflages.[8]

Uncanny and unlikely juxtapositions of images as well as sounds, in fact, make up a characteristic of Stevens' verse, often for surprise or comic effects. The incongruity of bathos is both witty and outrageous. This is especially the case with Stevens' titles, as his working notebook for titles and phrases, "From Pieces of Paper," illustrates over and over. But the poems themselves frequently employ the same technique: "Gloomy grammarians in golden gowns" ("Of the Manner of Addressing Clouds," *CPP* 44); "We enjoy the ithy oonts and long-haired / Plomets, as the Herr Gott / Enjoys his comets" ("Analysis of a Theme" *CPP* 305).

"Long and Sluggish Lines" (*CPP* 442–43) is a late poem (1952) told from the perspective of a poet "so much more / Than seventy." The title connects the sluggishness of the lines to the debility of the aging poet, and so the first two couplets recount the monotony of the wood smoke rising through the trees: "But it has been often so." The trees themselves emit a kind of squalor in their own repetitiveness. Suddenly, however, they give way to "an opposite, a contradiction," as the aging poet reawakens to youthful vigor:

The trees have a look as if they bore sad names	5
And kept saying over and over one same, same thing,	6
In a kind of uproar, because an opposite, a contradiction,	7
Has enraged them and made them want to talk it down.	8
What opposite? Could it be that yellow patch, the side	9
Of a house, that makes one think the house is laughing;	10
Or these—escent—issant pre-personae: first fly,	11
A comic infanta among the tragic drapings,	12
Babyishness of forsythia, a snatch of belief,	13
The spook and makings of the nude magnolia?	14

These middle five couplets set up for Stevens a competition of sounds and words as "wakefulness" overcomes sluggishness and newly found youth confounds age.

The first two couplets of the poem (not quoted above) are perfectly rhymed (more / before; flow / so), appropriate to a pattern of endless repetition ("it has been often so"). Line 6, the one that is the longest and most sluggish, is a congeries of rhymes: "And kept saying over and over one same, same thing" (And / and; over / over; say / same / same;-ing /-thing). The reader, too, almost nods. Even so, a subtle "contradiction" is already happening: the final words of each line of the couplet (lines 5 and 6) are no longer perfect rhymes (names / thing) and in all the succeeding couplets such rhyming is abandoned in the face of the poet's obtruding "opposite."

The trees, in fact, are not swaying in dreary and droning repetition but are "enraged" in an "uproar" of resistance to the tedious and tendentious "opposite" and "contradiction." It should be noted that internal rhymes linger: "uproar" in line 7 echoes "bore" in line 5 and "enraged them and made them want to talk it down" in line 8. The" talking" of the trees in long and sluggish lines is the talking of the poem itself, and the urge to "talk it down" occurs by lowering the vocalic pitch from "want" to "talk" to "down." The resistance of the trees to change is a noisy verbal one.

What exactly is the "opposite," the "contradiction," of lines 7 and 9? Through what images is such contradiction defined? It is the "yellow patch" on the side of the house, giving the house the appearance of a laughing face and canceling the "sad names" from line 5. That patch of light is a mere incipiency of spring, preliminary "—escent—issant pre-personae." The Latin suffix "escent" in English denotes a general state of being, as in pubescent or adolescent, for example, where he defines states of being as kinds of "pre-personae." The French "issant" is a present participial suffix, but the action is not yet captured in a complete word. From these inchoate "pre-personae" Stevens again aligns a succession of appositives: "first fly," "comic infanta," "Babyishness of forsythia," "snatch of belief," "spook and makings of the nude magnolia." The voluptuous sibilants and succession of unstressed syllables in "Babyishness of forsythia" (the flowering bush picks up the color of the patch on the side of the house) are reined in and balanced in the same line by the terse "a snatch of belief." All are fresh "makings," the creations of the contradictory force of spring, youth, and vitality. The word "makings" is itself a translation of the Greek word for poet and poetry; once again we are reminded of "lines," "names," "saying," and "talk" as reflexive of the poem itself. In the face of such beginnings and freshenings, the aging poet is "not born yet," and he indulges a new "wakefulness inside a sleep."

As both "The Motive for Metaphor" and "Long and Sluggish Lines" demonstrate, Stevens delighted in the play of sounds between the decorous, sensuous Latinate sounds and the earthier directness of the Anglo-Saxon. Marie Borroff has noted some of the exercises of this tendency throughout the poetry:

Odd verbal combinations were identified . . . as a hallmark of his [Stevens'] style; among these, we can single out one type as especially worthy of note: that in which Latinate (L) and sound-symbolic (s-s) words [onomatopoeia] appear side by side. The examples "A syllable (L), / Out of these gawky (s-s) flitterings (s-s), / Intones (L) its single emptiness"; "addicts (L) / To blotches (s-s), angular (L) anonymids (L), / Gulping (s-s) for shape"; and "the honky-tonk (s-s) out of the somnolent (L) grasses" . . . were cited earlier. (71)

Stevens defines this prosodic pattern himself—referring to "Heavenly labials in a world of gutturals" in "The Plot against the Giant" (*CPP* 6)[9] or his wish "To compound the imagination's Latin with / The lingua franca et jocundissima" (*CPP* 343) in "Notes toward a Supreme Fiction."

To his Cuban friend José Rodríguez Feo, Stevens once defined his own "frivolity": "All the interest that you feel in occasional frivolities I seem to experience in sounds, and many lines exist because I enjoy their clickety-clack in contrast with the more decorous pom-pom-pom that people expect" (*L* 485). Before anything else, Stevens wanted to draw his reader into the carnival of the poem, the antics of rhythm and sound. But of course sounds could also be decorous. The poet-actor-metaphysician described in "Of Modern Poetry" twangs his instrument upon a "new stage" and thereby "gives / Sounds passing through sudden rightnesses, wholly / Containing the mind" (*CPP* 219). At the conclusion of his essay "The Noble Rider and the Sound of Words," Stevens refers to the imagination as a "*violence* from within" (*CPP* 665; emphasis added), not unlike the "rage to order words" (*CPP* 106) in "The Idea of Order at Key West." Such violence and rage are necessary, he argues, because, reduced to language, they "have something to do with our self-preservation; and that, no doubt, is why *the expression of it, the sound of its words,* helps us to live our lives" (*CPP* 665; emphasis added). The expressiveness of language, almost the tactility of its surfaces rough and smooth, delighted Stevens all his life and defined him as a poet. The fund of language and the cadences into which it was cast were for him inexhaustible, never to be hoarded but spent prodigally, "Engaged in the most prolific narrative, / A sound producing the things that are spoken" (*CPP* 256).

PUBLICATION AND READER

Stevens Abroad

Stevens had the good fortune to have the steady loyalty of his publisher, Alfred A. Knopf. It was the novelist and music critic Carl Van Vechten who originally acted as intermediary on Stevens' behalf with Knopf for the publication of his first volume, and that house subsequently brought out all of Stevens' volumes up to and including *Collected Poems,* as well as *The Necessary Angel: Essays on Reality and the Imagination.* Four volumes, in limited and deluxe editions, were published by private presses during Stevens' lifetime with Knopf's approval—two in the 1930s with Alcestis Press (*Ideas of Order* and *Owl's Clover*) and two in the 1940s with Cummington Press (*Notes toward a Supreme Fiction* and *Esthétique du Mal"*); two poems, along with essays, appeared in Cummington's *Three Academic Pieces.* Knopf kept a close, proprietary eye upon Stevens' unfolding career and, every few years, would prompt Stevens with the suggestion that a new volume was in order, and Stevens always responded positively, immediately applying himself to the making of additional new poems. The overwhelming majority of Stevens' poems first appeared in little magazines and other outlets before being collected in the Knopf editions—often as the result of editors' solicitations. With a widening number of readers in mind, Stevens actively encouraged the publication of his poems in Spanish and Italian. He also had a special interest in the dissemination of his work in the United Kingdom. There, however, the path was not so smooth. The reasons for that recalcitrant reaction are many and complex and continue in varying degrees into the twenty-first century, but Stevens himself anticipated the very response that awaited him: "The truth is that American poetry is at its worst in England and, possibly in Ireland or in any other land where English is spoken and whose inhabitants feel that somehow our English is a vulgar imitation" (*L* 597).[1]

As a poet's work nears completion as he advances in age, his fate as a poet is increasingly left to the judgment of editors and critics. We have been trac-ing in loose fashion the evolution of Stevens' work from the external circum-stances of writing one particular poem ("Sea Surface Full of Clouds") to a detailed examination of a major and completed poem ("The Idea of Order at Key West") to discussions of Stevens work in the context of the political and social backgrounds out of which it emerged, and, in the previous chapter, in noting some of the qualities that make up his characteristic style. It remains to consider the evolution of his "audience" during his lifetime but especially since his death in 1955 and especially in Great Britain and Ireland, where that audience remained small even as it very gradually began to be more widely absorbed over the ensuing decades.

In our consideration of "The Idea of Order at Key West" we weighed in some detail the role of the addressee in the poem, Ramon Fernandez, and his role as the audience of the poem's speaker and as our own surrogate as hearers and witnesses of "song" and "voice" at various levels in that poem. The case was made for the necessity of Fernandez-as-audience as the means by which the speaker's own incantations escape the putative solipsism of the woman's song as it is overheard along the shores of Key West. I recollect that discussion here as we conclude with an account of the obstacles and setbacks to Stevens himself in gaining an Anglo-Irish audience and in the context of the emergent modernism of the first half of the previous century. As we will see, it was a matter that commanded a great deal of his attention in the last years of his life and led to no small amount of frustration and discouragement. Of course audience mattered for Stevens, in spite of his personal unwillingness to play the public role of agent or promoter. In the years since his death, while many British and Irish poets, theorists, reviewers, and editors have acknowledged a growing degree of admiration for his powers as a poet, much of their praise has continued to be guarded, equivocal, and qualified.

Publication

Thirty years separated the publication of Wallace Stevens' *Harmonium* (1923) and the first publication of a volume by him in England. A selection made by Stevens himself for Faber and Faber's *Selected Poems* (1953) marked the first authorized and representative collection of the American poet's work in that country. Until then, Stevens' poems were familiar only to a small circle of English and Irish readers through a few anthologies and magazines. An attempt to publish a book-length selection in the 1940s had been aborted by a series of charges and countercharges between two competing English publishing firms and their appeals and claims to publishing rights to Stevens' American publisher, Alfred A. Knopf, Inc. In exasperation and some fear of injuring his standing with Knopf, Stevens called a halt to the project in 1946. Six years later, however, only weeks before the publication of the Faber volume, a totally unauthorized collection published by the Fortune Press, one of the competing firms in the earlier imbroglio, suddenly appeared in England. Legal action initiated against that firm by Knopf led to the suppression of undistributed copies. I want to begin with that story, preceded by Stevens' earliest publications in Great Britain, leading up to the competing editions of a *Selected Poems*.

The various individuals involved in this publication drama include, in addition to Stevens, the son of the Cambridge philosopher George Edward Moore, Nicholas Moore, a poet himself, who offered to make a selection of poems by Stevens for the Fortune Press in 1944; and Tambimuttu, a Ceylonese who was an important publisher, editor, and early champion of T. S. Eliot. Faber's interest in Stevens had been endorsed by directors Peter du Sautoy and Eliot himself, in part through the beseechings of Marianne Moore. Moore also had a minor role in the final selection of Stevens' poems for Faber and Faber. Alfred Knopf, along with Herbert Weinstock and William Koshland of the Knopf publishing house, was actively involved in the various negotiations from America. Laurence Pollinger was Knopf's literary agent in England at the time.

The sequence of complications that blocked the publication of a Stevens volume in England before the early 1950s is extraordinary in itself. It undoubtedly complicated and delayed Stevens' access to a British audience. It also provides a revealing view of Stevens' own conception of himself as a poet and his ambition to enlarge the number of his readers abroad. However, the high value he placed on his association with his American publisher is perhaps the key factor in his own role in the long episode. Not until shortly before his death did he have the satisfaction of seeing a representation of his work, the Faber edition, available to an English audience.

Stevens' introduction to English readers antedates *Harmonium*, but the initial publication itself cannot have been entirely pleasing to him. Early in 1920 the American poet John Gould Fletcher, in a letter to the editor of the *London Mercury*, had singled out Stevens, along with Conrad Aiken, Carl Sandburg, Alfred Kreymborg, and Maxwell Bodenheim, as one of the young American poets who had shown "signs of genius, each in an entirely different and quite individual way" ("American Poetry" 330). A few months later in the same year, Fletcher presented a sample of Stevens' verse in the *Chapbook*, along with poems from a number of younger American poets and his own introductory essay. Stevens was represented by a four-stanza version of "Sunday Morning." In his commentary, Fletcher found "Sunday Morning" "deliberately cryptic,"[2] although he classified it as "another *Portrait of a Lady* better and more memorable than T. S. Eliot's" (29, 30). Harriet Monroe's famous five-stanza abbreviation of the eight-stanza "Sunday Morning" had already appeared in her magazine *Poetry* five years earlier, and the individual who made the selection for the *Chapbook* (Fletcher or editor Harold Munro?) used that version, but exercised further editorial liberties. Already cut by three stanzas in *Poetry*, the poem was now cut by one more.[3] The *Chapbook* numbered the stanzas I, II, III, and V, baldly inserting "(One stanza omitted)" between III and V. Only with the publication of *Harmonium* three years later was the much-shredded poem restored to its original order and length. Its publication in England, nonetheless, presages the challenging fate of the American poet's work in that country in the succeeding years and decades.

Stevens' first previously unpublished poem to appear in England, "Mandolin and Liqueurs," also appeared in the *Chapbook* in April 1923. It is a minor piece that was never collected later by Stevens and appears to owe something to Eliot's equally wry "The 'Boston Evening Transcript.'" A curious choice to lay before the British public, it ends with this insouciant and slightly flippant stanza:

> I love to sit and read the *Telegraph*,
> That vast confect of telegrams,
> And to find how much that really matters
> Does not really matter
> At all. (*CPP* 555)

About a year earlier, Conrad Aiken wrote to Stevens soliciting his permission to include five previously published poems ("Peter Quince at the Clavier," the five-stanza version of "Sunday Morning," "Le Monocle de Mon Oncle," "Thirteen Ways of Looking at a Blackbird," and "Domination of Black") in an anthology to be published in England. Aiken's remarkable keenness in selecting these major *Harmonium* poems before their publication in that volume is a tribute to his independent critical alertness. His anthology, *Modern American Poets*, was published by Martin Secker of London in 1922.[4]

The first detailed British response to Stevens came in an essay in the American journal *The Dial*—just preceding the first publication of "Sea Surface Full of Clouds" in the same issue in 1924. Llewelyn Powys identified the Stevens of *Harmonium* as a modern Symbolist: "And no poet, not Baudelaire, not Edgar Allan Poe even, has revealed with a surer touch, a surer ambiguity, the very shades and tinctures of this indefinable borderland than has this ultramodern supersubtle lawyer from the confines of Hartford, Connecticut." It would be many years before another British critic would seriously choose to evaluate the work of Stevens. Powys' admiration of Stevens notwithstanding, he set the tenor of future British responses, regretting what he called "Wallace Stevens' hermetic art and finicky preoccupations" (45, 48).

Stevens' poems appeared sporadically in English magazines throughout the 1930s and 1940s. All were directly or indirectly solicited by the editors. "Farewell to Florida," for example, first appeared in *Contemporary Poetry and Prose* in 1936. In 1937 Julian Symons, an early and enduring champion of Stevens in England, published two of the poems that were eventually to be absorbed into "The Man with the Blue Guitar" (V and XXVI). His *Twentieth Century Verse* also published "Connoisseur of Chaos" in 1938. When Cyril Connolly wrote to Stevens in April 1947 asking for a poem to be published in a special number of *Horizon* to be dedicated to the arts in America, Stevens sent him "The Owl in the Sarcophagus"; it appeared there later that year. Nicholas Moore, a key figure in the ensuing publishing controversies, was coeditor and copublisher in the late 1930s of a magazine called *Seven*. Stevens sent him three poems during this period: "The Blue Buildings in the Summer Air," "Thunder by the Musician," and "Yellow Afternoon."[5] Apparently the writing of the long poem "Owl's Clover" was stimulated by an invitation from Richard Church of J. M. Dent in London. In his correspondence of 1935, Stevens indicated that Church was collecting "a series of long poems" for publication and wanted one from him" (*L* 279). There is no evidence that the poem was ever used by Church, however.[6]

Besides the magazines and Aiken's early anthology, a few poems by Stevens began to appear in various British collections, but these never numbered more than a handful, often the same poems reappearing. The most popular of these early anthologies that included selections by Stevens was Oscar Williams' *A Little Treasury of Modern Poetry: English and American* that was distributed in England by Routledge and included "Peter Quince at the Clavier," "Thirteen Ways of Looking at a Blackbird," "Le Monocle de Mon Oncle," "Sunday Morning," and "So-and-So Reclining on Her Couch." Geoffrey Hill recalled receiving it from his father as a gift when he was about fifteen: "I think there was probably a time when I knew every poem in that anthology by heart" ("Geoffrey Hill" 78). Philip Hobsbaum recalled that "I owed a great deal [in learning about Stevens] to Oscar Williams' *Little Treasury of Modern Verse*, two copies of which I have worn out during my reading life."[7] Among the other more widely accessible of the anthologies that included poems by Stevens was the *Oxford Book of American Verse*, which was published in 1950 and contained twenty-five Stevens poems. B. Rajan's *Modern American Poetry*, published in London also in 1950, collected four poems by Stevens, including "Credences of Summer," and an essay by Louis Martz entitled "The World of Wallace Stevens." As a result of scattered publications such as these, poems by Stevens gradually found his first English admirers, though they remained small in number. The poet David Gascoyne, for example, wrote to Stevens in 1944, asking that copies of several of his American volumes be sent over, and Stevens quickly accommodated him. In 1951 another English poet, Charles Tomlinson, also posted laudatory remarks to Stevens and included an essay on "Credences of Summer," to which Stevens responded favorably.

Two of the anthologies containing poems by Stevens appeared in England in the early 1940s and signaled poet and editor Nicholas Moore's deepening interest in the poet. Having earlier published the poems by Stevens in *Seven*, Moore requested additional ones for a collection to be issued in 1942 by the Fortune Press, entitled the *Fortune Anthology*. Stevens arranged for him to use "Asides on the Oboe" and "Mrs. Alfred Uruguay," both of which had appeared in American magazines. In the notes on the contributors, Stevens is identified as "an elder American poet, well-known there, but not here" (80).

A year later, in August 1943, Moore again requested some poems for still another anthology that he was coediting, the *Atlantic Anthology*, also being published by Fortune Press. Ever wary of copyright complications, Stevens suggested that Moore consult his recently issued "Notes toward a Supreme Fiction." The Cummington Press in America had published the volume during the previous year, and the poet himself controlled the copyright. Stevens endorsed Moore's project by introducing him to Harry Duncan, editor of the Cummington Press, as "one of the younger English poets, very active, and potentially one of the best, if not the best of them."[8]

Moore's poems do not always measure up to Stevens' praise, but it is clear, as Carolyn Masel has shown (126–30), that Moore had absorbed certain qualities from the work of his newly found *maître*. In his volume published in 1944, with drawings by the young Lucian Freud, *The Glass Tower,* are two poems formally dedicated to Stevens: "Yesterday's Sailors" and "The Waves of Red Balloons." The latter had also appeared in his preceding volume, *"The Cabaret, The Dancer, The Gentlemen* (1942). Here is one stanza:

> But waving the red balloons, I saw him come,
> Magician of the blue word and the steely music,
> Making a mystery out of our time.
> I recognized in him the emperor's capers,
> The colossal sham of chocolate and ice. (64)

In *The Cabaret, The Dancer, The Gentleman* there is a poem called "Ideas of Disorder at Torquay" not so much in dialogue with "The Idea of Order at Key West" as a portrait of England in the throes of World War II. The ordered world of Torquay itself has succumbed to disorder: "Who would not / Protest that such order might be destroyed?" (31). Moore's poem happens to be first of a succession of such responses to Stevens' poem from British and Irish poets in the decades to come.[9]

In any case, Moore, having been licensed by Stevens, selected cantos from "Notes toward a Supreme Fiction" almost randomly, choosing finally eight from the thirty-one that comprise the complete poem. Again, Stevens was introduced in the *Atlantic Anthology* as a poet with "a considerable reputation in America, but comparatively little known in England" (vii). It was to remedy just that defect that the Fortune Press wrote to Stevens on March 20, 1944, offering to publish a volume of his verse in England, the poems to be selected by Nicholas Moore.

As early as 1927, three years after its founding by Reginald A. Caton, its publisher, Stevens had written to the Fortune Press requesting a list of its publications.[10] By 1944 he had seen his poems arranged by Nicholas Moore and published in the *Fortune Anthology*. Plans for the second anthology selection were underway. Stevens' personal library contained inscribed volumes of poetry by Moore, and, as we have seen, Stevens praised the poems lavishly. In his correspondence with Moore, Stevens fondly recalled occasional meetings with Moore's parents in America. Consequently, when the March 1944 letter from the Fortune Press arrived offering to publish a volume of his work selected by Moore, Stevens had no reason to accept the news in any way other than delight: "No doubt I owe this suggestion to your interest and kindness, for which I am sincerely grateful," he wrote to Moore on May 9. In the second paragraph of the letter, Stevens introduced the question of copyright and his own obligations to Knopf:

> It so happens that Mr. Knopf, who has published my books in this country, has a contract with me under which the permission would have to come from him. Let me say at once that my relations with Mr. Knopf have always been everything that I could possibly want them to be and that I feel that I am under obligations to him. But, in view of this arrangement, it is necessary for me to send the letter of The Fortune Press to Mr. Knopf; he will write directly to The Fortune Press. It would do no good for me to attempt to do so because I could agree to nothing.[11]

In his next letter to Stevens, Moore acknowledged that he had himself suggested to Caton that Fortune Press issue a volume by the American poet. The prospect of an early publication seemed favorable. Before the end of the summer, however, Stevens received another letter from a London publisher, a man who identified himself as Tambimuttu, editor of the influential *Poetry London*. Tambimuttu also proposed the publication of a volume of Stevens' poems and indicated a long-standing attempt on his part to purchase the British rights, although Stevens himself was unaware of such negotiations. A subsidiary of Nicholson and Watson, Ltd., but controlled editorially by Tambimuttu, *Poetry London* had been appearing since 1939. (The name itself was used to indicate both the firm and the magazine.) As a publishing house, the subsidiary had brought out volumes by Kathleen Raine, David Gascoyne, and a translation of Hölderlin by Michael Hamburger. The firm likewise had close ties with Nicholas Moore, publishing his volume of poems, *The Glass Tower* (1944), as well as an anthology of short fiction edited by him. Moreover, Tambimuttu's *Poetry London* was preparing to republish a poem by Stevens with an exegesis by Moore, "A Difficult Poem: 'The Woman That Had More Babies than That.'" It was in large part Nicholas Moore's divided loyalty between the Fortune Press and the firm of Poetry London that helped to erect the barriers that were ultimately to prevent the publication of a volume by Stevens in English during the 1940s.

When he received Tambimuttu's letter, Stevens sent a complete copy of it to Knopf, adding, "What I want to say in substance amount[s] to this, that I am very much interested in seeing something of this sort done and should, of course, be willing to waive payment of any sort."[12] Alfred Knopf's response to Stevens on September 21 made clear the distribution of publishing rights:

> In May of this year, at your request, we wrote the Fortune Press, Ltd. in London about your poems. In June they replied explaining on how small a scale they operated. In July we countered with the suggestion of a fee of ten pounds for an edition of one thousand copies. Meanwhile, in September '43, a London agent wrote about Tambimuttu's interest in your book. We replied to this letter and sent copies of the books, but up to July '44 neither letter nor books had been received on the other side. Then a few days ago we had a letter from the Fortune Press accepting our offer and last week an agreement was sent them. Thus, as matters stand, I do not see that we can do anything for Mr. Tambimuttu and I return his letter of August 10th to you herewith.[13]

The precise nature of the dealings at this time between Knopf's London agent at that time, Laurence Pollinger, and the Tambimuttu firm is unclear. Tambimuttu took the position that he had a prior claim upon the British publication rights, while Knopf and his agents found no justification for such a claim. The impact of Knopf's letter, however, did not disturb Stevens. Without reservation, he accepted Knopf's arrangement and responded to Tambimuttu on September 23 accordingly: "Since Mr. Knopf controls my things in England, I am very much afraid this eliminates you."[14] The controversy might very well have been averted at this point, as the Fortune Press, having signed the agreement with Knopf, proceeded with its own publication plans.

Tambimuttu, however, was not easily appeased. In an October letter to Stevens he proposed a compromise. Moore would go ahead with a small selection by the Fortune Press, but this would be followed with three more extensive selections for Poetry London. The letter concludes with Tambimuttu's promise to consult with Pollinger, the Knopf agent. Continuing to keep Knopf fully informed, Stevens forwarded Tambimuttu's letter on to his New York publisher.

Stevens' own association with Knopf since the publication of *Harmonium* had always been professionally cordial. Nonetheless, as noted earlier, Stevens had arranged to have a number of volumes published by small independent presses on the grounds that these presses were not commercial rivals of Knopf, and the latter always had the option of reissuing them for the wider market. As early as 1935, however, Knopf had tried to discourage Stevens' independent publishing ventures, though he never absolutely forbade them. It is clear that the poet was aware of potential strains with Knopf over the British rights, and he went out of his way to avoid them. Even so, he was also eager to exercise his own influence to expedite publication. To Tambimuttu, Stevens then wrote: "I hope that you and Mr. Pollinger [Knopf's agent] will be able to come to an agreement."[15]

For the next seven months Stevens' correspondence with the London publishers came to a halt. In the interim, he had negotiated both with the Cummington Press to publish *Esthétique du Mal* in a limited edition and with Knopf to reissue *The Man with the Blue Guitar*. On July 10, 1945, however, Nicholas Moore wrote to Stevens a long and angry letter. In it he made clear his own disenchantment with the Fortune Press, his personal animosity toward Laurence Pollinger of Knopf, and his newly directed loyalty to Tambimuttu and Poetry London, whose staff he was joining. The letter proposed an altogether new publishing strategy. The Fortune Press would be forgotten (the contract with Knopf notwithstanding), while Poetry London would proceed to publish three separate volumes of poems by Stevens: (1) *Parts of a World*; (2) a volume of fifty other poems, selected by Moore, the list of titles enclosed in the letter; and (3) a book of more recent poems, including "Notes toward a Supreme Fiction" and "Esthétique du Mal." In the first two cases, permission from Knopf would have to be secured, but a second letter from Moore to Stevens complained of Knopf's annoyance with him and with Poetry London arising from his (Moore's) *volte-face.*

Having received the second letter before the first, Stevens responded to Moore: "Mr. Knopf, who is ordinarily an amiable sort of person, seems to be a little on edge about Tambimuttu. Just what this is all about I do not know."[16] When the earlier letter arrived (quoted above) and Stevens began to perceive the rivalries and bickering at large, he can only have regarded the episode with dismay and no little incredulity. He did not, however, despair. Obviously believing that publication rights might yet be arranged with Knopf, Stevens found Moore's alternate plan for publication plausible. In an important letter to Moore, dated July 25, 1945, Stevens joined forces with Moore, Tambimuttu, and Poetry London:

> I like the plan outlined by you. PARTS OF A WORLD is, in my own judgment, my best book and I am glad to hear that you are going to publish it first and, apparently, in its entirety. The ESTHETIQUE is a small collection of related poems, which ought to run to not more than about 20 or perhaps 25 pages. It will contain illustrations of a sort. It happened to be just the right size for The Cummington Press.
>
> Mr. Knopf has no status as yet respecting NOTES TOWARD A SU-PREME FICTION; the same thing is true as to the ESTHETIQUE. Both of these books were published by the Cummington Press, which does not have nearly the acute sense of property that Mr. Knopf seems to have. However, I owe a good deal more to Mr. Knopf than I do to The Cummington Press, so I want to leave that subject alone.[17]

A copy of this letter was sent to Harry Duncan of the Cummington Press, who soon endorsed the plan of allowing publication of "Notes toward a Supreme Fiction" and "Esthétique du Mal" as Poetry London's projected third volume. Departing from his customary practice of keeping Knopf fully apprised of his own actions, however, Stevens did not forward a copy of this letter to his New York publisher, perhaps because of his judgmental reference to Knopf's "acute sense of property."

A few months later, on November 1, Knopf's increasing annoyance with Poetry London, as well as with Stevens' continuing association with the Cummington Press, came to a head. To Stevens he wrote:

I hope that some day you will visit me here in my office. When you do, I will show you the file of correspondence and cables that we have collected in connection with Fortune Press, Nicholas Moore, and Wallace Stevens. This has been so time-consuming, expensive, and exasperating that I think we ought to assign back to you any British rights, excluding Canada, which our contracts with you ever gave us, leaving you free to make your own arrangements over there as you would seem to be doing in any case. For example, I hear that Mr. Moore has arranged with you and the Cummington Press to publish next year in one volume your "latest two books." But I have not heard of this from you. In view of our long, and certainly not unpleasant, publishing relationship, I think we should be taken rather more fully into your confidence. After all, there could never be any money involved for anyone in connection with placing your books in England, and we only represented you as a matter of friendly service. But in thirty years of publishing, I give you my word I have never run into such a mess all around as arose, or so it seems to me, from these English people discovering they could deal with you and with us at one and the same time.[18]

Determined to make his peace with Knopf, Stevens replied immediately: "I know nothing about what is going on in England and know of nothing that would justify you or anybody else in saying that I have been dealing directly. Any letters that I have received from publishers over there have been sent to you and the writers have been referred to you." The poet then went on to quote to Knopf the tripartite publishing plan of Nicholas Moore and Poetry London and cited directly from the July 10 letter wherein Moore promised to arrange publication rights with Pollinger, Knopf's agent. He continued, "I wrote in reply: 'I like the plan outlined by you.' Mr. Moore has not written to me since, nor have I written to him."[19] At about the same time, Oscar Williams wrote to Stevens requesting "So-And-So Reclining on Her Couch" for his *A Little Treasury of Modern Poetry*. Stevens' reply of November 20 hinted at his continuing fears over Knopf's displeasure: "I am glad that you have applied to Knopf because I rather think that he regards the idea of using uncollected poems in anthologies as irregular. Naturally, I want to keep my relations with Knopf topside up."[20]

Knopf then sent to Stevens a lengthy memorandum summarizing the sequence of his communications with his agent in London and the two English firms. Its most pertinent disclosures account for some of the entanglements. Six months before Stevens received the first letter from the Fortune Press proposing publication of a volume, Tambimuttu had indeed approached Pollinger, expressed an interest in producing such a volume from his Poetry London. Books (Stevens' volumes, one assumes) were requested by him and, according to Knopf, dispatched. Tambimuttu later claimed never to have received them. In September 1944, a year after Tambimuttu's initial overtures to Knopf, the Fortune Press accepted an offer to purchase Stevens' publishing rights for a volume, although a final contract was not completed until the following year. By November 1944, Pollinger reported to Knopf, a falling out between Nicholas Moore and the owner of the Fortune Press had occurred. A testy letter from Reginald Caton, the owner, to Pollinger followed in January 1945, in which the publisher made clear his resolve, under no circumstances, to sacrifice his signed agreement with Knopf to publish the Stevens volume with or without Nicholas Moore as editor. These events understandably irritated Knopf and, as it turned out, eventually dashed Stevens' own hopes at that time for a publication in England.

On February 20, 1946, twenty-three months to the day after receiving his first letter from the Fortune Press, Stevens wrote to Moore withdrawing his endorsement of the plan. Foremost in his own thinking was the preservation of good feelings with Knopf, who was proceeding to publish *Transport to Summer*:

> Things in England have not been straightened out, and it would probably make it all the more difficult to straighten them out eventually if I were now to publish a book there. I am free to do so as far as Mr. Knopf's rights are concerned, but, in view of what has happened and of the possible effect of streightening [*sic*] things out in England eventually, and of the very good chance that he would take offense, *I think*

I shall not go any farther with this [emphasis added]. A poet must have a publisher and is fortunate to have a decent one after his first book or two. It is not the easiest thing in the world to persuade a publisher to publish one's sixth or seventh book. Knopf is as good a publisher as there is in this country and I value my connection with him. I think you will understand all this and I hope that you will think that I am doing the right thing. While I am doing it for my own welfare, nevertheless I think it is the right thing to do from any point of view. It is not necessary to say how much I regret having put you to so much trouble. I am grateful to you.[21]

A few weeks later, to his friend Henry Church, Stevens spoke of the British publication as "something that I have wanted very much to bring about," but he had withdrawn his approval "because of a possible conflict with Knopf."[22]

Where precisely to lay the blame for this outcome in 1946 is not immediately apparent. Nicholas Moore's personal alienation from the Fortune Press after his arrangements with them and his subsequent alliance with Tambimuttu and Poetry London were in part responsible. All the parties involved, including Stevens, Knopf, and Poetry London, persisted in the belief that Moore should be retained to make the selection of poems for the volume. (Stevens remained on friendly terms with Moore; in October 1949, responding to a request from Moore, the poet sent him "Angel Surrounded by Paysans," which first appeared in *Poetry London*.) The Fortune Press itself stubbornly but legally refused to give up its claim to publish, in spite of Moore's defection and daunting frowns from Knopf. By first refusing to make the selection of poems, Stevens sacrificed control of the venture, even as he greeted all publication proposals with epistolary encouragement. Communication, mostly by letter, with so many parties, and over such distances in wartime, led to minor misunderstandings that took on exaggerated importance. Such appears to have been the case with Stevens' letter to Moore of July 25, 1945, in which he endorsed the plan of Moore and Tambimuttu to publish three volumes, a letter that Knopf learned of only later, to his chagrin, and one that Poetry London took as a green light from America. (This is the letter that Stevens did not send as a copy to Knopf.)

As a coda to the two-year struggle for publication, the Fortune Press tried once again in October 1946 to interest Stevens in selecting poems himself for a volume, Nicholas Moore having removed himself from consideration. Advertisement for the volume had led to subscriptions, the letter informed Stevens, and there was need for a speedy resolution. Stevens sent the letter to Knopf, but with a disclaimer: "I think that if anything comes of it the selection should be made by someone in England. Taste in the two countries is quite different. Anyhow, I should not be willing to make the selection."[23] Nothing came of it for the next five years.

Efforts toward publication in England of a volume by Stevens resumed in the fall of 1951, five years after Stevens had called a halt to the earlier attempts. This time the initiative began with Faber and Faber, Ltd. That publishing house had already introduced poems by Stevens in Michael Roberts' influential anthology *The Faber Book of Modern Verse*. It first appeared in 1936 and allotted three pages to Stevens' work, all from the second edition of *Harmonium* ("Two at Norfolk," "Tea at the Palaz of Hoon," "The Death of a Soldier," and "The Emperor of Ice-Cream"). In subsequent editions of the anthology, the selections of poems by Stevens changed.[24]

Faber also published *The Little Book of Modern Verse* in 1941, and the editor, Anne Ridler, included Stevens with "The Emperor of Ice-Cream" and "Gray Stones and Gray Pigeons." T. S. Eliot wrote a brief introduction to the collection but did not single out Stevens for commentary.

It was Eliot, then a director of Faber and Faber, who formally proposed the publication of a Stevens *Selected Poems*. He had been aware of Stevens' poems for some time. A quarter-century earlier, he had recommended to Robert Graves the work of Stevens, among others, as one who should be included in a publishing venture proposed by Graves.[25] As editor of the *Criterion*, he also published a laudatory review of *Ideas of Order* by Marianne Moore.

As Peter Brazeau reports, "On November 22, 1950, Knopf's London agent . . . had sent a copy of Stevens' latest book, *The Auroras of Autumn*, to . . . Eliot's fellow director at Faber and Faber, pointing out that the author had recently received the Bollingen Prize and inquiring whether this English firm would like to publish the work. The matter was then brought to Eliot's attention. He proposed that, instead of publishing *The Auroras of Autumn*, it would be better to do a selection from Stevens' poetry as a whole as his debut volume in England. Eliot indicated that if that book sold well, his firm would also consider bringing out a volume of Stevens' collected poems at a later date" (155).

Free this time from recrimination and delay, arrangements were easily concluded with Faber the following October. When Herbert Weinstock, a senior editor at Knopf, wrote to Stevens in October announcing the plan, he conveyed the wishes of Faber that Stevens himself make the selection of poems. Though not unequivocal in his reluctance, Stevens still demurred: "I think that it would be a mistake for any one over here to make the selection."[26]

Eliot later recounted his own role in the publication of a Stevens volume: "I had taken for granted that some other firm had published his work [in England], and wondered at their incompetence in taking so little trouble to make the fact known: it was one of my fellow directors [Peter du Sautoy] who first called my attention to the fact that Stevens, although his name and some of his poems were very well known to the élite who really know, had had no book to himself" (Untitled remarks 9). Eliot, responding to Stevens' unwillingness, proposed the name of Marianne Moore as the one to make the selection for Faber. A close friend of Stevens, Moore had in fact been urging Peter du Sautoy to publish Stevens' work, though her importuning on Stevens' behalf apparently came after an agreement had been reached. Du Sautoy recalled that the suggestion to publish Stevens was his: "I think it would be true to say that the publication of Wallace Stevens' works by Faber and Faber resulted from my initiative, though T. S. Eliot was always consulted and fully approved."[27] Stevens at first agreed to the suggestion that Marianne Moore make the selection for Faber, but when he learned that Knopf would not be able to provide remuneration for her efforts, he agreed finally to make the selection himself.

The poet's role as self-editor, one he would exercise again when the *Collected Poems* was published three years later, was limited by the publisher's stipulation that the volume consist of 160 pages. In sending the list to Weinstock, Stevens insisted that it was "representative," but not "a list of things that are what 'the author wishes to preserve'" (*L* 732). Poems were chosen from all of Stevens' volumes, including the long poems "The Man with the Blue Guitar" and "Notes toward a Supreme Fiction" in entirety. *Harmonium* was the volume most widely represented, with thirty-four poems, though most of these were relatively brief lyrics including "Sea Surface Full of Clouds." *Ideas of Order*, on the other hand, was represented by only four poems, one of which was "The

Idea of Order at Key West." *Parts of a World*, once regarded by Stevens as his most distinguished collection, included five. In addition to "Notes toward a Supreme Fiction," *Transport to Summer* was also represented by "Credences of Summer" and six other shorter poems. A shorter version of "An Ordinary Evening in New Haven" was included, along with four other poems from *The Auroras of Autumn*. The title poem from that volume, however, was included only as an alternate and was not among the contents of the final determination.

Although Marianne Moore did not make the selection of poems, she took a keen interest in the project and persuaded Stevens and Peter du Sautoy to include "Final Soliloquy of the Interior Paramour," a poem that had recently appeared in the *Hudson Review* but not in any other collection. She exercised one *sub rosa* role for Stevens when she inquired of Faber and Faber the terms of tax exemption for Stevens on the publication of the volume abroad. (She reported back to him early in 1952 that the matter was to be treated directly with the publishers.)

Unknown both to Steven and his London publishers, Reginald Caton of the Fortune Press, now *sans* Nicholas Moore, was simultaneously and independently proceeding with his own publication of a *Selected Poems*. Peter du Sautoy learned of its completion from an announcement in the *Times Literary Supplement* on December 26, 1952. Stevens heard of it only when his friend John Sweeney sent a review by Austin Clarke, which had appeared in the *Irish Times* on February 14 in the following year. Stevens' astonishment must have been at least as great as Clarke's:

> Now, at the age of seventy-four, Wallace Stevens has achieved the minor success of having two selections from his poems published in London at the same time. Curiously enough, no explanation of this double celebration is given to us by either publisher. "Selected Poems," published by Messrs. Faber, is well set out and the book is pleasant to look at. "Selected Poems," issued by the Fortune Press, is closer set and contains more poems, page for page; the choice was made by Mr. Dennis Williamson and he has written an agreeable foreword. (6)

Dennis Williamson, himself a poet who had recently come down from Oxford, had just published the previous July *The Modern Genilon and Other Poems* through Caton's firm.[28] In introducing the Fortune Press's *Selected Poems*, he begins by acknowledging that Stevens, "one of the most skilled and stimulating of American poets, is generally known in this country only by a few 'anthology pieces.'" He makes clear his preference for *Harmonium*, and, indeed, thirty-five of the total eighty poems selected by him are from that volume. Though *Parts of a World* demonstrates a greater social awareness on Stevens' part, Williamson allows, he also discerns a "less finished technique" (10–12). The longest poem in the collection is "The Comedian as the Letter C"; none of the later longer poems reproduced in the Faber selection is included.

Upon receiving Sweeney's letter with the review from the *Irish Times*, Stevens wrote at once to Herbert Weinstock requesting further information. Weinstock's reply brought news of the resolution: "To our consternation we later heard that Fortune Press, despite the cancellation of the contract, was proceeding to publish. . . . When simple suasion failed, we had a firm of barristers take the matter in hand. . . . The barristers had some trouble locating the proprietor [Reginald Caton]. At last, he agreed to withdraw the book and destroy all copies of it except a few that had already gone out to reviewers."[29]

What had happened? The contract between Knopf and the Fortune Press, which had been signed in 1945, was later cancelled by Knopf. Peter du Sautoy recalls that "there had been a contract between Knopf and the Fortune Press for such a volume but the time limit for its publication had expired, so Knopf were fully entitled to make an agreement with us [Faber & Faber].[30] In fact, the contract had expired on December 31, 1946. Even as late as February 1951, Knopf had extended a final six-month grace period to Caton. With no publication forthcoming from the Fortune Press, negotiations with Faber commenced in August of that year. Had Caton heard of the proposed Faber volume and defiantly rushed into print his own collection six weeks in advance of the other? Did he somehow believe that he still enjoyed a valid contract with Knopf? Charles Skilton, a later proprietor of the Fortune Press, was unsure: "[Caton] ran the business entirely as a one-man show—very industriously but highly eccentrically—and most of the history of it died with him."[31] Weinstock's letter to Stevens indicates that Caton at first resisted "simple suasion," but on January 17 Caton informed Knopf's attorneys in London that the sale of his *Selected Poems* was being abandoned. By February 5 he had agreed to destroy all remaining copies. In the event, however, Caton did not do so. According to Timothy d'Arch Smith: "Never much one for contractual niceties, Caton had to be legally constrained from marketing his edition. Even then, he did not destroy it as requested but merely stuffed the books under some basement stairs" (85).

In the last weeks of his life Stevens suddenly resumed correspondence with one of the figures from the earlier publishing controversy. Tambimuttu, the editor of Poetry London who in the mid-1940s had vied with the Fortune Press in bringing out a Stevens collection, was resuming the publication of his magazine to be renamed *Poetry London-New York*, and wanted a poem from Stevens. There were certainly no lingering hard feelings on Stevens' part ("Greetings and welcome—just as if I owned the place"),[32] but surgery for cancer prevented him from sending a poem. Tambimuttu, ever resourceful and persistent, invited himself to Hartford for a personal meeting, but, writing from the Avery Convalescent Hospital a couple of months before his death, Stevens discouraged it.

At the time of his death, Stevens' reputation in America enjoyed a small but secure audience. But even in his native land, he had never attained the popularity or fame of other major American modernists. In reviewing Stevens' *Transport to Summer* in 1947, Robert Lowell noted that Stevens "has never had the popularity of Robert Frost, or the international reputation of T. S. Eliot or Ezra Pound" ("Imagination and Reality" 400). Even well into the twenty-first century one could make a similar claim, and the reasons for that lack of widespread popularity on both sides of the Atlantic are not unrelated.[33]

With the publication of the Faber edition, however, and in the last year of his life, Stevens enjoyed the satisfaction of accessibility to British readers for the first time and an emerging awareness of his work in England. As Irish critic Denis Donoghue has noted, however, in reflecting on the beginning of his own career in the 1950s while studying in Ireland and England, and with his focus on American literature, "It is hard to remember that American literature, during those years, had little footing in Europe, and that those European scholars who taught it and wrote of it had missionary zest to keep them going" (*Connoisseurs of Chaos* 4).

Nonetheless, the beginnings of an interest in Wallace Stevens in England was, in all its incipiency, underway after *Selected Poems*. Alan Pryce-Jones had written in 1954, requesting poems for the *Times Literary Supplement*. Stevens responded with two of his final poems, "Presence of an External Master of Knowledge" and "A Child Asleep in Its Own Life." More significantly, not only had *Selected Poems* gone on to receive a second printing, but the Faber edition of *The Collected Poems*—just as Eliot had anticipated—had been announced. It was to appear two months after Stevens' death. Eliot, writing in a brief tribute to Stevens about a year before his death, looked hopefully to a gradual emergence of interest in Stevens: "Now, his reputation is beginning to spread to the people who don't know. There is no compliment on my own work that gives me more pleasure than that of the man who says, 'I didn't know anything about this chap, but I picked up a volume of his the other day—and I found I *liked* it!' I have heard that said lately several times, about the book of Wallace Stevens" (Untitled remarks 9).

RECEPTION: The Critics

After all the decades that have elapsed since Eliot wrote the words quoted above, one invariably asks if Stevens did indeed go on to enjoy the success for which the poet and director at Faber was claiming to see the beginnings. The initial responses to the *Selected Poems* in the months following its publication in many ways demonstrate a pattern that would persist in the ensuing decades. John Wain, for example, composed an admiring review, "The Freshness of Ourselves," for the BBC Third Programme, which was broadcast on March 29, 1953, along with a reading of some of the poems. Stephen Spender, writing in *Encounter,* proclaimed Stevens "one of the half-dozen great representatives" of American poetry ("American Diction v. American Poetry" 65). For Donald Davie, Stevens was "a poet to be mentioned in the same breath as Eliot and Yeats and Pound. . . . He is a great poet indeed" ("Essential Gaudiness" 455, 462). William Empson noted that Stevens "has been highly acclaimed in America for thirty years, and it is time he was better known here" (521).

But these are scattered comments, typically accompanied by doubts, reservations, and—in some cases—reversals. Empson, for example, in the same review quoted above, went on to identify in the poems "a good deal of philosophising" that he finds "very airless": "One can't help wishing he had found more to say, if only because he could evidently say it" (521).[34]

Empson's case is a particularly interesting one because we have evidence of his somewhat defensive decision to omit the poems of Stevens from his teaching syllabus. Taking a leave from Sheffield University in order to lecture in Ghana in 1964, Empson permitted a Fulbright Fellow from the University of Michigan named James Gindin to take over his lectures in his absence. As John Haffenden describes the episode, Empson sent Gindin a list of poets to be covered:

> Some students were beginning to show an interest in the poetry of Wallace Stevens, Empson noted, but he himself did not find it interesting; all the same, if Gindin wanted to give a lecture of Stevens, he should feel free to do so. When Gindin arrived in London in mid-September, Empson took him out to an alcohol-fuelled lunch; and only when the meal was almost over did Empson announce that they must have another drink because they had not yet discussed Gindin's teaching. 'Of course,' Empson then declared, 'some of the students want to talk about Stevens. But I can't read him. Let's leave him off the course.' Gindin was taken aback by this sudden reversal. (518)

He chose to give the Stevens lecture in spite of Empson's discouragement.

Donald Davie, writing in 1953 and in spite of his placing of Stevens "in the same breath as Eliot and Yeats and Pound," finds much to disapprove: He discerns an "epistemology of excess" and that is consistent with "the best language [which] is excessive language, so the best, the noblest sort of conduct is action in excess" ("Essential Gaudiness," 1953, 455, 459-460). When the review-essay was republished in 1977, a quarter century later, Davie added a "Postscript" indicating a more extreme antipathy toward the American poet. He briefly refers to Harold Bloom's identification of Stevens as an heir of Emersonian romanticism, leading Davie to pronounce: "Accordingly I should now probably be more captious about Stevens than I was when I wrote this" ("Essential Gaudiness" 17).

Two longer reviews in the early 1950s, equally uncertain about Stevens, dealt with issues that were to restrict the appeal of Stevens more generally. The anonymous reviewer in the *Times Literary Supplement,* for example, acclaimed Stevens as "the best poet writing in America, and one of the best now writing in English" (396). Half of the review, however, chided the poet for deliberate obscurity: "the average man is going to find that—charmingly stated or not—confusion differs from order, and that these poems, if full of meaning, leave much of their meaning merely noted" (396). Writing in the same review in which he had ranked Stevens so highly, Stephen Spender saw him as "a poet whom most English critics would consider American to the point where his imagination even baffles the English reader" ("American Diction v. American Poetry" 61). For Bernard Bergonzi, Stevens' constant concern with a "poetic epistemology" isolated his work from more conventional themes and left it "lonely and depopulated." He concluded that Stevens' poetry "represents a life-time of magnificent achievement. But it is, alas, essentially a barren magnificence (which is not to imply that younger poets cannot learn much from Stevens about the art of poetry)" (50–51).

Charges of obscurity and dispassion were of course not limited to his British readers, but these purported handicaps contributed to an immediate hesitation about Stevens that his British readers would be slow to relinquish. Julian Symons, writing a year after the Faber publication, contended that Stevens was simply not widely read: "It remains true, however, that Stevens is held in no such esteem here as that accorded to T. S. Eliot and Ezra Pound; it is doubtful if he has even the small band of devoted admirers possessed by John Crowe Ransom and Conrad Aiken" ("Stevens in England" 43).[35] Of the thousand copies of the first edition of *Selected Poems*, 820 were sold in the first year, and fewer than 150 copies were sold annually during the next ten years.

The small number of sales notwithstanding, it is the loyalty of Faber and Faber to the publication of his work that assured steady access to Stevens' work in England continuing into the twenty-first century. In addition to the second printing of *Selected Poems* in 1954, followed in the next year by the *Collected Poems*, Faber went on to issue editions of *Opus Posthumous* (1959), *The Necessary Angel* (1960), and Holly Stevens' edition of *Letters* (1967). The third printing of *Selected Poems* in 1965 in a paperback edition appeared to launch a significant interest in Stevens in England. Peter du Sautoy, then chairman of Faber and Faber, reported that sales "really took off when the paperback appeared."[36] A separate edition of *Harmonium* was added to the list in 2001. In 2008, Faber issued *Wallace Stevens: Poems Selected by John Burnside,* the latter a distinguished Scottish poet and novelist. (Editorial errors, however, led to the withdrawal of the collection by Faber.)

Foundations for study of Stevens in Britain and Ireland were laid early by two distinguished critics, Frank Kermode and Denis Donoghue. Each quickly demonstrated his larger interest in the role of twentieth-century American poetry and its contribution to modernism as it had evolved in the previous decades. Their special interest in Stevens began early but would envelop the whole of their remarkable careers.

The growing attention to Stevens abroad was partly spurred by the 1960 publication of Kermode's pioneering critical study *Wallace Stevens* in the Writers and Critics series. It was the first detailed consideration of the whole of Stevens' work to be offered by a British critic: "Much commentary [on Stevens' work] . . . is bound to give the impression that this kind of pure poetry carries badly made bundles of ideas on its back. But it is genuinely the poetry of a man who thought poetry began where philosophy left off. . . . His fictions may result from feeling; but thought is felt. The poet's business is not merely to satisfy the lovers of truth, but to make brilliant the poverty on which their thoughts dwell. By altering the world he makes it acceptable to humanity" (126–27). But Kermode's Stevens is not a purveyor of the imagination alone: "The degree of attention to reality, the faithfulness of mind he required of poets, has rarely been so unflaggingly exercised as by Stevens" (127). Kermode went on to give detailed readings of representative poems over the whole of Stevens' career. As Ben Lerner has said of this book in 2012, "It was ahead of its time—and still largely ahead of ours—in its nuanced attention to a poet's attitude towards content, which is not reducible to content itself, and which allows us to treat the poem not just as the record of a person (Stevens), but as advancing a theory of personhood ('major man')" (no page-number indicated). *Wallace Stevens* was, in every way, an ideal introduction of the American poet to a British audience.

Writing a decade after Stevens' death, Donoghue too had absorbed not just *Selected Poems*, but the *Collected Poems*, *Opus Posthumous*, and the essays in that collection as well as those in *The Necessary Angel*. His work is informed by a close familiarity with the whole of Stevens' oeuvre—the poems of *Harmonium*, but also those from all the subsequent volumes, including both shorter and longer poems. He is attuned to the varieties of the poet's style. Devoting a chapter to Stevens in his *Connoisseurs of Chaos: Ideas of Order in Modern American Poetry* (1965), he is notably aware of the varieties of the imagination and reality in Stevens' work: "There is no authority but the poet himself, no structures of belief but the structures he makes for his own appeasement. The poet's act of faith is: I believe in the inventions of my own productive imagination" (191). Even the titles of some of his books betray the force of Stevens' influence: *Connoisseurs of Chaos: Ideas of Order in Modern American Poetry*" (1965), *The Sovereign Ghost* (1976), *Ferocious Alphabets* (1981), *The Pure Good of Theory* (1992)—all taken from poems by Stevens. In many ways, Stevens and Eliot were lodestars for Donoghue in the more than half a century of his analyses of American poetry generally.[37]

With the endorsement of Eliot, Kermode, Donoghue, and other poets and critics following the initial publication of *Selected Poems,* one might expect Stevens' "discovery" to have led to a steady growth of interest among his new readers. After all, with poems now at hand, there was nothing left to do but read them. In the decades that followed the publication of *Selected Poems* in 1953 and the early reviews that followed, however, it is apparent that that was not to be the case. Faber's John Bodley wrote in 2001: "We can't provide sales figures I'm afraid, but there is no question that for English readers Stevens, in all his richness and variety, remains one of the glories of modern poetry."[38] The question remains: who exactly were those readers and were they indeed significantly increasing in numbers?

As one surveys the responses of British critics and poets to the work of Stevens—beginning with the American publication of *Harmonium* but including the later responses to the Faber edition of the *Selected Poems* in the 1950s and subsequent reviews and essays throughout the remainder of the twentieth century and well into the twenty-first—a consistent ambiguity occurs. It is as if the critic cannot quite make up his mind. That indecisiveness is apparent in the early reviews of *Selected Poems* from which I quote above. British critics often eagerly acknowledge Stevens as a major modernist, a poet of exceptional power and importance, but almost at once certain demurrals follow. It is often these demurrals that give us an insight into a lingering hesitancy on the part of many British readers.

One of the most receptive of the anthology selections of Stevens in Britain appeared in the year after the Faber edition of *Selected Poems.* In his *The Penguin Book of Modern American Verse,* Geoffrey Moore reproduced the whole of "Sunday Morning" in its proper order and the whole of "Credences of Summer," with some shorter poems and two selections from "Notes toward a Supreme Fiction." In his "Introduction," Moore notes rather presumptuously that "it is only after thirty years of neglect that Mr. Stevens' stature has been fully recognized" (24). He adds, "One could not mistake Mr Stevens' style for that of an Englishman; his idiom is American, but naturally and not protestingly so" (24).

One of the most perceptive of Stevens' early British readers was A. Alvarez.[39] In his *The Alvarez Generation*, William Wootten writes, "Alvarez's taste in British, American, and Central European poetry was to become a significant factor in the writing, publishing and reading of poetry throughout the 1960s and into the early 1970s" (xvi). Alvarez's influential book *The Shaping Spirit* appeared in 1958 and included a chapter on Stevens. The essay begins with acclaim: "Eliot apart, Stevens is the most perfectly finished poet America has turned out" (124), and while "he might very easily have been a worse poet . . . it is hard to see that he could have been any better" (124). Nonetheless, Alvarez admits to "hesitations" (138) and perceives unevenness. He detects "disparity between his elaborate furnishings and the rather stringent bareness of the ideas" (136). The invariable label "dandyism" (135) emerges when discussing "Le Monocle de Mon Oncle."

Stevens as "dandy" was not a new claim even then. The American critic Gorham Munson had earlier launched the term in his 1925 essay "The Dandyism of Wallace Stevens." In this influential appraisal, he found Stevens' vocabulary expressive of the "lightness and coolness and transparency of French," and the poems themselves revealing "the discipline of one who is a connoisseur of the senses and the emotions." Removed from historical concerns, Stevens seems to "sit comfortably" and "to be conscious of no need of fighting the times" (42, 43). Munson's own observations were restricted, of course, to the poems of the recently published *Harmonium*, but the term "dandyism" quickly gained a currency that would be applied to the later volumes as well and that would become for many years a touchstone label for American as well as British critics.

The influential critic Philip Hobsbaum has pointed to the singular influence of a review of *Ideas of Order* written by Geoffrey Grigson in *New Verse*, the journal that Grigson edited. Entitled "The Stuffed Goldfinch," the essay became, in Hobsbaum's estimation, "the godfather of many ascriptions of dandyism to that great poet." He adds that the review "may have had a privative effect" among Stevens' readers in England."[40] Comparing Stevens' second volume with his first, Grigson's short review dismissed Stevens as "still the finicking privateer, prosy Herrick, Klee without rhythm, observing nothing, single artificer of his own world of mannerism, mixed-up of chinoiserie. . . . Too much Wallace Stevens, too little everything else" (18).

Alvarez himself, writing more than twenty years after Grigson's review, found in certain of the poems a point "with Stevens, and he reaches it often, at which profundity becomes blurred with rhetoric." His indictment becomes more sweeping: "It is a poetry of irritation. He [Stevens] seems to be continually baffled by the impossibility of describing anything at all with finality. A motion of the wrist, the slightest variation in light or in the mood of the observer, and the object is utterly different. The impossible endlessness of observation, then, is Stevens's creative premiss" (134, 129). Here Alvarez lays out the objections that would inform numerous iterations among the poet's British critics: a surface dazzle in vocabulary and image that seemed to belong more to the French tradition than the British or the American; a poetry that preferred thirteen ways of viewing the world over a single and final one; an aloof, ironical and dispassionate voice that played whimsically, teasingly and often obscurely with ideas. Unlike Stevens' American critics in the decades following the poet's death, many of his British critics seemed to have little interest in taking the poet beyond such categorizations. His critics might recognize an extraordinary poetic talent, but often relegated that talent to superfluity and irrelevance.[41]

John Malcolm Brinnin, in an interview in 1976, found that English readers saw Stevens more in the tradition of the French than American: "To go to England and talk about Wallace Stevens as I did was to go to the Sahara. They didn't know about him, didn't want to. This was not an American poet; this was a sophisticate out of Paris and other nefarious influences" (194).

Allied to the idea of dandyism was something that might be called American dilettantism. How, his British readers wondered, could a businessman be taken seriously as a poet, especially if he was a successful and apparently wealthy businessman? Stevens was not even a man-of-letters but an insurance executive who settled the claims of surety bonds. Surely only Americans could

breed such a contradiction, and to take seriously a poet from such a background seemed not just improbable but slightly preposterous.

A third reason for regarding Stevens with suspicion had to do with the
rather loose but negative association of the poet with the dominant figures of
American modernism generally: Eliot, Pound, Williams, Crane, the early Lowell, and others. To many, the dislodgements of poetry from traditional forms
and the radical innovations of style, the incongruous juxtapositions of images
and allusions, and the defiant turn upon English Romanticism by these poets
targeted American modernists as unified agents of poetic eccentricity and de-
viants from the sanctioned British tradition. Stevens himself once remarked in
a letter that "the English insist that Americans have no background" (L 614).
As Lee M. Jenkins has noted, when Stevens was published in England at *mid-
century* it was "a time when the 'Movement,' with its suspicion of modernism,
its 'Englishness,' its stance in favour of the purity of English diction and plain
speech, held sway in British poetry" (*Rage for Order* 2). The Irish-born poet
Justin Quinn, author of *Gathered beneath the Storm: Wallace Stevens, Nature
and Community*, finds it "unlikely" that Stevens will ever become accepted
in Britain: "The dominant tradition, stretching from Hardy through Larkin
to such contemporary practitioners as Thom Gunn, Carol Ann Duffy, Glyn
Maxwell, and Sean O'Brien, is essentially grounded in dramatic narrative and
unengaged by the type of philosophical interests that fuelled so much of Stevens's poetry" ("A Second Look" 53). Robert Conquest, whose anthology *New
Lines* (1956) collected the Movement poets and gave them their identity, found
Stevens privately obscure. In a 1963 interview, he says, "A lot of American stuff
seems to be written privately, not for themselves alone, but for themselves and
a friend they have taken the bother to explain it all to first. You get that with
Wallace Stevens, for instance" (48). Carolyn Masel agrees that poets like Philip
Larkin and John Betjeman satisfied a "preference for realism, especially auto-
biographically based work" (134), while Stevens' poetry seemed antithetical
to that.[42] Some of this bias continues to linger among English readers in the
present century.

Frank Kermode's early endorsement of the poet with his critical study in
1960 continued through the second half of the twentieth century. His *Wallace
Stevens* was reissued in 1979 with an added preface: "I have not changed my
opinion that he is among the greatest of twentieth-century poets" ("Preface"

unnumbered page). For a still later edition of the same book in paperback in 1989, Kermode continued to advance the case for the American poet, calling "the poems of the last years" to be "for me the greatest modern poems in English about death and old age, and possibly about anything" (xiv). Kermode consistently prefers the late and more meditative poems of Stevens over what he called in 1958 (and before the publication of his *Wallace Stevens*) "the dazzle caused by over-long attention to the fireworks of *Harmonium*" ("The Gaiety of Language" 51). In 1997 he coedited with Joan Richardson *Wallace Stevens: Collected Poetry and Prose,* the Library of America edition of Stevens' works.

Taking stock of the slowness with which Stevens seemed to be catching on in his native country, Kermode, in his 1989 edition of *Wallace Stevens,* went on to address a liability that he saw as arising from Empson's review of *Selected Poems* written more than thirty years earlier and already cited above ("One can't help wishing [Stevens] had found more to say, if only because he could evidently say it"). Here the charge of dandyism is resurrected, and Kermode seeks to explain its significance: "And by going on about Stevens being dandyish, American and rich, Empson may also have done something to strengthen an existing prejudice against him; the fifties in Britain being a bit dowdy and rather poor, people weren't altogether keen on the idea of a dandyish versifying American tycoon. For at this time the one thing everybody who had so much as heard of Stevens was sure of was that he was an insurance fat-cat" (xii).

When Faber published Stevens' *Collected Poems* in 1954, the Irish poet Thomas Kinsella reviewed it for the *Irish Press* under the title "Major American Poet." Pointing to the title, the opening sentence defines Stevens as "a product of this grotesque, successful country." He finds it "orthodox" to agree that, "after 'Harmonium,' Stevens produced nothing that increased his stature, nothing to show that his subsequent eloquence was any more than mere talkativeness." Kinsella adds, "Orthodox but not quite true." But he himself offers little to dispel such orthodoxy and immediately points to Stevens' "faults": a "talent for word-play which sometimes lets him down, a frequent successful resisting of the intelligence [that] persisted to the end, and . . . creative energy [that] failed to rise." Only the late poems merit his approval: "a subject which suited his voice perfectly and proved to be a source of serene beauty: age, the ending of life, and the anticipation of death" (4).

In an essay for the *Bulletin: British Association for American Studies* in 1962,

Malcolm Bradbury and F. W. Cook sounded the familiar theme: "Like the collector decorating with the horse-brasses his grandfather used as work-objects, Stevens collects words. He titillates the reader's appetite by the idiosyncratic obliqueness of his wit." He embraces, they claim, an aestheticism and "a cut-off one" at that, "the search of a vice-president of an insurance company, comfortably disposed, taking risks only with his soul, reflecting on aesthetics like a gentleman. One cannot help but suspect a certain lack of bite, a certain dilettantism in his vein" (37, 37–38).

A smaller number of critics were less daunted by apparent obscurity or a "certain dilettantism" in Stevens' work. Like the work of Kermode and Donoghue, their defense of the poet was indeed a response to the charges that had been lodged against him, but theirs were also ambitious attempts to see Stevens inclusively and more cumulatively.

Philip Hobsbaum, writing at the time of his professorship at Queen's University in Belfast, Northern Ireland, and at the very time of his weekly meetings there with young poets like Seamus Heaney, Michael Longley, and James Simmons (who would come to be called "the Belfast group" initially under Hobsbaum's sponsorship), also turned his attention to Stevens. As Alvarez would do after him, he asserted that "in many poems" Stevens was merely "a creator of the beautiful and a purveyor of rhetoric." He added, however, an important admonitory note to all of the poet's British readers: "Stevens' poems do not exist merely as word-collocations, texture to be enjoyed for texture's sake"; they are "usually *about* something." He regrets that the best poems tend "to be taken at their surface value, without consideration of the uses to which the surface may be put." The result is that "poems more rich in content, though less immediately colourful, may well be neglected" ("Critics at the Harmonium" 49).[43]

Like Hobsbaum, poet and critic Roy Fuller sought to convey some of the complexity of Stevens' work to his British readers. When he was elected chair of poetry at Oxford University in 1968, he dedicated one of his lectures there to Stevens' work. Basing his remarks upon a review that he had written earlier following the publication of Stevens' letters, he sought to lay out for his audience a sense of how life and work come together for Stevens. The letters he found immensely helpful in this endeavor, and he called the collection edited by Stevens' daughter "one of the great books of the twentieth century." He noted that the newly published correspondence "reveals sparse English interest in Stevens' work [during the poet's lifetime]" and, now in the late 1960s, "Stevens's English admirers have not been numerous." Fuller regrets this state of affairs and goes on to show that Stevens' poetry combines a love for the efficacy of the imagination and "poetic power of giving to nature names and significant associations," while, at the same time, showing "nature's other reality—the brute, alien reality which is essentially inimical or least indifferent to man." He adds, "I know of no other poet who in his work was so constantly alive to what I would characterize as poetry's supreme task—to delineate the life of man in relation to nature unconsoled by any supernatural idea" (73, 85, 72).

Toward the end of the century, the noted critic Michael Schmidt attempted to push Stevens beyond the facile categories to which many of his British *confrères* had assigned him. In his *Lives of the Poets* (1998), he places Stevens as one of "the big lights of the first half of the century" (600) and chides Eliot for his slowness in publishing Stevens before 1953 ("quite obviously his peer" [601]). He goes on to argue for the seriousness of Stevens' poetry beyond its "gaudy" surface:

> He is often gaudy, he is sometimes silly, his forms hold in the way that pre-Modernist form was required to hold. Yet Stevens *chose* his forms, fully understanding what was afoot in modern verse, and he chose them because what he wanted his poetry to hold was not an historical, political, theological or contingent world but a world that was unassistedly 'real.' . . . His work is of a piece, and if there are longueurs in the later poetry, where he seems to jump up and down on more or less the same spot, or advance very slowly on his quarry, there is no point where the verse is untrue to its—and his—objectives. (605)[44]

Stevens was also taken up by British painters, David Hockney in particular. In the summer of 1976 Hockney was given a copy of "The Man with the Blue Guitar" by a friend. "When I first read it," he later noted, "I wasn't quite sure what it was about, like all poems like that, but I loved the rhythms in it and some of the imagery, just the choice of words is marvellous. Then, when I read it out loud . . . I loved it even more, because I got the music that it has" (in Charles Ingham, *Words in Pictures* [A89]. He eventually completed a set of twenty colored etchings as a portfolio and book—with the poem and, in particular, Picasso's "The Old Guitarist" as a basis for the drawings. As Glen MacLeod has observed, "The imagery in Hockney's etchings comes from Picasso, not from the poem" (162). The portfolio was published in 1977. Later that year two additional paintings directed toward Stevens, "Self Portrait with Blue Guitar" and "Model with Unfinished Self-Portrait,"[45] followed.

As the century came to an end, Ian Hamilton included Stevens in his *Against Oblivion: Some Lives of the Twentieth-Century Poets*. He begins his introductory essay with this: "Although it is commonplace nowadays for Wallace Stevens to be ranked as one of the major modern poets, it is rare to hear him or his works spoken of with great affection" (32). Nor has Hamilton great affection for the poet, and here he falls back into a recitation that echoes so many of the critics of the previous half-century. He notes his "monotony, or repetition, or an obscurity which even the most finely tuned eavesdropper will not find easy to decipher. His critics have continued to complain, with some justice, that he had little or no interest in the dramatic, the social, the autobiographical." Stevens is guilty of "a modish Francophilia." What rescues Stevens for Hamilton is the very late poems toward which "we are likely to respond . . . to the unexpectedly heartfelt final act" and to find them "touchingly courageous" (32, 35, 33, 35). Hamilton's summary, coming some half-century after the publication of Faber's *Selected Poems*, shows how slowly, but, by now, predictably, the response typically unfolds: general endorsement—often in superlative terms—but followed by begrudging and exasperating reservations.

RECEPTION: The Poets

The response of the British poets themselves is often of a different quality from that of the critics. Stevens' voice, his traits of style, and, invariably, certain individual poems have been impressed onto their sensibilities as practicing craftsmen themselves. It is worth noting that four poems in particular, "Thirteen Ways of Looking at a Blackbird,"[46] "The Snow Man," "Sunday Morning," and "The Idea of Order at Key West," have become paradigmatic touchstones for many British and Irish poets (and critics as well). In several instances, one notes an initially reluctant absorption of the strange poet from across the Atlantic who nonetheless remains difficult, if not impossible, to dismiss. Upon occasion, they extol the strengths of Stevens' verse and even, in many cases, acknowledge his direct influence upon them. At the other extreme, a few feel compelled to debunk him as though he posed a wayward path.

Among those who make up the latter category are two poets who discovered Stevens early and to their dismay. Laura Riding and Robert Graves, with only *Harmonium* as a specimen and writing in 1927, pointed in passing to a "frivolousness" and, placing Stevens in association with Aldington, Pound, and Williams, found the four of them guilty of "parasitical inter-imitativeness" (166, 216).

When William Butler Yeats's edition of *The Oxford Book of Modern Verse* appeared in 1936, in his "Introduction" he offered an excuse for his omission of American poets except for Eliot and Pound:

> A distinguished American poet urged me not to attempt a representative selection of American poetry; he pointed out that I could not hope to acquire the necessary knowledge: "If your selection looks representative you will commit acts of injustice." I have, therefore, though with a sense of loss, confined my selections to those American poets who by subject, or by long residence in Europe, seem to English readers a part of their own literature. (*"Introduction"* xlii).

More candidly, he explained in a letter to Charles Williams in the previous year his reasons for the omissions, though he never mentions the name of Stevens:

> You speak of my ommissions [sic.] of certain Americans; H.D., Robert Frost, and Benet. . . . I am acting on the advice of T.S. Eliot who said 'dont *[sic]* attempt to make your selection of American poets representative, you cant [sic.] have the necessary knowledge and will be unjust; put in the three or four that you know and like'—or some such words. I am taking his advice and am explaining so in my introduction. As a matter of fact this will be far better for the popularity of the book as I shall not have to condemn certain popular figures. (in "Yeats as Anthologist," Stallworthy, 181).

Edward Clarke, in his *The Later Affluence of W. B. Yeats and Wallace Stevens*, admits that "we do not know if Yeats ever read Stevens, there is no indication that he did." He adds that "neither poet seemed especially important to the other" (7, 8), though he notes Stevens' use of "The Lake Isle of Innisfree" in his poem "Page from a Tale." The generation of Irish poets after Yeats would take Stevens far more seriously.

In his *W. H. Auden, A Commentary*, John Fuller, discussing Auden's poem "In Praise of Limestone," reproduces a piece of doggerel that Auden had privately sent to Ursula Niebuhr in 1947 but never otherwise published. Liesl Olson reproduces the note which accompanied Auden's dispatch of the poem to Ursula Niebuhr: "Have been reading the latest Wallace Stevens, some of it is very good, but he provoked me to the following little snoot" (253). The "snoot" is a poem, entitled "Miss God on Mr Stevens," as Fuller transcribes it from the letter:

> Dear, O dear. More heresy to muzzle.
> No sooner have we buried in peace
> The flightier divinities of Greece,
> Than up there pops the barbarian with
> An antimythological myth,
> Calling the sun, the sun,
> His mind "Puzzle." (408)[47]

Auden appears to be referring to the first canto of "Notes toward a Supreme Fiction" in which Stevens ambiguously presents the sun, declaring that it "Must bear no name" other than to be itself, even though he calls it "gold flourisher" (*CPP* 330). Three cantos later in the same poem, he depicts a kind of anti-mythological myth, the origin of the "first idea" in a "muddy centre before we breathed." That "centre" he calls "a myth before the myth began" (*CPP* 331).

Here are the relevant lines from "In Praise of Limestone," Auden's more formal reference to Stevens:

> The poet,
>   Admired for his earnest habit of calling
> The sun the sun, his mind Puzzle, is made uneasy
>   By these solid statues which so obviously doubt
> His antimythological myth. (*Selected Poems* 186)

The "solid statues" who go on to respond negatively to the poet, "rebuke his concern for Nature's / Remotest aspects" (*Selected Poems* 186).

In his commentary on these lines, Tony Sharpe, the English biographer of Stevens, calls attention to the American poet's "appetite for abstraction which tends to reduce life to a merely mental event ["Nature's / Remotest aspects"], combining with a scepticism about religious accountings of reality that overlooks its own mythic status" ("Final Beliefs" 65).

Whatever Auden's referents, his Stevens-poet is jokingly presented as a maker of "heresy" who must be muzzled. The "flightier divinities of Greece" have been discarded, but Stevens, the "barbarian," has imposed his own "antimythological myth" in "Calling the sun, the sun." (Auden anticipates a phrase Stevens himself would use in 1953 in describing his description of a different poem, "The Comedian as the Letter C": "There is another point about the poem to which I should like to call attention and that is that it is what may be called an anti-mythological poem" [*L* 778].) Sun-as-sun replaces a flightier divinity like Apollo but installs a new myth in opposition to the old. In any case, Stevens' mind in the end is "Puzzle" (The word is used in both "Miss God on Mr Stevens" and the lines quoted above from "In Praise of Limestone")—as if to say, "Who can say what the puzzling Stevens myth is anyway?" Moreover, Auden's title, "Miss God on Mr Stevens," itself implies that all seven lines make up a campy, insiders' joke—whatever else it is that the puzzle master and barbarian poet might otherwise finally represent. (In "Analysis of a Theme," Stevens describes, not a "Miss God" but "Herr Gott": "We enjoy the ithy oonts and long haired / Plomets, as the Herr Gott / Enjoys his comets" [*CPP* 305].) Taken in its entirety, it should also be noted, "In Praise of Limestone" defines the humanly imperfect lives of those living in the limestone country, including the unnamed poet associated with Stevens as well as the speaker, who are different from the more extreme examples of virtue and evil in the world. As a result and for all its waywardness, the limestone country willfully "calls into question / All the Great Powers assume: it disturbs our rights."

When in Chapel Hill, North Carolina, in 1971, Auden confided to me that he regarded Stevens as a poet of secondary importance, a conclusion that he widely shared with others throughout his life, obviously a fixed opinion. But, in spite of his personal dismissal of the poet, in the year following Stevens' death Auden included a generous selection from his poems in his *Faber Book of Modern American Verse.*[48] In his introduction, he purports to offer "a broad picture of American poetry" in order to introduce "less familiar work" (*Faber Book* 21). Only Frost and Moore are allotted more pages than Stevens.

One of the young poets who gathered around Auden during his Oxford years, C. Day Lewis, would later become poet laureate. In his Charles Eliot Norton Lectures delivered at Harvard in 1964–65, he deplored Stevens as a lyric poet. Of "The Snow Man," he is quick to say that "I have studied this poem very attentively, and come to the conclusion that the poet is attempting the impossible. He has tried to put himself into the mind, not even of an animal, but of an artifact—a snow man which has no sentience whatsoever . . . Side-stepping the pathetic fallacy, he has tumbled into another pitfall—let us call it the noetic fallacy" (110–11).

Writing several years later, Ted Hughes, acknowledging Stevens' influence upon Sylvia Plath, found the American poet's work an enthusiasm he could not share with his wife: "He was a kind of god to her, while I could never see anything at all in him except magniloquence" (210). The poet Roy Fisher, committed to the presentation of "fictive things" in his own poetry, apparently found Stevens' own poetic fictions too airy: "At the same time I don't want ever to go over into an elaborated set of fictions like Wallace Stevens's, I'd not find that congenial" (32).

The novelist, poet, and close friend of Philip Larkin from their Oxford days Kingsley Amis breezily dismissed Stevens in a letter to Larkin in 1953. John Wain had just introduced Stevens on the radio Third Programme about which Amis was curious: "By the way, did you hear him on Wallace Stevens last night? I missed it unfortunately. Do let me have a report on it. Because apart from some bits of *Le monocle do mon oncle* oh go and get *interfered with,* man I think W.S. . . . is a very bad writer. I can't see how he means all the time, and I have to do that before I think a man is any good, don't you" (313)? [Note to reader: I have checked the accuracy of this quotation.] There is no evidence of Larkin's immediate response ("Do let me have a report on it"). Nine years later, however, Larkin responded caustically in a letter responding to some comments by Cyril Connolly in his essay "E.E. Cummings." Connolly had noted, "The total silence surrounding Cummings's death [that] made me wonder if it were not part of a larger ignorance, if today the two alienated cultures are not art and science but British and American. I began to consider how many people in this country have read, as well as Cummings, Wallace Stevens, [William Carlos] Williams or Hart Crane" (235). Stevens, he added, was "a poet of great intelligence and exquisite fancy" (236). In a letter to Robert Conquest, Larkin registered his own derisive response to the comment: "And C[yril] Connolly asking rhetorically why the British haven't read e.e.c., Stevens, W.C. Williams & co.—hasn't it occurred to him that we've read them, & don't think them worth mentioning" (*Selected Letters* 348)?[49] As we have seen, the poetry of the "Movement" and its reaction to Modernism, including the work of Amis and especially Larkin, contributed to a certain antipathy to Stevens. Robert Conquest, one of the critics and anthologists who first identified "Movement" poetry and already cited above as an antagonist to Stevens, is quoted by Larkin in a letter: "The very existence of people like Stevens, Pound, Eliot & Yeats seems to fill him [Conquest] with dancing fury: he has written denouncing them all to the *Obs*[erver], but they refuse to print it" (*Letters to Monica* 274).

In spite of himself, Larkin continued to read Stevens and even recommended three lines to Monica Jones in 1967: "Talking of poetry, have you ever come across these three enigmatic lines from Wallace Stevens? 'And to feel the light is a rabbit light, / In which everything is meant for you / And nothing need be explained . . .' Rather nice, isn't it? From *A Rabbit as King of the Ghosts*, complete bunk otherwise. But doesn't the extract sound deeply sympathetic to you?" (*Letters to Monica* 374–75).[50]

On the centennial of Stevens' birth in 1979, the English poet Craig Raine wrote an assessment in which he found little to like. Comparing Stevens with Whitman, he defined him as "self-made" and "almost inevitably uneven." "Read in bulk," he could be "profoundly monotonous" (62) and his obscurity had an "element of riddling . . . , something to be solved" (64). Finally and inevitably, Stevens is made to succumb to his own "grand manner": "Tempted by metaphysical pathos, the victim of his own grand manner, he substituted a choir of sounding phrases for the simply sensuous" (62). The critic Neil Corcoran points to Raine's fellow poet of the so-called Martian School, Christopher Reid, as one revealing "explicit responses" in some of his poems to Stevens' "Sunday Morning": "that classic post-Arnoldian statement of transcendental absence and sublunary repletion" (239). In his *English Poetry since 1940*, Corcoran nonetheless notes that the influence of Stevens in contemporary

British poetry is "unusual" (142). Unusual or not, Stevens may have had some influence on the early poetry of James Fenton; Michael Schmidt finds that the British poet admired Stevens "briefly to the point of idolatry" (*Lives* 719). However, by 1990 Fenton found Stevens excessively happy: "Unhappiness . . . seems to be a colour missing from Stevens's palette." Fenton is "not sure" he can "believe in a happiness in the absence of unhappiness" (16). (He might have consulted poems, even titles of poems like "Depression before Spring," "Domination of Black," "In a Bad Time," "Esthétique du Mal," and any number of other poems, especially from among those set in autumn and winter.)

Other poets have been more generous in their praise, even as they invariably feel compelled to put some distance between themselves and the American poet. Such distancing, when it is employed, emerges variously. Parody is one such device; accusations of an outdated romanticism a second; and even the frequent begrudging and only partially tempered resistance makes up a third.

In an essay published in 2006, Michael Schmidt opines that Stevens' influence on some British poets has been hazardous—not an exercise of resistance so much as a too easy imitation: "His curious enchantment wrecked many a poet whose voice and ear were not strong enough to resist the siren that Stevens quite clearly can be." He adds that "it is hard for the specifically English ear not to mishear Stevens, not to read in him a relatively regular iambulator." Schmidt does not identify these poets, but for himself, however, Schmidt finds that in hearing Stevens' own recorded voice reading his poems he discovers a different poet. The poet's spoken iambs, his "metrical poison so many poets imbibe with their Stevens is not *his* poison" and is "quite unmechanical" ("Wallace Stevens: Arranging, etc." [54, 55]).

In a special issue on American writing in the *Times Literary Supplement* in 1954, Edith Sitwell singled out Stevens by quoting six lines from the poem "Nomad Exquisite" followed by these remarks: "Those lovely lines . . . seem to embody the life of the best American poets of our age whose poetry 'angers [sic] for life' and moves with an entirely natural ease, an inborn athleticism [sic]" (i).

Reviewing Faber's new edition of *Collected Poems* for *London Magazine* in 1965, the twenty-seven-year-old poet Thom Gunn was already established in America under the tutelage of Yvor Winters at Stanford. Gunn had been told to read Williams and Stevens by his mentor. Having done so, one presumes, he begins the review by heralding Stevens as "one of the most considerable poets of the last hundred years, but still too little read both in his own country and here." He anticipates the problems British readers will have with Stevens: "His work is voluminous, and his style seems elaborate, even pretentious—two reasons why an unprepared reader may feel discouraged." He adds another "difficulty" to the list: "Admittedly the esoteric vocabulary, the made-up onomatopoeic words, the French phrases, and the extraordinary proper names can suggest a tiresomely finical writer." In spite of these rather formidable liabilities, he assesses Stevens as "a serious and coherent writer searching for positive values." Going on to introduce readings of "Sunday Morning," "Notes toward a Supreme Fiction," and "The Snow Man," Gunn values Stevens' mastery of the blank-verse line, "a subtle sureness of movement for which we have to look back hundreds of years to equal." He then puts Stevens squarely in the English tradition: "He learned, as few others have learned, not only from Jacobean blank verse, but from Milton's, Wordsworth's, and Tennyson's" (81, 84).

Perhaps most lavish in his commendation of Stevens' earliest work was the Scottish poet Hugh MacDiarmid (then writing as C. M. Grieve, his given name). In reviewing *Harmonium* in 1924, when Stevens was all but unknown even in America, he found only adulation: "We have absolute faith in Mr Stevens's perseverance, and in his ultimate success. But in the meantime we are more than content that his incessant efforts should continue. They provide a spectacle unique in contemporary literature—a series of unparalleled efforts, conceived with an adroitness that borders on the miraculous" (178). It was the dazzling showiness of these first Stevens poems that so amazed him: "In the meantime let us follow every movement with gratitude—magnified and given to our eyes in the 'slow motion' of a verbalism that does not permit the tiniest absurdity, the most elusive impossibilism, to escape" (179) MacDiarmid's fellow Scot, the poet Norman MacCaig, later acknowledged Stevens as one of two discernible influences in his own poetry.[51]

Hardly influenced by Stevens, Dylan Thomas was familiar with his poetry and informed a correspondent in 1939 that he was going to "read poems" at the English Club at Cambridge and intended to include "one decorative Wallace Stevens" (428) in his selections. One wonders which poem he chose. But Thomas hardly held a great and abiding interest in Stevens. His agent for his four trips to America and author of *Dylan Thomas in America*, John Malcolm Brinnin, later recalled, "Thomas had no sense of Stevens whatsoever;

we talked a lot privately about poetry. If I mentioned Stevens—and I must have—there was no recognition" (194).

Geoffrey Hill admitted an attraction "towards an idea by which it [my argument] would much prefer to be repelled"—namely, Stevens' "magnificent agnostic faith" (*Lords of Limit* 16). Hill points to Stevens' affirmation of faith in poetry as, in Stevens' words, "life's redemption" after "one has abandoned a belief in god" ([*CPP*] 901).[52] Hill's nine-line poem "An Order of Service" seems to be in dialogue with Stevens' "The Snow Man," although neither poet nor poem is directly named. Hill's poem begins with the "nothing" of a surveyor's "ice-world":

> He was the surveyor of his own ice-world,
> Meticulous at the chosen extreme,
> Though what he surveyed may have been nothing.

Unlike Stevens' "nothing," however, this one seems to possess little in the way of affirmation or gain. Rebuking Stevens' "mind of winter," who chooses to forfeit his very humanity by becoming the snow man ("concede / His mortality"), Hill's poem disdains such "renunciation." The poem ends with the empty "Blank" of his implied snow man's gaze:

> In such a light dismiss the unappealing
> Blank of his gaze, hopelessly vigilant,
> Dazzled by renunciation's glare. (*Collected Poems* 68)

Hill's admiration of Stevens extended beyond a single poem. Lee Jenkins, a student of Hill's at Cambridge, reports that in a seminar there he played the Caedmon recording of Stevens reading "The Idea of Order at Key West," "over and over again."[53]

The English poet who is first on the lips of everyone in making a connection with Stevens is Charles Tomlinson. Tomlinson was one of Stevens' first admirers in England, exchanged letters with him, and sent him a copy of his essay on "Credences of Summer" that has never been published, though Stevens found it "a very fair and perceptive job" (*L* 719). As poet and critic, Tomlinson absorbed the works of Stevens over decades of reading and writing.

Donald Davie has noted: "In *The Necklace,* Tomlinson's second collection [1955] but the first where his writing is assured, everyone acknowledges the presence of Wallace Stevens" ("Foreword" 4). The tone and style of "Thirteen Ways of Looking at a Blackbird" are evident, for example, in certain poems from that volume like "Nine Variations in a Chinese Winter Setting" and "Eight Observations on the Nature of Eternity." Tomlinson has recalled that in these and other poems Stevens' blackbird poem "led me for a while to look from different angles at separate instances of the meticulous" (*Some Americans* 10).

But the influence is more pervasive. As Tomlinson has stated in reference to his poem "The Art of Poetry" (also from *The Necklace*), "I was also arguing with one of my mentors [Stevens] and with a certain aspect of his eloquence [in "The Snow Man"] as a "playful demur" on Tomlinson's part. Playing upon the last line of "The Snow Man" ("Nothing that is not there and the nothing that is"), "The Art of Poetry" argues ambiguously for "nothing which is not elegant / And nothing which is":

Proportions

> Matter. It is difficult to get them right.
> There must be nothing
> Superfluous. Nothing which is not elegant
> And nothing which is if it is merely that. (*Collected Poems* 11)

Tomlinson, in fact, is not merely echoing Stevens. He tells us that these lines make up a reaction against Stevens as one who sponsors "rather self-conscious writing": "I was arguing for a kind of exactness in face of the object, which meant an exactness of feeling in the writer. It meant that you must enter into a relationship with things, that you must use your eyes and see what they were offering you" ("Words and Water" 25). The American poet's innate romanticism, of which he saw his "elegance" as part, led him to conclude in a different essay in 1982 that "Stevens is a poet of evocations rather than patterned inscapes. He hovers above and about his subjects rather than entering into their life co-extensive with his own." That observation appeared in an essay well-informed of both the poetry itself and criticism of it. "Wallace Stevens and the Poetry of Scepticism" (405), appeared in *The New Pelican Guide to English Literature.* It was Stevens, his sometimes "inexactness" notwithstanding, and Marianne Moore, Tomlinson acknowledged in an interview, "who saved me from the Dylan Thomas infection" ("Words and Water" 26).

Gareth Reeves has argued that the presence of Stevens in the background of Tomlinson's later poetry is greater than the poet himself and his critics have acknowledged. The sixth part of the longer poem *Antecedents* (1960), for example, is called "Something: A Direction" and presents a dissociation of sun from its beholder ("Sun is, because it is not you; you are / Since you are self, and self-delimited / Regarding sun" [*Collected Poems* 54]. Reeves sees the poem as "an implicit reply to 'Not Ideas about the Thing [But the Thing Itself]'": "Tomlinson's sun exists by reason of its being other than human consciousness; conversely, human consciousness exists by reason of its being other than sun" (64). Another poem by Tomlinson, "Swimming Chenango Lake" (1969), describes the lone swimmer as one able to "take hold / On water's meaning, to move in its embrace / And to be, between grasp and grasping, free." The water in his wake recalls the concluding images in Stevens' "Sunday Morning": it is "lifting and lengthening, splayed like the feathers / Down an immense wing whose darkening spread / Shadows his solitariness" [*Collected Poems* 155].

In 1944, the poet David Gascoyne had written Stevens introducing himself as "an ardently enthusiastic admirer," one who had encouraged Tambimuttu to publish an edition of his poetry, and who had recently given "a programme of contemporary American poetry" and "was privileged to introduce to an English audience altogether unfamiliar with your work the wonderful 'Montrachet-le-Jardin' (from 'Partisan Review') which aroused the greatest interest and warmth of appreciation."[54]

Around the time of the letter, Gascoyne composed his "With a Cornet of Winkles" as both "a tribute to Wallace Stevens" and, as the poem itself confesses, "this perfectly awful attempt at a parody." The difficulty of enjoying the parody when the object of the parody (Stevens' verse) was largely unknown by Gascoyne's British readers accounts perhaps for the poem's deliberately over-inflated style. The poem begins:

> O bravo! For a maladif, mandarin-miened, mauve melody-man
> With a glittering, lissome, pat-prattling lute—
> *Que c'est beau!* as he lo! hums and haws,

And soon again haws, then heigh-ho! how he hums
And whilom most becomingly strums
On his poignantly Quince-flavoured lute! (174)

Henry Reed, known for his World War II poems such as "Naming of the Parts," reviewed *The Necessary Angel* and *Opus Posthumous* in 1960; he noted that Stevens was a poet "who has often been called a dandy and a hedonist: the terms have not always been consciously dismissive: but they do in fact belittle him, even if indulgently." Then, somewhat indulgently, he defends Stevens' "idiosyncrasies" as something more than "endearing perversities," if for no other reason than the fact that he "pleads his agnosticism so earnestly." Reed notes that British readers of Stevens remain "in a peculiar position": "Most of us don't, quite simply, know him well enough" (675), and he charges that ignorance to the "insularity of English culture" (675).

Peter Redgrove's first response to Stevens occurred four years after the death of the American poet. In his first volume in 1959 he published "Thirteen Ways of Looking at a Blackboard." The title immediately suggests playful parody, and such is the case: the eighth "way of looking" is the following: "I dream. / I am an albino." But the poem also bears a more serious intent as it rewrites each of Stevens' thirteen "ways." Redgrove's third section, for example, adapts Stevens' first: "Among twenty silent children / The only moving thing / Is the chalk's white finger" (*The Collector* 12), suggesting the motion of the poet's pen.

Thirteen years later, Redgrove's "The Idea of Entropy at Maenporth Beach" showed a more complex engagement with "The Idea of Order at Key West." Both poems present a woman walking along the seashore and interacting with it—Stevens' woman through song—but Redgrove's through immersion of her white dress and skin into mud and muck. Her erotic assumption of a different racial identity swerves the poem, partly by bathos, away from Stevens' woman:

Now that I am all black, and running in my richness
And knowing it a little, I have learnt
It is quite wrong to be all white always. (*Selected Poems* 31)

The poem speaks more of an "idea of empathy" than an "idea of entropy" (title). Erik Martiny sees the poem somewhat differently: "Redgrove's mud figure is the ultimate lubricant that connects man to nature. Its melding of the two elements of earth and water makes it into a trope for undissociated harmonious interaction between the human and the non-human" (82). Besides "The Idea of Order at Key West," Redgrove's poem seems to owe something both to Stevens' "Mud Master," as well as "The Paltry Nude Starts on a Spring Voyage" ("And then the blackness breaks open with blue eyes / Of this black Venus rising helmeted in night / Who as she glides grins brilliantly" (*Selected Poems* 31).

Martin Bell, who joined the London "Group" of poets organized by Philip Hobsbaum in London in the 1950s came to know Redgrove there, as well as Edward Lucie-Smith, George MacBeth, Peter Porter, and others. In editing Bell's poems, Porter connects Bell to Stevens, "who felt simple emotions voluptuously, and a similar fondness for 'essential gaudiness' informs Bell's verse" (18). His six-line "Wallace Stevens Welcomes Doctor Jung into Heaven" makes Stevens into Jung's jovial comrade of earthly sensations transported to heaven: "saffron ice cream cones / Topped up with glacé cherries and chopped cashew nuts." Stevens exclaims, "Doggone, they've let you in at last, Doc!'" (185). (The title perhaps owes something to Stevens' title "Lytton Strachey, Also, Enters into Heaven.")

The poet R. S. Thomas—Welshman, Anglican clergyman, and country dweller—concluded an interview—twenty-six years after Stevens' death—with these words, "I'd be the first to, I would hope I would be the first, to welcome some great new voice in English poetry, I can't honestly say there's one about . . . I think Wallace Stevens comes nearest to expressing the situation, in poetry" (Lethbridge 56). Thomas's biographer reports that Thomas "once claimed to have read a poem by Wallace Stevens on every day of his adult life" (Byron Rogers 8). As early as 1963, Thomas included Stevens' first poem, "Common Soldier," from the "Lettres d'un Soldat" sequence in *The Penguin Book of Religious Verse* that he was editing.[55] Three of Thomas' own poems appear to be in direct dialogue with Stevens, as even the titles suggest: "Wallace Stevens" (1963), "Thirteen Blackbirds Look at a Man" (1983), and "Homage to Wallace Stevens" (1995). Stevens is mentioned by name in two other poems, "Negative" (1995) and "Anybody's Alphabet" (1995).[56]

Thomas' first two Stevens poems cast the poet in a distant, hardly appealing light. In four brief stanzas, "Wallace Stevens" traces the American poet from conception to death, but sees only the darker side of Stevens' autumnal poems. ("His one season was late fall," he incorrectly declares.) The poem ends, "He limped on, taking despair / As a new antidote for love" (*Collected Poems* 135). The poem echoes some of the language from "Stars at Tallapoosa" and "Sailing after Lunch," as well as Eliot's "Gerontion." Written twenty years later, "Thirteen Blackbirds Look at a Man" has, in this case, nothing of Redgrove's parody, but continues in the same darker vein as "Wallace Stevens"—fixing this time not on Stevens the poet but upon "man" himself. The loftier blackbirds speak in each of the thirteen sections and look down with dismay on the unnamed figure who occupies Eden just after the fall but before his expulsion. Unlike the liberating rejection of Eden proclaimed in Stevens' "Sunday Morning," the birds here register only scorn for bungling and befouling "man":

> 6
> We wipe our beaks
> on the branches
> wasting the dawn's
> jewelry to get rid
> of the taste of a man. (*Collected Poems* 408)

It is not until "Homage to Wallace Stevens" ("I turn now / not to the Bible / but to Wallace Stevens") that Thomas unabashedly embraces the poet as a congenial figure. Instead of the "despair" described in the earlier "Wallace Stevens," he now associates the poet with "hope," but only through his use of the "imagination":

> We walk a void world,
> he implies for which
> in the absence of the imagination,
> there is no hope. (*Collected Later Poems* 266)

Thomas, the Anglican parish priest, struggled with his own inconstant religious faith and found in Stevens a poet whose religion of the earth was a powerful magnet: "He burned his metaphors like incense, / so his syntax was as high / as his religion." The poem concludes with Thomas' personal benediction: "Blessings, Stevens; . . . celebrating the sacrament / of the imagination whose high-priest / notwithstanding you are" (*Collected Later Poems 266*).

It was the same "fictions" over "faith" that Thomas also singled out in "Anybody's Alphabet," a poem from the same volume:

> For Stevens fictions
> were as familiar
> as facts and if far-
> fetched preferable.
> Forfeiting for faith
> fable, he feasted on it. (*Collected Later Poems* 293)

In the estimation of Andrew Rudd, Thomas found in Stevens' skepticism an example that proved highly beneficial to Thomas' own "gaze at emptiness and doubt" as he otherwise adhered to an "affirmative and life-enhancing faith" (51).

The contemporary British poet Sean O'Brien published in the 1990s a poem with the comic title "Reading Wallace Stevens in the Bath." It pulls images and phrases from a variety of Stevens' poems, including "The Snow Man," "Credences of Summer," "Of Mere Being," and "The Idea of Order at Key West" ("Bookless Fruiterers, tell me if you can / What he may find to sing about" [144]). Set in O'Brien's own Newcastle upon Tyne it mocks the town, its river and Forest Hall. With interjections of the local exclamation "Howay"—which can mean by context either encouragement or discouragement (Here it seems one with the poem's mockery)—a Stevens-like "large pink man / Is reading Stevens in the bath." He is also singing, "Half-audible and howling," baying to the indifferent moon, *"Say it's only a paper moon"* and then ends "Howay. Howay. Howay!" The clever poem combines parody and pastiche, winking all the while to those who know their Stevens!

Stevens' linkings with Irish poets, as a general rule, were more immediate and congenial than those with the British, and this recognition begins with the generation following Yeats. In 1948, Stevens began a personal connection with an Irish correspondent, Thomas MacGreevy,[57] the poet, art critic, and later director of the National Gallery in Dublin. He would correspond by mail with

Stevens for the rest of Stevens' life and became the first Irish reader to take a serious interest in his work. It might be noted, however, that MacGreevy's own poems owe more to Eliotic modernism than to the influence of Stevens. Mac-Greevy's correspondence with Stevens and his mention of places like Mal Bay and Tarbert in his own poems ("Recessional" and "Homage to Hieronymus Bosch") led to Stevens' writing the poem "Our Stars Come from Ireland."[58]

The first part of Stevens' poem "Our Stars Come from Ireland" is subtitled *"Tom McGreevy, in America, Thinks of Himself as a Boy."* Just as Ireland touches Stevens in his writing of the poem, so does MacGreevy, now placed in America, reverse the process as he remembers Ireland (Mal Bay, Tarbert, Kerry) and his present life in Pennsylvania (Swatara, Schuylkill). Justin Quinn sees Mac-Greevy "by synecdoche," as a stand-in for all Irish immigrants and, indeed, all European immigrants: "This poem goes down to the foundations of our idea of nation—direct human perception—and attempts to interpret the New World through them" (*Gathered beneath the Storm* 133). The words "Tom McGreevy, in America, Thinks of Himself as a Boy" are appended under the poem's title. The speaker, however, appears to be Stevens himself. The identities of the poem's "I" somehow consist of both MacGreevy and Stevens, what Tara Stubbs calls "a kind of symbiotic fusion between the two countries, but also hints that this fusion extended to him—as the American poet—and to McGreevy, as his Irish correspondent" (86). MacGreevy's own response cements the "fusion": "And to say I should feel honoured [in having Stevens publish the poem] would be inadequate because there is more than feeling honoured to it. The true answer would be a poem. Say a prayer that I may write it some day."[59] The MacGreevy correspondence and friendship is the first major linking of Stevens with the transatlantic shores to occur.[60]

Stevens has held a notably strong appeal for poets of Northern Ireland dating back to the 1960s.[61] Edna Longley, the critic and wife of Northern Irish poet Michael Longley, has observed that "Northern Irish poetry of the 1960s, I would argue, initiated such a [new aesthetic] cluster in the tradition of the English lyric, and these American poets . . . influenced its formation" (*Poetry and Posterity* 260). She lists Stevens along with Frost, Crane, Lowell, Wilbur, and Roethke.

"Rage for Order,"[62] a forty-line poem by the Northern Irish poet Derek Mahon, has become what Hugh Haughton calls "one of the poems that helped define the temper of Northern Irish poetry" (79). It is at first a begrudgingly restive response to "The Idea of Order at Key West." The "poet" of the poem is usually taken to be Mahon himself or any Northern Irish poet. I take him to be Stevens. The poem begins: "Somewhere beyond the scorched gable end and the burnt-out buses / there is a poet indulging / his wretched rage for order." The burnt-out gables and buses suggest the Troubles of Northern Ireland but Stevens is the stand-in for such a poet. The poem calls Stevens' work and that of others like him "a dying art, / An eddy of semantic scruple / In an unstructurable sea." Such a poet is "far / From his people," and "His posture is / Grandiloquent." But for all these familiar gestures, as we have seen, of accusation hurled at Stevens, Mahon finds himself unable to dismiss him out-of-hand, as well as his fellow aesthetes. He concludes:

> Now watch me
> As I make history,
> Watch as I tear down
>
> To build up
> With a desperate love,
> Knowing it cannot be
> Long now till I have need of his
> Terminal ironies. (*New Collected Poems* 47–48)

Whatever Mahon meant by "terminal ironies," he reverted to the same terminal lines of Stevens' poem in an assessment of his work up to 1978. The poem is called "The Sea in Winter," one stanza signaling Stevens as a stepping-stone to his future as a poet:

> And will the year two thousand find
> Me still at a window, pen in hand,
> Watching long breakers curl on sand
> Erosion makes for ever finer?
> I hope so, for the sake of these
> Subsidized serendipities.
> 'Ghostlier demarcations, keener
> Sounds' are needed more than ever. (*Poems 1962–1978* 113)

Mahon's interest in Stevens reasserts itself from time to time in his poetry without necessarily implying a dialogue with the American poet. His own Key West poem is called "Key West" where Stevens' "striding" along the shore becomes Mahon's strolling ("this wintry night, that summery place— / how we strolled out there on the still-quaking docks / shaken but exhilarated" [*New Collected Poems* 189]); or his nod to "The House Was Quiet and the World Was Calm" in "Harbour Lights": "It's one more sedative evening in Co. Cork. / The house is quiet and the world is dark" (*New Collected Poems* 281); or his own "Sunday Morning" with no more than a glance at an evocation of Stevens via the title.

Edna Longley has also noted—as has Seamus Heaney—the importance of a recording to certain young Irish poets: "A Caedmon record of American poets reading their work was endlessly played by Mahon and Longley at Trinity College, Dublin in the early 1960s. Top of the pops was Wallace Stevens reading 'The Idea of Order at Key West'" (*Poetry and Posterity* 263).

Michael Longley, husband of Edna and close friend of Mahon, remembers inhaling side-by-side with Mahon "our untipped Sweet Afton cigarettes" when they were undergraduates and "inhaling" also the poetry of Stevens, Crane, Cummings, Wilbur, Lowell, and others ("Empty Holes of Spring" 53). Of his own work, he says "I was homing in with radar-accuracy on the weaknesses of good poets, combining the tweeness [*sic*] of E. E. Cummings, for instance, with the "portentiousness [*sic*] of Wallace Stevens" (52). In his inaugural lecture as Ireland Professor of Poetry, Longley began by distributing a copy of "A High-Toned Old Christian Woman" to his audience and citing the first line: "Poetry is the supreme fiction, madam." He hails the poem as the work of "the great American poet Wallace Stevens" ("A Jovial Hullabaloo" 7) and in fact, names the lecture "A Jovial Hullabaloo," another phrase from the poem. Edna Longley finds the Stevens influence (along with that of Crane and Lowell) evidenced in the first volumes of both Longley and Mahon.[63]

Mahon's contemporary Seamus Heaney has scattered references to Stevens in his formal essays, but in an interview in 1988 he admits to a great attraction to the poet,[64] even as he finds him "difficult" and (though he recognizes a "deep mind-current") elusive in demonstrating a unifying "gestalt." Heaney's puzzled ambivalence is apparent:

Wallace Stevens I am helplessly in awe of but my response is as helpless as it is awed. When I open the door into that great cloudscape of language, I am transported joyfully. And I have got to a stage of reading Stevens where—to mix the metaphor—I can feel the bone under the cloud. I love his oil-on-water, brilliant phantasmagoria. And there is deep mind-current under the water, and a kind of water-muscle mind at work, but I find it difficult to hold that in my own reader's mind. I find it difficult to see a Stevensian gestalt in the way that I can see Frost as a whole. I can see Frost defined against a sky or landscape. Somehow with Stevens, I cannot see the poetry defined. It is coterminous with the horizon. That says a lot for him but it also means he is difficult to think about. (Randy Brandes, An Interview 15–16)

In his Nobel lecture, "Crediting Poetry," Heaney confesses that he "went for years half-avoiding and half-resisting the opulence and extensiveness of poets as different as Wallace Stevens and Rainer Maria Rilke" (*Opened Ground* 418).

In spite of its being "difficult to think about," it is obvious that the poetry of Stevens came to mean a great deal to the Northern Irish poet. In his poem "The Bookcase" from *Electric Light* (2001) the Irish poet remembers fondly his volumes by MacDiarmid, Bishop, Hardy, and Yeats, volumes that rested colorfully on the bookcase's shelves. To his personal and unofficial canonization, he goes on to add: "Voices too of Frost and Wallace Stevens / Off a Caedmon double album, off different shelves" (60).

As we have seen in the chapter "The Social Context," Heaney begins one of his best-known essays, "The Redress of Poetry," by implicitly identifying his own views of the role of politics in poetry with those of Stevens. Stevens defended the social content of the imagination by calling it "a violence from within that protects us from a violence without" (*CPP* 665), words quoted multiple times by Heaney. But for some would-be political and "disaffected heckler," he imagines, such interior violence would never be sufficient: "The heckler . . . is going to have little sympathy with Wallace Stevens." Heaney, however, mounts his defense of both Stevens and, implicitly, his own poetry: "Such an operation does not intervene in the actual, but by offering consciousness a chance to recognize its predicaments, foreknow its capabilities and rehearse its comebacks in all kinds of venturesome ways, it does constitute a beneficent event, for poet and audience alike. It offers a response to reality which has a liberating and verifying effect upon the individual spirit, and yet I can see how such a function would be deemed insufficient by a political activist" (*Finders Keepers* 281, 282).[65]

Heaney has one direct allusion to Stevens, and it occurs in a poem called "Fosterage." The poem is dedicated to Michael McLaverty, a writer of short stories and principal of an intermediate school where Heaney, as his career was getting underway, had taught for a year. McLaverty is one of the figures who "fostered" the young Heaney, and, through McLaverty, the writer Katherine Mansfield was another, as was "poor Hopkins," whose personal copy of Hopkins' notebooks he gave to Heaney. Stevens is implicitly one other such fosterer. The poem begins with these words in quotation marks: "'Description is revelation'" (*Opened Ground* 134). The words occur in Stevens' poem "Description without Place," words which can only be taken as advice from one writer to another:

> Description is revelation. It is not
> The thing described, nor false facsimile.
>
> It is an artificial thing that exists,
> In its own seeming, plainly visible,
>
> Yet not too closely the double of our lives,
> Intenser than any actual life could be. (*CPP* 301)

Stevens' counsel to Heaney is that the poet can only reproduce the imaginative "seeming" of things and thereby attain a realism that is "Intenser than any actual life could be." Unlike Mansfield and Hopkins, Stevens remains unnamed in the poem, but his voice as an implicit sponsor of the "seemings" of reality introduces a fosterage that is not completely consistent with that of Mansfield, who seems less "seeming" and more sensuously real: "Remember / Katherine Mansfield—*I will tell / How the laundry basket squeaked*" (134). Another late poem by Heaney, "The Door Was Open and the House Was Dark," appears indebted to Stevens' "The House Was Quiet and the World Was Calm."[66]

By the end of his life, Heaney was placing Stevens with Shakespeare, Yeats, and Milosz as "great poets" of old age: "you sense an ongoing opening of consciousness as they age, a deepening and clarifying and even a simplifying of receptivity to what might be awaiting on the farther shore . . . No poet can avoid hoping for that kind of old age" (*Stepping Stones* 466).

Delivering the Inaugural Lecture as Professor of Poetry at Oxford in November of 1999, the Irish poet Paul Muldoon declared that "Most late twentieth-century agonizing over the 'purpose' of poetry goes back to Wallace Stevens, it would seem, particularly to his essay "The Noble Rider and the Sound of Words." He cites the "poet's role" in Stevens' essay, "to help people live their lives," even as he also dismisses the "sociological or political obligation of the poet" by saying "*He has none*" (*The End of the Poem* 3).

Stevens himself once said—just after the end of World War II: "At best it is difficult for an American poet to make his way in England. With all the realism of their situation over there, my sort of thing might find itself terribly out of place and, if so, given the freedom with which Englishmen discuss American books, would probably have no chance at all" (*L* 524). Though at the time of writing these remarks, when his poetry had been given little such chance, he seems to have been remarkably prescient in the observation. As noted, in another letter two years later to an Irish correspondent, he added, "The truth is that American poetry is at its worst in England and, possibly in Ireland or in any other land where English is spoken and whose inhabitants feel that somehow our English is a vulgar imitation" (*L* 597). In the ensuing years, many of his British and Irish critics, taking him at his word, as it were, seem to have adopted judgments not altogether unlike these: they continue to find much to marvel at in his poetry and to regret that he is not better known and yet to feel a distance, a separation, as if the sensibility of this American poet remains excessively disguised in ornamentation and obfuscation. It is not that so many of these writers, critics, and poets find fault with Stevens, but that they do so on such limited evidence. As we have seen, there have been important critics—Donoghue, Kermode, Hobsbaum, Schmidt—who have not fallen into this pattern and have themselves disdained the indifference and aloofness of some of their peers. The poets, however, are less troubled than the critics with the issue of a merely exterior spangle in Stevens' poems accompanied by their dispute over the presence of a discernible interior content. The poets have surely proved that there are more than thirteen ways of looking at "Thirteen Ways of Looking at a Blackbird!" In these various verses—and others making reference to, especially, "The Idea of Order at Key West," "The Snow Man," but many others—their responses are vibrant, sometimes joking or even ridiculing, but giving ample evidence of dialogue and engagement with the American poet who has pressed upon their sensibilities with a force that continues to attract them.

Twenty-First Century

Early in the present century it became apparent that a new group of critics, largely British, but with a special interest in Stevens, were emerging. The seriousness with which the poet was beginning to be recognized by them did not mean that the old reservations and qualifications had dissolved, but newer readers were beginning to read him more deeply and comprehensively, to consider him beyond a handful of anthology specimens, and to value him for more than a superficial congeries of dazzling diction and preciosity. Nor could they overlook the mounting evidence of Stevens' influence on British and Irish poets in the last decades of the previous century and continuing into the present one.

Philip Hobsbaum's own interest in Stevens remained fervid in the new century, contributing to the Blackwell Publishers' *A Companion to Twentieth-Century Poetry* in 2001 with his essay that centers on *Harmonium*. That volume, "the most attractive of all [Stevens'] books," he avers, "can be read, quite lazily, for the snap, crackle and pop of its words; or it may be studied as representing the first major phase of one of the very few genuinely philosophical poets in English" (421). At the time of Hobsbaum's death in 2005, he was at work on a book-length study of Stevens. Carolyn Masel, an Australian then lecturing at the University of Manchester, concluded that "Stevens' influence has extended all over the English-speaking literary world" (134), even if he is "rarely if ever mentioned in the same breath as Yeats, Eliot, and Pound" (123). In 2008 Faber introduced a new collection entitled *Wallace Stevens* and edited by the Scottish poet and novelist John Burnside. In his introduction Burnside charts the new direction in Stevens studies: "Far too many of us still see Stevens as the poet of 'Thirteen Ways of Looking at a Blackbird' and 'The Snow Man' but, as fine as these are, he was much more than that. I hope the great sequences included here—twentieth-century masterpieces like 'Esthétique du Mal,' 'An Ordinary Evening in New Haven' and, of course, 'Notes Toward a Supreme Fiction'—will send readers to those marvellous sequences" (xiv). By the end of the century and all the decades that followed the first Faber publication of *Selected Poems,* Stevens was no longer being ignored or simply dismissed with summary and impressionistic conclusions by his British and Irish audience, even if his newly sympathetic readers were mostly among the poets and a growing number of academic critics.

In August 2005, a group of international Stevens scholars convened at the Rothermere American Institute at Oxford to present and hear presentations focusing upon "Fifty Years On: Wallace Stevens in Europe," the first major European conference on the American poet. It was organized by Belgian scholar Bart Eeckhout and a recent graduate of Cambridge University, Edward Ragg. The essays were later collected under the title *Wallace Stevens across the Atlantic* with a preface by Frank Kermode; it included an essay by poet and critic Mark Ford called "Nicholas Moore, Stevens and the Fortune Press."[67] In 2006, a special issue of the *Wallace Stevens Journal* was more narrowly dedicated to "Wallace Stevens and British Literature," again edited by Eeckhout and Ragg. It was followed by another special issue in 2013 focusing on Wallace Stevens and W. H. Auden. In 2014, another conference, organized by the ubiquitous Eeckhout, this time in Belgium, took as its theme "Poetry after Wallace Stevens," including European poetry; this conference became the basis for the publication of *Poetry and Poetics after Wallace Stevens* published by Bloomsbury in 2016 and edited by Eeckhout and Lisa Goldfarb.

Tony Sharpe, then senior lecturer and head of the Department of English at Lancaster University, published *Wallace Stevens: A Life* in 2000, appearing simultaneously in England and the United States. In his "Preface," he defines himself as "a British critic beholding an American poet, and my reading is on occasions adversarial" (ix), though the biography as a whole is highly sympathetic and well-informed.[68] Lee M. Jenkins' *Wallace Stevens: Rage for Order,* appearing in the same year, is the work of another Cambridge-educated critic, lecturing at University College Cork, who sees Stevens in terms of region and place. Her introduction takes notice of early and guarded reactions to Stevens by critics like William Empson and Donald Davie.[69] As the century turns, however, she claims that "the people [British and Irish critics] who don't know

[Stevens]" have since remedied their ignorance, and cites figures like Geoffrey Hill, Craig Raine, Frank Kermode, Denis Donoghue, and others (*Rage for Order* 5–6)

English critic Michael O'Neill's *The All-Sustaining Air: Romantic Legacies and Renewals in British, American and Irish Poetry since 1900*, cites Stevens and Hart Crane as "determinedly ambitious as post-Romantic poets" (10), and, in spite of "arabesques" and "preciosities," Stevens "hungers after what he calls 'the normal'" (106). But the normal does not preclude suffering and pain, a theme O'Neill pursues at length in Stevens' "Esthétique du Mal."

Philosopher Simon Critchley's *Things Merely Are* appeared in 2005. In his opening remarks he says, "I am trying to show two things: first, that Stevens's poetry . . . contains deep, consequent and instructive philosophical insight, and second that this insight is best expressed poetically" (4). Five years later, Edward Ragg's *Wallace Stevens and the Aesthetics of Abstraction*" concurs with Critchley but points to Stevens' use of abstraction as "based on an ideal ['idea' derived from an impersonal I] that is nonetheless part of 'reality'" and is "central to Stevens' work and practice." It also "comprises a misunderstood aesthetic that actually defines the poet's contact with life at large" (29). Two years following Ragg's study, Daniel Tompsett's *Wallace Stevens and Pre-Socratic Philosophy* views the ontological Stevens from the earliest Greek philosophers, through Plato and Kant, and absorbing Heidegger, Gadamer, and other twentieth-century theorists. These British critics-aestheticians have defined the foundations of the "ontological Stevens" for the new century.

Other important monographs from British and Irish readers would follow. Eeckhout, with his hand on the pulse on all things Stevensian across the Atlantic, gave an account in the *Wallace Stevens Journal,* Spring 2015, of an evening he witnessed in London dedicated solely to appraisals of Stevens' work.[70]

In his *Irish Poetry and the Construction of Modern Identity* (2005), Stan Smith places Stevens as an established influence on Irish poets. In his comment on Northern Irish poet Gerald Dawe's poem "Supreme Fiction" (with the poet's own "rage for order, / standing like a scarecrow when mists / swept off the broad Atlantic" [22]), Smith notes "a significantly recurrent reference point for Irish poets in this lineage [of "supreme fiction"], Wallace Stevens" (157). Commenting later on Paul Muldoon's poem "Tea" and its reference to Key West, he finds the mere mention of that town "now forever associated with (yet again!) Wallace Stevens's reflections on the maker's rage to order words of the sea" (195). "Tea" seems otherwise to owe little if anything to Stevens. Tara Stubbs's *American Literature and Irish Culture, 1910–1955* (2013) singles out Stevens for an important "transatlantic Celticism" through his epistolary friendship with Thomas MacGreevy and the poem "Our Stars Come from Ireland" (83–91), as we have seen. One of Stevens' late poems, "The Irish Cliffs of Moher," based upon a postcard he had received with a picture of the cliffs in County Clare, is evidence of what Stubbs calls the American poet's "transatlantic translation" of the actual Ireland into a personal mythology (119). Because Stevens claimed Ireland, she concludes, Ireland, in turn, has claimed him.

The editor of the *Wallace Stevens Journal,* appraising the ten issues under his responsibility from 2011 to 2015, notes that "nearly a third" of the contributors "came from outside the United States"—thirteen countries. He adds, "The ten issues have included a remarkable number of books that come from outside the United States: individual studies by a Polish, an Indian, and an Irish critic, one by a critic working in Switzerland, two by French scholars, and no less than six by British writers" (Eeckhout, *Wallace Stevens in Context* 178). This is a late but welcome trend that will no doubt continue and add immeasurably to all our readings of the poet.[73]

Every great poet teaches us how to read poetry anew. In a sense, I think this is what the English poet, novelist, and essayist John Wain meant when recalling his first reading of Stevens:

> I remember that when Wallace Stevens was first published in England, in the early fifties, and we had the job of coming to terms with his poetry and assimilating it into the tradition we were working from, most people adopted this simple approach ["going through his prose utterances, letters, recorded conversations, etc., and then turn to the poems and spot every line in which those ideas seemed to crop up"] to begin with; I certainly did myself. But as soon as the poems are familiar, and we begin to move towards a more sensitive and intimate approach, we have to realize that a poet may use his ideas in a number of ways. (327)

What Wain seems to be saying is that, instead of imposing our initial impressions and personal standards upon the poet, we ought otherwise to adapt ourselves to the larger terms of the poet's individual and unique art. Writing these words in 1977, Wain suggests how difficult this had proved to be with the British reception of this particular poet. Stevens is not as alien to the tradition of British poetry as many of his critics have suggested. It is perhaps not sufficiently appreciated among British readers that, as a poet, Stevens can be as sensuous as Keats; as absorbed by the natural world as Wordsworth;[71] with as much ostentation in style, at least in his early work, as Hopkins; as committed as Arnold to the eminent role of poetry in a post-Christian world. In a tentative way, his early, apprentice work began under the influence of poets like Sidney and Herrick (*SP* 50–51, 28), and the English Romantics. Although Stevens' struggle, first, to find publication in England and then to be read seriously there, was and has continued to be indisputably difficult, his work has never been antithetical to the English tradition.

When American poets generally and Stevens in particular earn the status and respect of British critics and other readers—both within British universities (and they have not yet fully done so)[72] and beyond—Stevens' standing there will evolve toward a fuller and richer transatlantic validation. The struggle in the twenty-first century to define and come to terms with the "modernism" of the first half of the previous century has undoubtedly mandated a closer look at Stevens—both in the United States and, especially, in the United Kingdom. To know Stevens as a modernist, a high priest of the imagination but also a classical disavower of the same imagination in favor of the rigorous, even ascetic demands of reality—all played out in his poetry's progression through the symbolism of the four seasons—has made it increasingly clear that this poet cannot be reduced to a handful of poems or to a quick reckoning of the poet's style as baroque and foppish. Stevens' style, as we have seen in the previous chapter, is not uniform and speaks in many voices, but it is consistent with the content that informs a given poem and in unpredictably creative ways. Moreover, his poetry is far more deeply engaged with the political upheavals and economic crises of his lifetime than is sometimes recognized.

To come to terms with Stevens asks much of us—at least as much as it does in reading Eliot, Pound, and other modernists. After many decades, it can now be said that the poetry of Stevens, however inchoately, increasingly possesses an acknowledged canonicity in the United Kingdom and Ireland. In the years that lie ahead all readers of this poet will benefit as that critical consolidation expands within an ever-widening historical, cultural, and geographical heterodoxy. For all his readers, Stevens' various makings of his poems, as we continue to discover and construe them and even to find ourselves confounded at times by them, remain, as Stevens hoped they would and even foretold: a complete planet on the table, extraordinary references, creations of sound, spoken words of self and origin.

NOTES

1. Hi Simons to Wallace Stevens, January 14, 1940, in Folder 8, Box 1, Hi Simons Papers, University of Chicago Library. Reproduced with permission.

CHAPTER ONE

1. Elsie Stevens to Mrs. Lehman W. Moll, June 1939, Huntington Library. Reproduced in George S. Lensing, *Wallace Stevens: A Poet's Growth*, 148–49: "This is the view of the Atlantic ocean from our rooms in Holly Inn. The water between the islands along the 'rock bound' coast of Maine, as far as we can see from here—and farther—is called the Thread of Life—the islands are mostly rocks that are very white in the sunlight and the brilliantly green spruce trees seem to grow right out of them. Many birds are here: gulls, terns, kingfishers and we saw some herons on the island the other day when we passed in a boat."

2. Elsie Stevens' *Sea-Voyage* is reproduced here and is located at the Huntington Library, Art Gallery and Botanical Gardens, San Marino, California. It was first published: "Mrs. Wallace Stevens' *Sea Voyage* and 'Sea Surface Full of Clouds'" *American Poetry* 3 (Spring 1986): 76–84.

3. The Personnel Department of the Hartford Accident and Indemnity Co. is unable to identify the names here cited. As to the Mr. Marvin (mistakenly cited as "Mr. Marion" in *Letters*) who had served as Stevens' host during his visit to Havana the previous February, Stevens identifies him as "one of the representatives of the Hartford Fire" (*L* 235).

4. The novel had been published the previous August by Alfred A. Knopf.

5. Mrs. Stevens would surely have noted with personal interest (in light of the evolving strains in her own marriage) this rejoinder from one of the novel's characters: "You are cheerful and amusing and decorative. I'm glad I didn't marry you. No husband can be cheerful and amusing and decorative to his wife, and a man who is cheerful and amusing and decorative to the world, but who ceases to be so to his wife, soon loses his self-confidence, and fails to interest anybody" (62).

6. For a more complete account of Stevens' early association with Van Vechten, see Carl Van Vechten, "Rogue Elephant in Porcelain," *Yale University Library Gazette* 38 (October 1963): 41–50.

7. With minor alterations the poem appeared again in *Hound and Horn* (Fall 1929), now entitled "Academic Discourse at Havana," and later in *Ideas of Order*.

8. For the best treatment of the Symbolist influences in the poem, see Lisa Goldfarb, *The Figure Concealed: Wallace Stevens, Music, and Valéryan Echoes*, especially her emphasis on "Stevens' sonic and rhythmic changes" throughout the poem (101).

9. Shane Murphy has suggested that a poem called "Ark of the Covenant" by Northern Irish poet Ciaran Carson imitates Stevens' poem in this mode of framing: "[Carson's] suspicion of, and playful attitude towards, language becomes evident in 'Ark of the Covenant' in which he imitates Wallace Stevens's 'Sea Surface Full of Clouds,' having each section as a variation of the other: using synonyms gleaned from a Thesaurus, Carson constructs four differing narratives based on a single text" (206). Carson's poem is more a tour de force than Stevens,' anti-lyrical in its densely layered coat of language. See chapter 5 for a fuller discussion of Stevens' influence on other Irish and Northern Irish poets.

10. The use of the word "Sambo" obviously is a stock name for an African American stereotype and suggests slightly the butt of a joke. See Stevens' letter to his fiancée dated December 7, 1908, in which he used the word ("Marse Sambo [CS 109],") in a private tale in which he plays Sambo and Elsie plays a "pretty maid." In another, dated December 2, 1908 (CS 106), he signs his name at the end of the letter as "Sambo" without commentary.

11. Stevens to John Paulker, June 3, 1941: "Then about Chinese chocolate: It may be that this is what may be called an embryo for charivari. The words are used in a purely expressive sense and are meant to connote a big Chinese with a very small cup of chocolate: something incongruous" (L 389). Of course in the poem there is no indication of the size of the Chinese or even that the word indicates a person.

12. Wallace Stevens, Letter to Renato Poggioli, June 10, 1953, The Huntington Library, Art Gallery and Botanical Gardens.

CHAPTER TWO

1. See, for example, "Infanta Marina," "Hibiscus on the Sleeping Shores," "Fabliau of Florida," "Homunculus et la Belle Etoile," part I of "The Comedian as the Letter C," "The Place of the Solitaires," "Stars at Tallapoosa," "To the One of Fictive Music," "Sea Surface Full of Clouds," "Farewell to Florida," part XXVII of "The Man with the Blue Guitar," "Variations on a Summer Day," part I of "Asides on the Oboe," "Somnambulisma," "Two Versions of the Same Poem," "Page from a Tale," "The Woman that Had More Babies than That," Part VIII ("It Must Be Abstract") of "Notes toward a Supreme Fiction," "part XXVII of "An Ordinary Evening in New Haven," "The Irish Cliffs of Moher," "The Poem that Took the Place of a Mountain," "Prologues To What Is Possible," and others.

2. In another essay, Vendler has indicated a different stylistic complexity: "The structure of the poem is ostensibly one of logical discrimination, but actually the complicated progressions ('even if . . . since . . . it may be . . . if . . . or . . . ') simply serve to implicate the various alternatives even more deeply with each other so that the sea, the girl, the water, the song, the wind, the air, the sky and cloud, the voices of the spectators, all become indistinguishable from each other, as Stevens wants them to be" ("The Qualified Assertions,"175).

3. See letter from Gerard Previn Meyer, an associate of Latimer, to John Gould Fletcher, dated August 17, 1933, quoted in Filreis's *Modernism from Left to Right*, 325.

4. The missing first card, omitted in *Letters*, is now at the Huntington Library and provides

the exact date of Stevens' visit there and makes clear that he is describing the Mardi Gras celebration.

5. The poem originally contained an extra line. In the sixth stanza, the line "As the night descended, tilting in the air," was written, "As the night descended, tilting up and down," followed by the line that was subsequently omitted: "Why the tilted lanterns dangling in the air." The poem's first line was set off from the first stanza. In a line in the second stanza, "Since what she sang was uttered word by word," originally employed "she" in place of "was." The ensemble of poems in *Alcestis,* though eight in number, was titled "Seven Poems."

6. Jonathan Wordsworth connects the woman singer in "The Idea of Order at Key West" with the woman "who bore a pitcher on her head" in Book XI of *The Prelude.* "The Mind as Lord and Master," 183–91.

7. Mervyn Nicholson has suggested that "sound alone" is a kind of pre-text to meaning: "To say that it is sound 'alone' is to remove from it all abstract meanings, while at the same time allowing the ground of all meanings to emerge. Hearing not only precedes meaning: it makes meaning possible, and hence contains meaning within itself in potential form" (67).

8. J. Hillis Miller has defined the conflict in the poem between "sea" and "she" somewhat differently: "The conflict between the singer and the genius of the sea is worked out as a kind of singing competition" (267). He goes on: "The woman's song is not just uttered 'word by word.' It is also 'sung,' that is, modulated in pitch. Song adds to the rhythms and cadences of speech the articulations of melody. The voices of sea and sky have no such divisions. They have no marked beginnings and endings. They are just one single, meaningless sound repeated endlessly in a summer without end" (272).

9. John Knight points out, "'Mere' in Old English and modern French derives from the Latin word, *mare,* and refers to the sea or a large body of water. Taken in this sense, 'merely' ['The ever-hooded, tragic-gestured sea / Was merely a place by which she walked.'] becomes a pun which tends to diminish the implication of division between the singer's song and the sea and suggests, somewhat comically, that a certain affinity exists between them." Knight, "Mimetic and Expressive Theories of Poetry," 50.

10. Wallace Stevens to Robert G. Tucker. February 15, 1954. WAS 2428. Huntington Library, Art Collections, and Botanical Gardens.

11. To some this "dismissal" of the woman from a presence in the poem has seemed an exertion of a patriarchal speaker silencing (though she is never heard directly) the female singer. This, however, is the poet Adrienne Rich's response to the female presence of the singer: "But 'The Idea of Order at Key West' offered me something absolutely new: a conception of a woman maker, singing and striding beside the ocean, creating her own music, separate from yet bestowing its order upon '*the meaningless plunges of water and the wind.*' This image entered me, in the 1950s, an era of feminist retrenchment and poetic diminishment, as an image of my tongue-tied desire that a woman's life, a poet's work, should amount to more than the measured quantities I saw around me" (199).

12. For further connections between Nietzsche's *The Will to Power* and "The Idea of Order at Key West," see B. J. Leggett, *Early Stevens: The Nietzschean Intertext,* 184–86.

13. Edna Longley has referred to this god-like power in the song of the woman: "In 'Idea of Order' the relation between the singer and the sea enacts that of the Creator—God or poet—to formless waters" (*Poetry and Posterity* 263).

14. See chapter 4 for further discussion of the world's sounds in the poem "The Creations of Sound."

15. James Longenbach has also noted the importance of an audience in the poem: "Just as the woman's song is meaningless in 'The Idea of Order' until it is heard by someone else, so does this work of art ["The Old Woman and the Statue"] require an audience" (166).

16. In stanza xix from "Like Decorations in a Nigger Cemetery," Stevens uses the word "portals" with the same theatrical association: "An opening of portals when night ends, / A running forward, arms stretched out as drilled. Act I, Scene I, at a German Staats-Oper" (*CPP* 123). Another poem, "Of Modern Poetry," directly associates the making of poetry with dramatic enactment:

> It [the "poem of the mind'] has
> To construct a new stage. It has to be on that stage
> And, like an insatiable actor, slowly and
> With meditation, speak words that in the ear,
> In the delicatest ear of the mind, repeat,
> Exactly, that which it wants to hear, at the sound
> Of which, an invisible audience listens. (*CPP* 219)

17. Jacqueline Brogan has pointed out the implications of gender at work here, as the presumed male voice of the speaker turns away from the woman, thereby imposing and affirming a more masculine view: "lights 'master' the night, 'portion' out the sea, 'arrange' and 'deepen' night, so that the words, in a kind of phallic 'mastering,' ironically create the 'fragrant portals,' essentially create the feminine" (103).

18. Joan Richardson, among others, mistakenly refers to him as a "Spanish critic" (117).

19. For references to Fernandez's collaboration with the Germans during World War II, see: Lottman, *The Left Bank*, and Dominque Fernandez. *Ramon*. In his *The Modern Dilemma*, Canadian Leon Surette adds, "Although the circumstances of his [Fernandez's] death remain obscure, it is thought that he committed suicide after being called before the *épuration* committee, whose mandate was to investigate and prosecute those who had collaborated with the Nazis during the occupation" (201).

20. The first critic to discuss this essay in the context of Stevens' poem was Joseph Riddel in his 1965 study, *The Clairvoyant Eye: The Poetry and Poetics of Wallace Stevens*. Here he cites one paragraph from the essay with the comment that it "should reveal something about Stevens' allusion, even if it was a happy coincidence" (117).

21. In his essay "Three Academic Pieces," Stevens differentiates between *seeing* the world and *begetting* or *making* it through "resemblance," such as, one might surmise, song resembling sea: "What the eye beholds may be the text of life. It is, nevertheless, a text that we do not write.

The eye does not beget in resemblance. It sees. But the mind begets in resemblance as the painter begets in representation, that is to say, *as the painter makes his world within a world* [emphasis added] (*CPP* 689).

22. From "Of the Principles of Human Knowledge" (259). Stevens in all likelihood takes Berkeley's quotation cited above from its reproduction in Arthur Kenyon Rogers' *A Student's History of Philosophy* (315–16). (He acknowledges this work as a general source for many of his quotes in "A Collect of Philosophy" [858].) Stevens also quotes from Berkeley in one of his "Adagia": "The imagination of the blind man cannot be the extension of an externality he has never seen" (*CPP* 921)).

23. In his book *Molière: The Man Seen through the Plays*, Fernandez restates the same danger of a kind of excessive imagination separated from the real as it is worked out in Molière's play *Les Prècieuses Ridicules*. Such is the object of the dramatist's satire: "At another moment the trick is to the Prècieuses [those who deny instinctual life] speeches in which they recoil from laying a finger on whatever object they are mentioning, even on things no more repulsive than a chair or a mirror. Again, the light will be focused on 'imaginings'—on the fancy of making life over and daydreaming it according to the conventions of fiction" (56).

24. Coleridge hints at such a residual memory in these words from his 1805 *Journal*: "In looking at objects of Nature while I am thinking, as at yonder moon dim-glimmering thro' the dewy window-pane, I seem rather to be seeking, as it were *asking,* a symbolical language for something within me that already and forever exists, than observing any thing new. Even when that latter is the case, yet still I have always an obscure feeling as if that new phaenomenon were the dim Awaking of a forgotten or hidden Truth of my inner Nature / It is still interesting as a Word, a Symbol! It is Λογος the Creator! (and the Evolver!)" (2546).

CHAPTER THREE

1. Writing on March 6, 1898, Garrett Stevens wrote: "Everybody wants war—Colleges are offering to defend the flag—become a bold buccaneer—bleed for glory—but it is a darned prosy career unless one is an Officer—for the privates spend 9/10 of the time cleaning up their arms and the quick ones must brush up the clothes of the Officers—and they get so infernally tired of that, that the prospect of getting shot is quite a relief—The West Point + other Military fellows get the offices—so that the Martial Spirit while a good thing should be confined to the fellows out of jobs." Reprinted from the Huntington Library, WAS 2138.

2. Margaret Leech in *In the Days of McKinley* reports that when the War broke out, "The expansion of the Navy, which somewhat more than doubled its personnel of about 12,000 officers and men, was on a far smaller scale than that of the Army, enlarged from a force of 28,000 men to more than a quarter of a million" (234–35).

3. Ezra Pound to Parker Tyler, dated February 14, 1933, and March 19, 1933, as quoted in George Bornstein. "Eight Letters from Ezra Pound to Parker Tyler in the 1930s." *Michigan Quarterly Review* 24 (1985): 1–17.

4. See Stanley Burnshaw, "'Turmoil in the Middle Ground," 41–42.

5. See *Marjorie Perloff, "Revolving in Crystal,"* 41–64.

6. See Frank Lentricchia, *Ariel and the Police.*

7. The harsh intrusion of the solider upon a scene of domestic peace was repeated in "The Bouquet":

> A car drives up. A soldier, an officer,
> Steps out. He rings and knocks. The door is not locked.
> He enters the room and calls. No one is there.
>
> He bumps the table. The bouquet falls on its side.
> He walks through the house, looks round him and then leaves.
> The bouquet has slopped over the edge and lies on the floor. (*CPP* 387)

8. As Friedrich Schlegel, in a different context, concluded: "Every honest author writes for nobody or everybody. Whoever writes for some particular group does not deserve to be read" (430).

9. The eleven-part sequence was first reassembled by A. Walton Litz in his *Introspective Voyager: The Poetic Development of Wallace Stevens* in 1972; and it is reproduced in Stevens' *Collected Poetry and Prose,* 525–29.

10. Milton Bates indicates that the sequence as it appears in *Opus Posthumous* was "reproduced in A. Walton Litz, *Introspective Voyager,* pp. 310–15, with minor variations based on Stevens' typescript in the Harriet Monroe Library of Modern Poetry" ("Notes" 319). As Litz observes, the sequence may originally have contained seventeen poems . . . Sections I–VI and VII–XI were published in the May 1918 issue of *Poetry.* Sections VI, VII, IX, and XI (the last under the title 'The Death of a Soldier') are reprinted without their epigraphs in the *Collected Poems.* In Morse's edition of *Opus Posthumous,* he reproduces the nine poems that had appeared in *Poetry: A Magazine of Verse* with the accompanying epigraphs. In *Wallace Stevens: Collected Poetry and Prose* (1997) the poem is reproduced with epigraphs in the thirteen poems reproduced by Litz, including the four that appeared in *Poetry: A Magazine of Verse.*

11. Stevens was sparing in his use of epigraphs throughout his career, and the *Lettres d'un Soldat* collection as it appeared in *Poetry* is his most extensive adoption of the device. See my "Epigraphs" (pp. 201–225) in *Wallace Stevens: A Poet's Growth.*

12. In letters dated November 15, 23, and 29, Lemercier refers to outdoor shrines as "calvaries."

13. One of Stevens' first assignments as a reporter for the *New York Tribune*—shortly after he had completed a three-year residency at Harvard and had moved to New York—was to cover the funeral of Stephen Crane in 1900.

14. "Ah, Yes, desire" (1ine 7) and "God and all the angels sing the world to sleep" (line 1) are transcribed into the poem from Stevens' notebook of titles, *From Pieces of Paper* in George S. Lensing, *Wallace Stevens: a Poet's Growth,"* 174. These entries must have been in some way a source for the poem's writing.

15. I have always thought of this poem as a kind of companion poem to "The Emperor of

Ice-Cream," a poem from Stevens' previous volume. Both poems consist of a series of commands instructing the listener in how to respond to the presence of a corpse and the grief that accompanies it. If for the earlier poem the conclusion is, "Let be be finale of seem," in this poem, one might say, the conclusion is "Let seem be finale of be."

16. I am grateful to Stefan Holander for noting these errors in Powell's reproduction of Stevens' drafting notes (197).

17. Clara Schumann, the recently widowed wife of musician-composer Robert Schumann, whose life had ended tragically, found assuagement from her grief in the music performed for her by Brahms. She describes it in a letter: "The day after my return, Brahms rejoiced me by a visit. He is with me now, and plays to me a great deal, which gives me real delight, and prevents me from so often feeling painfully conscious of my loneliness" (158).

18. Emily Anderson, in her annotations for this passage, indicates "K. 413–415, composed in 1782" (1242) as the concerto to which Mozart is referring.

19. See Michael Stegman, "Wallace Stevens and Music," 79–97.

20. Stevens' repeated apostrophe to "Be thou" echoes, as many critics have noted, the "Be thou, Spirit fierce, / My spirit! Be thou me, impetuous one!" (Shelley, "Ode to the West Wind," 414). In the echo, there is, as Walton Litz notes, "a nice irony in the contrast" between Stevens' poet and Shelley's spirit: "The 'thou' of Shelley's 'Ode' is all that is left of the old romanticism, but in its own way the new conception of the poet as realistic nightingale reaches just as far" (198)

21. Arthur Schlesinger, Jr., describes Roosevelt's fondness for poker games at the White House: "At the poker table . . . he adored reckless variations like seven-card stud with deuces and one-eyed jacks wild or improbable improvisations like 'spit in the ocean'" (579).

22. James Longenbach notes, "The president was Roosevelt; the director of his Office of Facts and Figures was the poet [Archibald MacLeish] whose most famous lines ordained that 'a poem should not mean / But be'" (262).

23. Jonathan Alter offers a similar view of the earlier response to Mussolini in America: "After all, the Italian Fascist Benito Mussolini, in power for a decade, had ginned up the Italian economy and was popular with everyone from Winston Churchill to Will Rogers to Lowell Thomas, America's most influential broadcaster. 'If ever this country needed a Mussolini, it needs one now,' said Senator David Reed of Pennsylvania, outgoing President Hoover's closest friend on Capitol Hill" (5–6).

CHAPTER FOUR

1. Eleven years earlier, Stevens made this entry in his journal: "A few Sundays ago I noticed a number of pigeons sitting out the rain on one of the ledges of Washington Bridge; and as I passed there this morning I heard their rou-cou-cou" (SP 175)

2. See unpublished dissertation: Karen Helgeson, "'For a Moment Final,'" 21.

3. Of "The Old Woman and the Statue" Stevens reported that it was "a carefully worked thing." That quality of being "carefully worked" and reworked perhaps accounts for the weightiness and abstraction of parts of "Owl's Clover."

4. Letter to Ronald Lane Latimer, May 27, 1935. Reprinted with permission of University of Chicago Library, Box 1, Folder 16, Ronald Lane Latimer Papers.

5. A few months before Stevens' death and in the middle of the twentieth century, Randall Jarrell looked back on the influence upon American poets of major Modernists: "If someone had predicted to Pound, when he was beginning his war on the iambic foot; to Eliot, when he was first casting a cold eye on post-Jacobean blank verse; to both, when they were first condemning generalization in poetry, that in forty or fifty years the chief—sometimes, I think in despair, the only—influence on younger American poets, would be this generalizing, masterful, scannable verse of Stevens', wouldn't both have laughed in confident disbelief?" ("Collected Poems of Wallace Stevens" 348).

6. Harvey Gross, "Hart Crane and Wallace Stevens," 225–46. Donald Justice, "The Free-Verse Line in Wallace Stevens," 51–76. Dennis Taylor, "The Apparitional Meters of Wallace Stevens," 209–28.

7. Lisa Goldfarb has connected Stevens to Valéry through their mutual conviction that the sounds of words in poetry draw the reader beyond discursive rational meaning: "By repeating the familiar sounds of the argument, Stevens, like Valéry's poet, dislocates the rational meaning that the reader expects the words to convey, hoping to draw his reader closer to the truth of his proposition" ("The Figure Concealed" 53).

8. To some degree, "The Motive for Metaphor" illustrates the conclusion of Anca Rosu that certain poems by Stevens possess "an overload of metaphors" that work against "an appetite for intelligibility and conclusiveness." But she then adds: "Yet once the function or representation is abandoned, reality does not have to be renounced, since language can generate that which for us counts as real" (148). Harrison DeSales defines the "A B C" and "X" of being in terms of parentage: "What 'The A B C of being' stands for is a primary parentage, or meaning's primal scene, on which one cannot look without risking the steel and the flash of the X. This X I take to be the first point of origin, without form and void, from which these original parents first sprang: the X that begat the A B C that begat all the words of the world" (79). To which I would add one final clause: " . . . and [words] that begat all the metaphors of the world."

9. This line is often cited among commentaries on Stevens' sound system. Charles Altieri cautions, however, that the "Third Girl" who utters this line to the "maundering . . . yokel" (*CPP* 5) will, in fact, "undo him" by whispering her "heavenly labials" (*CPP* 6): "A new poetry might find the *true* [emphasis added] giant by dwelling on the gutterals that undo his preferred self-image" (64). Labials and gutturals remain elements in contention and contrast, each with its own phonic claim.

CHAPTER FIVE

1. As he indicated in a letter to an Irish correspondent, Stevens resented the "insults" that came from the British to Americans: "But most of the insults that we get from the British are the sort of thing that we have been getting regardless of when or why and having nothing to do with economics and politics as they exist between the British and the Americans. . . . The truth

is that the British flatter themselves at the expense of the world, always have and always will" (*L* 646–47).

2. Many years later (1978), the American novelist Henry Miller expressed a similar response in a letter to the British novelist Lawrence Durrell: "Someone recently gave me a line from a poem by Wallace Stevens (an American poet I can't read). It goes like this: 'Death is the mother of Beauty.' Do you make anything out of it? I don't." (Durrell and Miller 500).

3. The four stanzas in the *Chapbook* correspond to Stanzas I, VIII, IV, and VII of the original and final version.

4. In "A Letter from America," published in the *London Mercury* 4 (June 1921): 199, Aiken had quoted approvingly from the first stanza of "Sunday Morning" and predicted that "slowly will come a hearing" for Stevens in England, as well as for Fletcher and Bodenheim.

5. For a more detailed account of Moore's own work and his relation to Wallace Stevens, see Mark Ford, "Nicholas Moore, Stevens and the Fortune Press," 165–85. It should be noted that when the essay was reproduced in Ford's *Mr and Mrs Stevens and Other Essays* (2011), the annotations and acknowledgments were omitted.

6. Holly Stevens' note in *Letters*, 311, that "the book was not published by the Dent firm; no correspondence relating to that possibility has been found by Mr. Church or the editor" is corroborated by a letter from Peter Shellard, director of J. M. Dent & Sons Ltd., to George S. Lensing, August 13, 1976.

7. Hobsbaum to George S. Lensing, September 15, 2004.

8. From the Wallace Stevens–Cummington Press Correspondence, 1941–51. John Rylands University Library of Manchester. Cited by Carolyn Masel, "Stevens and England," 126. Eight years after Stevens' death and through the initiative of Frank Kermode, the John Rylands Library at the University of Manchester purchased the 191 letters exchanged between Stevens and his editors at the Cummington Press in Cummington, Massachusetts.

9. Other poems by Moore—including "Pepe-le-Moko au Montrachet-le-Jardin," "L'Eau Verte du Lethe," and "In Memory of Wallace Stevens"—would reveal his continuing dialogue with Stevens.

10. Caton and his Fortune Press published Philip Larkin's first volume of poetry, *The North Ship* (1945), and his first novel, *Jill* (1944)—as well as works by Dylan Thomas, Kingsley Amis, Roy Fuller, C. Day-Lewis, and Nicholas Moore. For a complete index of Caton's publications, see Timothy D'Arch Smith, *R. A. Caton and the Fortune Press.*

11. Wallace Stevens to Nicholas Moore, May 9, 1944, The Huntington Library and Art Museum, San Marino, CA. (References to correspondence below are to the archives of the Huntington, unless otherwise indicated.)

12. Stevens to Alfred A. Knopf, September 14, 1944.

13. Knopf to Stevens, September 21, 1944. (For permission to quote from this unpublished letter and the one from Knopf to Stevens of November 1, 1945, I am grateful to William A. Koshland of Alfred A. Knopf, Inc.)

14. Stevens to Tambimuttu, September 23, 1944.

15. Stevens to Tambimuttu, December 1, 1944.

16. Stevens to Moore, July 20, 1945.

17. Stevens to Moore, July 25, 1945.

18. Knopf to Stevens, November 1, 1945.

19. Stevens to Knopf, November 15, 1945.

20. Stevens to Oscar Williams, November 20, 1945.

21. Stevens to Moore, February 20, 1946. Moore later recalled the disappointment in a brief tribute to Tambimuttu after his death in 1983: "I negotiated with Wallace Stevens for a selected poems, as I was already friendly with him, but his American publisher Knopf wouldn't sanction it. He had something against Tambi, I don't know what. Later Stevens wrote to me, 'You have taken a bad beating'" ("Tambi the Knife" 63).

22. Stevens to Henry Church, March 11, 1946.

23. Stevens to Knopf, November 8, 1946.

24. After Roberts's death, the edition of 1951, edited by Anne Ridler, omitted "The Death of a Soldier" and added part vii of "Esthétique du Mal" ("How red the rose that is the soldier's wound") along with the other three poems. The third edition of the *Faber Book of Modern Verse* appeared in 1965, now edited by the American poet Donald Hall. Hall retained "Tea at the Palaz of Hoon" and "The Emperor of Ice-Cream," but now added five late poems by Stevens: "The Rock," "Not Ideas about the Thing But the Thing Itself," "The World as Meditation," "The Course of a Particular," and "Of Mere Being." In a note, Hall added, "I would like to have printed Wallace Stevens' *Sunday Morning*, but of course it was available to Roberts [in the 1936 edition], and not chosen by him, and so if I used it I would be revising his opinions. Instead, I have added later (and I think excellent) poems by the same poet" (30).

25. Letter by T. S. Eliot to Robert Graves, October 27, 1925. In *Letters of T. S. Eliot*, II, 764.

26. Stevens to Herbert Weinstock, October 10, 1951.

27. Peter du Sautoy to George S. Lensing, August 3, 1976.

28. The Fortune Press had earlier issued *Poetry from Oxford, Michaelmas 1948 to Michaelmas 1949* in 1950, edited by Williamson and including three poems by him.

29. Weinstock to Stevens, February 27, 1953. These remarks were quoted in J. M. Edelstein, *Wallace Stevens: A Descriptive Bibliography* (Pittsburgh: University of Pittsburgh Press, 1973), 100. Edelstein incorrectly attributes the letter to Alfred A. Knopf instead of Weinstock.

30. Du Sautoy to George S. Lensing, August 3, 1976.

31. Charles Skilton to George S. Lensing, August 3, 1976.

32. Stevens to Tambimuttu, April 13, 1955.

33. For a discussion of the early critical response to Stevens in America, see my "The Early Readers of Wallace Stevens," 49–73.

34. Stevens himself seems to have responded to the earliest reviews with a mixed reaction. Writing to Richard Eberhart on April 17, 1953, he noted: "My book in England is doing well although the first two reviews that I saw were silly things. Faber sent me some clippings, however, which were really based on the book and had nothing to do with the reviewer's particular bias and I have sent them on to Knopf." ("Six Stevens Letters" 23).

35. Fourteen years earlier in 1940, Symons had written an essay commending "The Man

with the Blue Guitar" as "one of the most notable poetic achievements of the last twenty years, an achievement that may be compared with 'The Waste Land' or 'Mauberley'" ("A Short View" 219–20). Such encomia notwithstanding, he goes on to fault Stevens: "His work does not contain an objective view of life, nor does it express a philosophy of life; it gives instead an objective view of Mr. Stevens in various attitudes" ("A Short View," 222). The added remarks in *Trinity Review*, coming fourteen years later, conclude: "But not even an English view must end with such ungracious or ungrateful words. I am ready to bow the head, more than that, to go down on bended knee, in homage to the beautiful structure of Stevens's poems and the elegance and grace of his writing; and if a young poet were looking for a model (as almost all young poets unconsciously always are) he might gain much more, and with much less chance of harm, from Stevens than from Eliot or Pound. He is the most charming and accomplished of poets; and it is only the solemn scholasticism of some of his American admirers (dare I say?) that makes one question so sharply the accomplishment and charm" ("Stevens in England" 44–45).

36. Du Sautoy to George S. Lensing, August 3, 1976. In a letter dated February 21, 2002, John Bodley summarizes Faber's edition up to that point: "Collected edition in hardback was printed five times, and then superseded by the paperback which was printed seven times from 1984 to the present. Selected Poems had three printings as a hardback and as a paperback fourteen so far." Bodley to George S. Lensing, February 21, 2002.

37. See especially chapter 9, "Stevens and Eliot" in his *Words Alone: The Poet T. S. Eliot* (2000).

38. E-mail from John Bodley to George S. Lensing, November 20, 2001.

39. When Robert Lowell's *Life Studies* was reviewed by Alvarez in 1959, Lowell wrote to I. A. Richards: "I got rather a rave review from Alvarez in the *Observer*, so my book is off beyond my dizziest hope in England," April 18, 1959, 346. Such was the extent of Alvarez's reputation as critic.

40. E-mail from Philip Hobsbaum to George Lensing, August 5, 2004.

41. The charge of rhetorical superfluity proposed by Stevens' British readers in the 1950s and 1960s was not an isolated one. David Wright, for example, in his "Introduction" to his Penguin anthology, *The Mid-Century: English Poetry 1940–1960*, generalizes: "Contemporary American poetry—which, thanks to the excessive interest taken in it by American universities, is now an industry rather than an art—seems to be wandering off in the direction of the decorative, where style and technique is all and thought, if anything, a peg on which to hang a Chinese box of semantic ingenuities" (17).

42. Elizabeth Jennings, one of the poets identified with the Movement, saw Stevens more sympathetically: "Yes, Wallace Stevens, but more for ideas than forms, because I was almost obsessed at one point with the idea of what one made of a thing and what was reality, with objectivity and subjectivity, and then one day I picked up an anthology and found some Wallace Stevens and I thought, 'Ah, this person has done it, but maybe one can do something else like this or take it further'; though not quite as ambitious as that, but he was a big influence at one period, yes" (93–94).

43. In 2001 Hobsbaum was still writing on Stevens. The poet's "self-regarding dandyism" was

something out of which "Stevens managed to develop." He was "one of the very few genuinely philosophical poets in English," and "Sunday Morning" succeeds by "an original rehandling of blank verse; a remarkable achievement, aesthetic as well as technical, for this late stage in the history of literature. The working out of this great poem guarantees its philosophy" ("Wallace Stevens: *Harmonium*" 418, 421, 425).

44. In introducing the poets included in his *New Poetries II* (1999), Schmidt registers the American poet's appeal at the turn of the century—that dangerous Stevensian "iambulator" notwithstanding: "I am surprised once more to note the impact of Wallace Stevens on several of these writers: Stevens himself, not Stevens via Ashbery (though Ashbery has a place in their firmament); and Stevens, not Pound" (9).

45. On the dust jacket of the book *The Blue Guitar: etchings by David Hockney who was inspired by Wallace Stevens who was inspired by Pablo Picasso,* Hockney further explains the connection between the etchings and Stevens' poem: "The etchings themselves were not conceived as literal illustrations of the poem but as an interpretation of its themes in visual terms. Like the poem, they are about transformations within art as well as the relation between reality and the imagination, so these are pictures within pictures and different styles of representation juxtaposed and reflected and dissolved within the same frame."

46. Note, for example, the large number of British and Irish poets referred to below with titles that play upon Stevens' title "Thirteen Ways of Looking at a Blackbird."

47. Liesl Olson adds that "three drafts of the poem, under the title 'Art History,' appear in Auden's notebook, Poems 1947[-49], also housed in the Berg Collection of the New York City Public Library, showing the poem in its various stages of composition." Auden also wrote out the poem in his copy of one of Stevens' volumes: "Although Auden's copy of *Transport to Summer* has not been found, Alan Ansen—Auden's late amanuensis—reports that Auden's poem was written in a copy of the Stevens volume" (253, 252). Olson identifies several possible connections between individual poems by Auden and Stevens. In my *Wallace Stevens and the Seasons,* I suggest a noted similarity between Auden's "O What Is That Sound" and Stevens' later poem "Contrary Thesis (I)." See pp. 73–74.

48. The poems included in Auden's anthology are: "The Snow Man," "Disillusionment of Ten O'Clock," "Sunday Morning," "Dry Loaf," "Woman Looking at a Vase of Flowers," and, from "Notes toward a Supreme Fiction," two cantos: "Be thou me, said sparrow, to the crackled blade" and "We reason of these things with later reason."

49. In one interview, Larkin casually identified himself with Stevens as a poet who was not a professional poet: "You can earn your money talking about poetry in universities or hopping from one foundation to another or one conference to another—or you can go away and be something very different like an accountant—I believe Roy Fuller is something like that, Wallace Stevens was an insurance man. I'm a librarian" ("A Conversation," 28).

50. Dennis O'Driscoll has linked the two poets, not in poetic terms, but personal ones: "For men like Wallace Stevens and Philip Larkin who were not gregarious by nature, the daily contact with colleagues provided a social life which did not cut across the nocturnal poetry life. Stevens would be found at the Canoe Club on Wednesdays, enjoying cold-beef luncheon with Hartford

Accident colleagues. And if the Hermit of Hartford could be bibulously high-spirited enough to kick a tray of hors d'oeuvres from the hands of a Canoe Club waitress, we should not be surprised to catch a glimpse of the Hermit of Hull as he emerged from the bookstacks 'behind the leader of a conga in which everyone had joined' at the library's Christmas party" (219).

51. The remark is referred to by Mary Jane W. Scott in her essay "Neoclassical MacCaig," *Studies in Scottish Literature* 10 (January 1973), 142. She refers to an unpublished interview with MacCaig conducted by M. J. Wittstock on January 12, 1972.

52. After his comparison with Stevens, Hill goes on to give an adumbration of his own "theological view of literature": "The major caveat which I would enter against a theological view of literature is that, too often, it is not theology at all, but merely a restatement of the neo-Symbolist mystique celebrating verbal mastery; an expansive gesture conveying the broad sense that Joyce's *Ulysses* or Rilke's *Duino Elegies* 'must, in the splendor of its art, evoke astonishment at the sheer magnificence of its lordship over language.' If an argument for the theological interpretation of literature is to be sustained, it needs other sustenance than this" (*Lords of Limit* 17).

53. Jenkins to Lensing, February 17, 2017, e-mail message.

54. David Gascoyne to Wallace Stevens. August 5, 1944. Huntington Library and Art Museum.

55. "Common Soldier" did not appear in the original "Lettres d'un Soldat" selected by *Poetry: A Magazine of Verse* in 1918 but in *Opus Posthumous* in 1963 where Thomas must have encountered it in time for his anthology.

56. In his *The Poetry of R. S. Thomas*, J. P. Ward identifies two additional poems by Thomas as coming under the influence of Stevens, "Winter Starlings" and "Mrs Li." Of the latter, he says, "But 'Mrs Li' is so clearly an antiphonal poem to Stevens's "To the One of Fictive Music,' that one feels Thomas exploring Stevens during this period and half-hoping to find the direction he so desperately wants. . . . But with Stevens I feel Thomas senses an opportunity. The sensuous qualities Thomas finds at times almost unbearably in matter itself, can be lifted forward into the poetry that would—as Stevens himself once put it—'suffice.' But Thomas has not the same formal and equable philosophical temperament as Stevens, such that an overall poetic philosophy could emerge from several poems" (62–63). Tony Brown, in his essay "R. S. Thomas and Wallace Stevens," connects "Mrs Li" to "The Idea of Order at Key West": "One might contend that 'Mrs Li' owes at least as much to the 'Key West' poem, in which the female figure is again present and the sea with its 'grinding water' is more prominent" (123). One should note the important work of William V. Davis on the Thomas-Stevens connection, especially two essays in the *Wallace Stevens Journal*. See Works Cited.

57. In his "Wallace Stevens, in America, Thinks of Himself as Tom MacGreevy," William Fogarty clarifies: "McGreevy changed his name to MacGreevy in the 1930s" (57). Stevens refers to him throughout as "McGreevy," even though the spelling of the name had been changed at the time of his correspondence with the Irish poet. Apparently, MacGreevy never corrected the spelling, even for the reference to him by name in his poem "Our Stars Come from Ireland."

58. See my essay on Stevens, "Correspondence," in *Wallace Stevens: A Poet's Growth*, 228–30.

59. MacGreevy to Stevens, August 4, 1948, Huntington Library, WAS 145.

60. The Irish poets of MacGreevy's generation had little contact with Stevens' work. It was

poet Austin Clarke (1896–1974) who wrote the review in the *Irish Times* of the Fortune Press unauthorized *Selected Poems*. It was by Clarke's review that Stevens first learned of that edition. Clarke mentions having a copy of *Harmonium* (1931), but there is little evidence of Stevens' influence in his own poetry. Poet Denis Devlin (1908–1959) has a poem, "The Statue and the Perturbed Burghers," that appears to have been influenced by Stevens' "Mr. Burnshaw and the Statue," part II of the Alcestis Press edition of *Owl's Clover*. See Alex Davis, *Broken Line*, 43. In an interview with Parkman Howe, poet Brian Coffey (1905–1995) registers his difficulty in reading Stevens: "Now about an enormous amount of Wallace Stevens' work I still find myself just unable to get it going. I partly think it is because he has made the poem itself the subject of his poetry—and I believe that is a false step, that that is short-circuiting self-awareness" (Howe 114).

61. Stevens' "Irish connection" is greater than one might suspect. As Lee M. Jenkins has pointed out in a footnote: "The 'Irish connection' with Stevens extends beyond [Thomas] MacGreevy to MacGreevy's friend and fellow modernist, the poet Denis Devlin, author of the Stevensian sounding poem 'The Statue and the Perturbed Burghers,' whose 'Lough Derg' Tate and Penn Warren compared with 'Sunday Morning.' . . . Stevens' *[sic]* owed *[sic]* a copy of Devlin's *Lough Derg and Other Poems*. . . . The 'Irish connection' extends, too, to the novelists Brian Moore and John Banville: Moore takes 'The Emperor of Ice-Cream' as the title of one of his novels, while Banville's *Dr. Copernicus*, which takes its opening epigraph from 'Notes toward a Supreme Fiction,' is about Stevens as much as it is about Copernicus. . . . And the Irish connection extends to poets like Derek Mahon (and his poem 'Rage for Order,' which was written in response to 'the *[sic]* Idea of Order at Key West'), to Austin Clarke (whose review brought the existence of the unauthorized Fortune Press edition of Stevens' *Selected Poems* to Stevens' attention), to Seamus Heaney, who has lectured on late Stevens and late Yeats, and to Beckett (whose liminal poetry offers points of comparison with Stevens' late work)" (*Rage for Order* 169–70). In addition to his novels noted above, the Man Booker Prize recipient John Banville published *The Blue Guitar* in 2015, and Colum McCann published a collection of shorter fiction under the Stevensian title *Thirteen Ways of Looking* in the same year.

62. The title *Rage for Order: Poetry of the Northern Irish Troubles*, edited by Frank Ormsby, is an anthology of political poems in response to the "troubles" of the second half of the twentieth-century in that country. (The anthology appeared in 1992.) Mahon's poem of the same title is included among the selections.

63. "[Mahon's] 'Day Trip to Donegal' appears in [his] sea-named *Night Crossing* (1968); 'The Hebrides' in Longley's also fluidly entitled *No Continuing City* (1969). If both first collections abound in sea-imagery (and they do), this is not wholly due to the effects of reading Crane, Lowell and Stevens. Nonetheless, these American voices reverberate at moments of oceanic intensity, moments close to the poetry's Romantic reach, its visionary and mythic ambition, its symbolic pitch" (*Poetry and Posterity* 264).

64. Heaney attributes to the critic Helen Vendler his increased attention to Stevens: "I have learned from her to pay a lot more attention to Wallace Stevens" (*Stepping Stones* 348).

65. The impression of Stevens upon another poet of Northern Ireland, Paul Muldoon, seems

less discernible. His early poem "I Remember Sir Alfred" echoes Stevens' "Earthy Anecdote." The dislodged hare in the fifth and final stanza recalls Stevens' bucks that "swerved" both "To the right" and "To the left" in the face of the firecat. Here is the final stanza of Muldoon's poem: "Now Sir Alfred has dislodged a hare / That goes by leaps and bounds / Across the grazing, / Here and there, / This way and that, by singleminded swervings" (18).

66. For a fuller treatment of the Stevens-Heaney connections, see my "Stevens and Seamus Heaney" in *Poetry and Poetics after Wallace Stevens*, ed. Bart Eeckhout and Lisa Goldfarb (London: Bloomsbury, 2016), 103–15.

67. The essay was reproduced in Ford's *Mr and Mrs Stevens and Other Essays* (2012). The title refers to a review-essay that originally appeared in the *London Review of Books*.

68. Sharpe has found British resistance to Stevens partially explained by his being labeled a "philosophical poet" and by the preemptive presence of Eliot: "But I suspect the resistance has been partly due to Eliot's getting in the way, as a model of the serious modern poet, and an intemperate suspicion that Stevens was a fraud as a thinker—actually, I think the 'philosophical' Stevens has been a great burden. And when Eliot didn't get in the way, perhaps Frost did." E-mail message to George Lensing, July 4, 2016.

69. Jenkins' references have been an invaluable source for this study as I have examined the early reactions to Stevens in the United Kingdom.

70. The presentations occurred at King's Cross in London on November 17, 2014, with presentations by Sarah Churchwell, a well-known "literary journalist"; the British poet Lachlan Mackinnon; and Christopher Le Brun, president of the Royal Academy of Arts and a painter, sculptor, and printmaker. In spite of ironical interjections, the presentations, according to Eeckhout, are largely commending. (See "A Ghostly Visit to London" 1–14.)

71. In his 1983 essay, Jonathan Wordsworth set out to compare Stevens and Wordsworth as "two great Romantic poets" (183): "Both equally were forced to be tentative, because each in his way was making the biggest claim for imagination, and for the human mind, that he knew how to make" (184). J. Wordsworth goes on to make revealing comparisons between "The Solitary Reader" and "The Idea of Order at Key West," between Wordsworth's Leech Gatherer and the old woman in Stevens' "The Old Woman and the Statue" in "Owl's Clover"; between Wordsworth's and Shelley's belief in the "god-like potential in man" (190) and the "glass man" in Stevens' "Asides on the Oboe." James Applewhite in "The Mind's Lyric and the Spaces of Nature: Wordsworth and Stevens" develops the connection between Stevens and his Romantic predecessors through "site lyric" and "muse figure": "Remarkably, from the earliest poems of *Harmonium*, Stevens was able to acknowledge his immersion in Wordsworth, Keats and Shelley through the precise demarcations of his language of assimilation. He was able to use and to reinscribe the romantic site-lyric, their human muse-figure, the romantic singing bird—even romantic blank verse" (*Mind's Lyric* 129).

72. As Carolyn Masel has noted: "Thus, we must turn to the treatment of American letters in English universities to see what has happened to [Stevens]. While some universities run joint programs in English and American literature, by far the predominant tendency is to separate the two literatures, confining American letters to interdisciplinary American Studies departments.

Of course there are good pedagogical reasons for both arrangements, but each has its drawbacks. It is difficult for students to understand *As I Lay Dying* if they have no knowledge of *Ulysses*. The student who appreciates Henry James's debt to Hawthorne may never realize the debt he also owes to George Eliot. The highly allusive Stevens, who draws on both English and American writers, is likely to suffer a diminution of context whichever arrangement is deployed" (133).

73. Addressing a meeting in Rhode Island of the American National Governors Association in July of 2017, Canadian Prime Minister Justin Trudeau included these remarks: "I have to tell you, Wallace Stevens is my favorite American poet. By day, he worked in insurance, up the road in Hartford, Connecticut, and by night he wrote some of the most thoughtful poetry this country, and indeed our world, has ever seen. As I get to know this beautiful historic corner of America a little better . . . , I've been thinking a lot of Wallace Stevens. In his poem "Theory," he declares, 'I am what is around me.' That makes me think of the concept of home—what it means and how we define it." (In "News and Comments," *Wallace Stevens Journal* 41 (Fall 2017), 308.)

WORKS CITED

Abel, Lionel. Untitled introduction to Ramon Fernandez, "An Open Letter to André Gide." *Modern Monthly* 8 (June 1934): 271–74.

Aiken, Conrad. "A Letter from America." *London Mercury* 4 (June 1921): 197–99.

Alter, Jonathan. *The Defining Moment: FDR's Hundred Days and the Triumph of Hope.* New York: Simon & Schuster, 2006.

Althusser, Louis. "Ideology and Ideological State Apparatuses." In *Critical Theory since 1965.* Ed. Hazard Adams and Leroy Searle. Tallahassee: Florida State University Press, 1986.

Altieri, Charles. *Wallace Stevens and the Demands of Modernity.* Ithaca, NY: Cornell University Press., 2013.

Alvarez, A. *The Shaping Spirit: Studies in Modern English and American Poets.* London: Chatto & Windus, 1958.

Amis, Kingsley. *Letters of Kingsley Amis.* Ed. Zachary Leader. London: HarperCollins Publishers, 2000.

Anderson, Emily (editor and annotator). *The Letters of Mozart & His Family.* London: Macmillan & Co. Ltd., 1938.

[Anonymous.] "Contributors." *Partisan Review* I (September–October 1934): 2.

[Anonymous.] "The Poetry of Wallace Stevens." *Times Literary Supplement* (June 19, 1953): 396.

Applewhite, James. *Seas and Inland Journeys: Landscape and Consciousness from Wordsworth to Roethke.* Athens: University of Georgia Press, 1985.

———. "The Mind's Lyric and the Spaces of Nature: Wordsworth and Stevens." *Wallace Stevens Journal* 29 (Spring 2005): 117–30.

Arensberg, Mary B. "'A Curable Separation': Stevens and the Mythology of Gender." In *Wallace Stevens & the Feminine.* Ed. Melita Schaum. Tuscaloosa: University of Alabama Press, 1993: 23–45.

Auden, W. H. *The Enchafèd Flood: or The Romantic Iconography of the Sea.* New York: Random House, 1950.

———. *The Faber Book of Modern American Verse.* Ed. W. H. Auden. London: Faber & Faber Ltd., 1956.

————. *Selected Poems.* Ed. Edward Mendelson. New York: Vintage Books, 1979.

Barthes, Roland. *The Pleasure of the Text.* Trans. Richard Miller. New York: Hill & Wang, 1975.

Bates, Milton J. "Notes." "Lettres d'un Soldat (1914–1915)." Wallace Stevens. *Opus Posthumous.* New York: Alfred A. Knopf, 1989: 319.

————. *Wallace Stevens: A Mythology of Self.* Berkeley: University of California Press, 1985.

Bell, Martin. *Complete Poems.* Ed. Peter Porter. Newcastle upon Tyne: Bloodaxe Books Ltd., 1988.

Benda, Julien. "Of the Idea of Order and the Idea of God: Study for a System of Metaphysics." Trans. J. F. Scanlan. *Criterion* 10 (October 1930): 75–94.

Berger. Charles. *Forms of Farewell: The Late Poetry of Wallace Stevens.* Madison: University of Wisconsin Press, 1985.

Bergonzi, Bernard. "The Sound of a Blue Guitar." *Nine* 4 (Winter 1953–54): 48–51.

Berkeley, George. "Dialogue II, Three Dialogues between Hylas and Philonous." In *Berkeley: Essay, Principles, Dialogues.* Ed. Mary Whiton Calkins. NY: Charles Scribner's Sons, 1929.

————. "Of the Principles of Human Knowledge." In *The Works of George Berkeley.* Vol. I. Edited by Alexander Campbell Fraser. Bristol: Thoemmes Press, 1994.

Blackmur, R. P. "Examples of Wallace Stevens." *Form and Value in Modern Poetry.* New York: Doubleday Anchor, 1957: 183–212.

Blasing, Mutlu. *Lyric Poetry: The Pain and Pleasure of Words.* Princeton, NJ: Princeton University Press. 2007.

Bloom, Harold. *Wallace Stevens: The Poems of Our Climate.* Ithaca, NY: Cornell University Press, 1976.

————. *Wallace Stevens: Bloom's Major Poets.* Philadelphia: Chelsea House Publishers, 2003.

Borroff, Marie. *Language and the Poet: Verbal Artistry in Frost. Stevens, and Moore.* Chicago: University of Chicago Press, 1979.

Bradbury, Malcolm, and F. W. Cook. "Whose Hoo? A Reading of Wallace Stevens' 'Bantam in Pine Woods.'" *Bulletin: British Association for American Scholars* 4 (August 1962): 36–41.

Brazeau, Peter. *Parts of a World: Wallace Stevens Remembered.* New York, Random House, 1983.

Brinnin, John Malcolm. "John Malcolm Brinnin." In *Parts of a World: Wallace Stevens Remembered.* Ed. Peter Brazeau. New York, Random House, 1983.

Brogan, Jacqueline Vaught. *The Violence Within, The Violence Without: Wallace Stevens and the Emergence of a Revolutionary Poetics.* Athens: University of Georgia Press, 2003.

Brown, Tony. "'Blessings, Stevens': R. S. Thomas and Wallace Stevens." In *Echoes to the Amen: Essays after R.S. Thomas*. Ed. Damian Walford Davies. Cardiff: University of Wales Press, 2003: 112–31.

Burnshaw, Stanley. "Turmoil in the Middle Ground." *New Masses* 17 (October 1, 1935): 41–42.

Burnside, John. "Introduction." *Wallace Stevens: Poems Selected by John Burnside*. London: Faber & Faber, 2008.

Carroll, Joseph. *Wallace Stevens' Supreme Fiction: A New Romanticism*. Baton Rouge: Louisiana State University Press, 1987.

Clarke, Austin. "Sky Shades and Lamp Shades." *Irish Times*, February 14, 1953, cols. 3–4, 6.

Clarke, Edward. *The Later Affluence of W. B. Yeats and Wallace Stevens*. New York: Palgrave Macmillan, 2012.

Cleghorn, Angus J. *Wallace Stevens' Poetics: The Neglected Rhetoric*. New York: Palgrave, 2000.

Cole, John. *The Casa Marina: Historic House by the Sea*. Key West: Scarma Bay Publishing, 1992.

Coleridge, Samuel Taylor. *The Notebooks of Samuel Taylor Coleridge*. Vol. 2. Ed. Kathleen Coburn. New York: Pantheon Books, 1961.

Connolly Cyril. "e.e. Cummings." *The Selected Works of Cyril Connolly, I*. Ed. Matthew Connolly. London: Picador, 2002: 233–36.

Conquest, Robert. "Robert Conquest." In *The Poet Speaks: Interviews with Contemporary Poets*. Ed. Peter Orr. London: Routledge & Kegan Paul, 1966: 45–50.

Cook, Eleanor. *Poetry, Word-Play and Word-War in Wallace Stevens*. Princeton, NJ: Princeton University Press, 1988.

Corcoran, Neil. *English Poetry since 1940*. London: Longman, 1993.

Crane, Stephen. *Poems and Literary Remains*. Ed. Fredson Bowers. Charlottesville: University Press of Virginia, 1969.

Critchley, Simon. *Things Merely Are: Philosophy in the Poetry of Wallace Stevens*. New York: Routledge, 2005.

Culbertson, Signe. "An Interview with Wallace Stevens: One Angry Day-Son." *In Context* 3 (1955): 11–12.

Cummings, E. E. In Richard S. Kennedy. *Dreams in the Mirror: A Biography of E. E. Cummings*. New York: Liveright Publishing Co., 1980.

Davenport, Marcia. *Mozart*. Garden City, NY: Garden City Publishing, 1932.

Davie, Donald. "'Essential Gaudiness': The Poems of Wallace Stevens." *Twentieth Century* 153 (June 1953): 455–62.

———. "'Essential Gaudiness': The Poems of Wallace Stevens." *The Poet in the Imaginary*

Museum: Essays of Two Decades. Ed. Barry Alpert. Manchester: Carcanet Press, 1977: 11–17.

———. "Foreword." In *Charles Tomlinson: Man and Artist.* Columbia: University of Missouri Press, 1988: 1–8.

———. "Milosz and the Dithyramb." In *Czeslaw Milosz and the Insufficiency of Lyric.* Knoxville: University of Tennessee Press, 1986.

Davis, Alex. *A Broken Line: Denis Devlin and Irish Poetic Modernism.* Dublin: University College Dublin Press, 2000.

Davis, William V. "'An Abstraction Blooded': Wallace Stevens and R. S. Thomas on Blackbirds and Men." *Wallace Stevens Journal* 13 (Fall 1984): 79–82.

———. "Wallace Stevens and R. S. Thomas: Influence *sans* Anxiety." *Wallace Stevens Journal* 30 (Spring 2006): 86–97.

Dawe, Gerald. *Early Poems.* Londonderry: Lagan Press, 2015.

Doggett, Frank. *Wallace Stevens: The Making of the Poem.* Baltimore: Johns Hopkins University Press, 1980.

Donoghue, Denis. *Connoisseurs of Chaos: Ideas of Order in Modern American Poetry.* New York: Macmillan, 1965. (Second Edition: New York: Columbia University Press, 1984.)

———. *Words Alone: The Poet T. S. Eliot.* New Haven, CT: Yale University Press, 2000.

Durrell, Lawrence, and Henry Miller. *The Durrell-Miller Letters 1935–1980.* Ed. Ian S. MacNiven. London: Faber & Faber, 1988.

Editors. "Contributors" [Ramon Fernandez]. *Partisan Review* I (September–October 1934): 2.

Eeckhout, Bart. *Wallace Stevens and the Limits of Reading and Writing.* Columbia: University of Missouri Press, 2002.

———. "A Ghostly Visit to London (Enter Stevens in a 500-Year-Old Bavarian Tree.)" *Wallace Stevens Journal* 39 (Spring 2015): 1–14.

———. "International Reputation." In *Wallace Stevens in Context.* Ed. Glen MacLeod. Cambridge: Cambridge University Press, 2017: 176–84.

Eliot, T. S. "Books of the Quarter." *New Criterion* 4 (October 1926): 751–57.

———. Untitled remarks. *Trinity Review 8 (May 1954): 9.*

———. *Letters of T. S. Eliot, II.* Ed. Valerie Eliot and Hugh Haughton. London: Faber & Faber, 2009.

———. *Letters of T. S. Eliot, V.* Ed. Valerie Eliot and John Haffenden. New Haven, CT: Yale University Press, 2012.

Empson, William. "An American Poet." *Listener* 49 (March 26, 1953): 521.

———. *Faber Book of American Verse.* Ed. Donald Hall. London: Faber & Faber, 1965.

Fenton, James. "Ars Poetica 19: Happiness." In *The Independent* (London), June 3, 1990: 16.

Fernandez, Dominque. *Ramon*. Paris: Bernard Grasset, 2008.

Fernandez, Ramon. "A Note on Intelligence and Intuition." Trans. T. S. Eliot. *New Criterion* 6 (October 1927): 332–39.

———. "On Classicism." Trans. A. Hyatt Mayor. *The Symposium* I (January 1930): 33–44.

———. "An Open Letter to André Gide." Trans. Lionel Abel. *Modern Monthly* 8 (June 1934): 271–74.

———. *Molière: The Man Seen through the Plays*. Trans. Wilson Follett. New York: Hill & Wang, 1958.

———. *Messages: Literary Essays*. Trans. Montgomery Belgion. Port Washington: Kennikat Press, 1964.

Filreis, Alan. *Wallace Stevens and the Actual World*. Princeton, NJ: Princeton University Press, 1991.

———. *Modernism from Left to Right*. Cambridge: Cambridge University Press, 1994.

Fisher, Roy. "An Interview with Roy Fisher." Conducted by Jed Rasula and Mike Erwin. In *Nineteen Poems and an Interview*. Pensnett: Grosseteste, 1977: 12–38.

Fletcher, John Gould. "American Poetry." *London Mercury* 3 (January 1920): 329–30.

———. "Some Contemporary American Poets." *Chapbook* 2 (May 1920): 1–31.

Fogarty, William. "Wallace Stevens, in America, Thinks of Himself as Tom MacGreevy." *Wallace Stevens Journal* 35 (Spring 2011): 56–78.

Fónagy, Iván. "Communication in Poetry." *Word* 17 (1961): 194–218.

Ford, Mark. "Nicholas Moore, Stevens and the Fortune Press." In *Wallace Stevens across the Atlantic*. Ed. Bart Eeckhout and Edward Ragg. New York: Palgrave Macmillan, 2008: 165–85.

———. *Mr and Mrs Stevens and Other Essays*. Oxford: Peter Lang, 2012.

Fortune Anthology. London: Fortune Press, 1942.

Frost, Robert. *Letters of Robert Frost, I*. Ed. Mark Richardson and Robert Faggen. Cambridge, MA: Belknap Press of Harvard University Press, 2014.

Frye, Northrop. *Anatomy of Criticism*. Princeton, NJ: Princeton University Press, 1957.

Fuller, John. *W. H. Auden: A Commentary*. London: Faber & Faber, 1998.

Fuller, Roy. *Owls and Artificers: Oxford Lectures on Poetry*. London: André Deutsch Limited, 1971.

Gascoyne, David. *Collected Poems 1988*. Oxford: Oxford University Press, 1988.

Gerber, Natalie. "Stevens' Mixed-Breed Versifying and His Adaptations of Blank Verse Practice." *Wallace Stevens Journal* 35 (Fall 2011): 188–223.

Goldfarb, Lisa. "'The Figure Concealed': Valéryan Echoes in Stevens' Ideas of Music." *Wallace Stevens Journal* 28 (Spring 2004): 38–58.

———. *The Figure Concealed: Wallace Stevens, Music, and Valéryan Echoes*. Brighton: Sussex Academic Press, 2011.

Grigson, Geoffrey. "The Stuffed Goldfinch." *New Verse* 19 (February–March 1936): 18–19.

Gross, Harvey. "Hart Crane and Wallace Stevens." *Sound and Form in Modern Poetry*. Ann Arbor: University of Michigan Press, 1964.

Gunn, Thom. [Untitled Review]. *London Magazine* 3 (April 1956): 81–84.

Haffenden, John. *William Empson: Against the Christians*. Vol. 2. Oxford: Oxford University Press, 2005.

Hamilton, Ian. *Against Oblivion: Some Lives of the Twentieth-Century Poets*. London: Viking, 2002.

Harel, Kay: "Again Is an Oxymoron: William James's Ideas on Repetition and Wallace Stevens' 'Sea Surface Full of Clouds.'" *Wallace Stevens Journal* 26 (Spring 2002): 3–14.

Harrison, DeSales. *The End of the Mind: The Edge of the Intelligible in Hardy, Stevens, Larkin, Plath, and Glück*. New York: Routledge, 2005: 67–102.

Hartman, Geoffrey F. *Beyond Formalism: Literary Essays 1958–1970*. New Haven, CT: Yale University Press, 1970.

———. "Geoffrey Hartman." In *Criticism in Society*. Ed. Imre Salusinszky. New York: Methuen, 1987: 75–96.

Haughton, Hugh. *The Poetry of Derek Mahon*. Oxford: Oxford University Press, 2007.

Heaney, Seamus. "An Interview." Conducted by Randy Brandes. *Salmagundi* 80 (Fall 1988): 4–21.

———. "Sounding Auden." *The Government of the Tongue: Selected Prose: 1978–1987*. New York: Noonday Press, 1988: 109–28.

———. "Frontiers of Writing." In *The Redress of Poetry*. New York: Farrar, Straus & Giroux, 1995.

———. *Opened Ground: Selected Poems 1966–1996*. New York: Farrar, Straus & Giroux, 1998.

———. *Electric Light*. New York: Farrar, Straus & Giroux, 2001.

———.*Finders Keepers: Selected Prose 1971–2001*. New York: Farrar, Straus & Giroux, 2002.

———.*Stepping Stones: Interviews with Seamus Heaney*. Ed. Dennis O'Driscoll. New York: Farrar, Straus & Giroux, 2008.

Heidegger, Martin: "Hölderlin and the Essence of Poetry." In *Critical Theory since 1965*. Ed. Hazard Adams and Leroy Searle, Tallahassee: Florida State University Press, 1986: 758–65.

Helgeson, Karen. "'For a Moment Final': Metaphor as Form in the Closures of Wallace Stevens' Poems." Unpublished dissertation, University of North Carolina at Chapel Hill, 1996.

Henderson, Alice Corbin. "The Late Edward Thomas." *Poetry: A Magazine of Verse* 12 (May 1918): 102–5.

Heringman, Bernard. "Bernard Heringman." In *Parts of a World: Wallace Stevens Remembered*. Ed. Peter Brazeau. New York: Random House, 1983: 198–205.

Hill, Geoffrey. "Geoffrey Hill." *Viewpoints: Poets in Conversation with John Haffenden*. London: Faber & Faber, 1981: 76–99.

———. *The Lords of Limit: Essays on Literature and Ideas*. New York: Oxford University Press, 1984.

———. *Collected Poems*. New York: Oxford University Press, 1986.

Hobsbaum, Philip. "The Critics at the Harmonium: Blackmur and Winters on Stevens." *British Association for American Studies Bulletin*, n.s.11 (December 1965): 43–57.

———. "Wallace Stevens: Harmonium." In *A Companion to Twentieth-Century Poetry*. Ed. Neil Roberts. Oxford: Blackwell, 2001: 414–26.

Hockney, David. *The Blue Guitar*. New York: Petersburg Press, 1977.

Holander, Stefan. *Wallace Stevens and the Realities of Poetic Language*. New York: Routledge, 2008.

Honig, Edwin. "Meeting Wallace Stevens." *Wallace Stevens Newsletter* 1 (1970): 11–12.

Hughes, Ted. "Ted Hughes and *Gaudete* (1977)." [Interview]. In Ekbert Faas. *Ted Hughes: the Unaccommodated Universe: With Selected Critical Writings by Ted Hughes & Two Interviews*. Santa Barbara: Black Sparrow Press, 1980: 208–15.

Howe, Parkman. "An Interview with Brian Coffey." *Éire-Ireland* 13 (Spring 1978): 113–23.

Ingham, Charles. *Words in Picture: The Manifestation of Verbal Elements in the Work of Kurt Schwitters and David Hockney*. Unpublished Master of Philosophy thesis, University of Essex, 1985.

Jameson, Fredric. "Wallace Stevens." *New Orleans Review* 11 (Spring 1984): 10–19.

Jarrell, Randall. "The Poet and His Public." *Partisan Review* 13 (September–October 1946): 488–500.

———. "The Collected Poems of Wallace Stevens." *Yale Review* 44 (March 1955): 340–53.

Jenkins, Lee Margaret. *Wallace Stevens: Rage for Order*. Brighton: Sussex Academic Press, 2000.

———. "The Strands of Modernism: Stevens beside the Seaside." *Poetry and Poetics after Wallace Stevens*. Ed. Bart Eeckhout and Lisa Goldfarb. New York: Bloomsbury, 2016: 27–42.

Jennings, Elizabeth. "Elizabeth Jennings." In *The Poet Speaks*. Ed. Peter Orr. London: Routledge & Kegan Paul, 1966: 91–96.

Johnson, Barbara. *Mother Tongues: Sexuality, Trials, Motherhood, Translation.* Cambridge, MA: Harvard University Press, 2003.

Johnston. Sara Andrews. *"Life's a Beach": The Shore-Lyric from Arnold to Ammons.* Unpublished dissertation, University of North Carolina at Chapel Hill, 1991.

Justice, Donald. "The Free-Verse Line in Stevens." *Oblivion: On Writers & Writing.* Ashland: Story Line Press, 1998: 13–38.

Kant, Immanuel. *Critique of the Power of Judgment.* Trans. Paul Guyer and Eric Matthews. Cambridge: Cambridge University Press, 2000.

Kaplan, Alice. "Ghostly Demarcations: On Ramon Fernandez." *Nation* 129, February 15, 2010, 29–32.

Kennedy, Richard S. *Dreams in the Mirror: A Biography of E. E. Cummings.* New York: Liveright, 1979.

Kermode, Frank. "The Gaiety of Language." *Critical Essays on Wallace Stevens.* Ed. Steven Gould Axelrod and Helen Deese. Boston: G. K. Hall & Co., 1988.

———.*Wallace Stevens.* Edinburgh: Oliver & Boyd Ltd., 1960; reprinted: New York: Chip's Bookshop, Inc., 1979; London: Faber & Faber, 1989.

———. "Preface." *Wallace Stevens across the Atlantic.* Ed. Bart Eeckhout and Edward Ragg. New York: Palgrave Macmillan, 2008, xv–xvii.

Kinsella, Thomas. "Major American Poet." *Irish Press* (June 23, 1956), Section 9: 4.

Knight, John R. *Mimetic and Expressive Theories of Poetry in the Writing of Wallace Stevens.* M.A. thesis, University of North Carolina at Chapel Hill, 1980.

Larkin, Philip. *Selected Letters of Philip Larkin.* Ed. Anthony Thwaite. London: Faber & Faber, 1992.

———. "A Conversation with Neil Powell." *Further Requirements: Interviews. Broadcasts, Statements and Book Reviews.* London: Faber & Faber, 2001.

———. *Letters to Monica.* Ed. Anthony Thwaite. London: Faber & Faber, 2010.

Leech, Margaret. *In the Days of McKinley.* New York: Harper & Brothers, 1959.

Leggett, B. J. *Early Stevens: The Nietzschean Intertext.* Durham, NC: Duke University Press, 1992.

Lemercier. Eugène. *A Soldier of France to His Mother: Letters from the Trenches on the Western Front.* Trans. Theodore Stanton. Chicago: A. C. McClurg & Co., 1917.

Lensing, George S. "Wallace Stevens and Stevens T. Mason: An Epistolary Exchange on Poetic Meter." *Wallace Stevens Journal* 4 (Fall 1980): 34–36.

———. *Wallace Stevens: A Poet's Growth.* Baton Rouge: Louisiana State University Press, 1986.

———. "The Early Readers of Wallace Stevens." *Order in Variety: Essays and Poems in Honor of Donald E. Stanford.* Ed. R. W. Crump. Newark: University of Delaware Press, 1991: 49–73.

———. *Wallace Stevens and the Seasons.* Baton Rouge: Louisiana State University Press, 2001.

Lentricchia, Frank. *Ariel and the Police: Michel Foucault. William James, Wallace Stevens.* Madison: University of Wisconsin Press, 1988.

Lerner, Ben. "'The World That Suffices: Frank Kermode and Wallace Stevens." *Critical Quarterly* 54 (April 2012): 35–42. DOI:10.1111/j 1467–8705, 2012,0231x. online.

Lethbridge, J. B. "R. S. Thomas Talks to J. B. Lethbridge." *Anglo-Welsh Review* 74 (1983): 36–56.

Lewis, C. Day. *The Lyric Impulse.* Cambridge, MA: Harvard University Press, 1965.

Litz, A. Walton. *Introspective Voyager: The Poetic Development of Wallace Stevens.* NewYork: Oxford University Press, 1972.

Longenbach, James. *Wallace Stevens: The Plain Sense of Things.* New York: Oxford University Press, 1991.

Longley, Edna. *Poetry and Posterity.* Highgreen: Bloodaxe Books Ltd., 2000.

———. *Yeats and Modern Poetry.* Cambridge: Cambridge University Press, 2013.

Longley, Michael. "The Empty Holes of Spring: Some Reminiscences of Trinity & Two Poems Addressed to Derek Mahon." *Irish University Review* 24 (Spring/Summer 1994): 51–57.

———*A Jovial Hullabaloo: Inaugural Lecture as Ireland Professor of Poetry.* London: Enitharmon Press, 2008.

Lottman, Herbert R. *The Left Bank: Writers, Artists, and Politics from the Popular Front to the Cold War.* Boston: Houghton Mifflin Co., 1982.

Lowell, Robert. "Imagination and Reality." *The Nation* 164 (April 5, 1947): 400–402.

———. *Letters of Robert Lowell.* New York: Farrar, Straus & Giroux, 2005.

Lyttle, Richard B. *II Duce: The Rise and Fall of Benito Mussolini.* New York: Atheneum, 1987.

MacCaig, Norman. Quoted in Scott, Mary Jane W. "Neoclassical MacCaig." *Studies in Scottish Literature* 10 (January 1973): 135–44.

MacDiarmid, Hugh. "*Wallace Stevens, 'Harmonium.'*" In *The Raucle Tongue: Hitherto Uncollected Prose I.* Ed. Agnus Calder, Glen Murray, and Alan Riach. Manchester: Carcanet Press Ltd., 1996: 178–81.

MacLeod, Glen. "The Influence of Wallace Stevens on Contemporary Artists." *Wallace Stevens Journal* 20 (Fall 1996): 139–80.

Maeder, Beverly. *Wallace Stevens' Experimental Language: The Lion in the Lute.* New York: St. Martin's Press, 1999.

———. "Stevens and Linguistic Structure." In *The Cambridge Companion to Wallace Stevens.* Ed. John N. Serio. Cambridge: Cambridge University Press, 2007: 149–63.

Mahon, Derek. *New Collected Poems.* Loughcrew: Gallery Press. 2011.

————. *Poems 1962–1978*. Oxford: Oxford University Press, 1979.

Martiny, Erik. "'From this collision were new colors born': Peter Redgrove's Reversionary Swerves from Wallace Stevens' Iconic Texts." In *Wallace Stevens Journal* 31 (Spring 2007): 73–85.

Masel, Carolyn. "Stevens and England: A Difficult Crossing." *Wallace Stevens Journal* 25 (Fall 2001): 122–37.

McRobbie, Angela. "Post-Marxism and Cultural Studies: A Post-script." In *Cultural Studies*. Ed. Lawrence Grossberg, Cary Nelson, Paula A. Treichler. New York: Routledge, 1992: 719–30.

Miller, J. Hillis. "The Ethics of Topography: Stevens." In *Topographies*. Stanford, CA: Stanford University Press, 1995: 255–90.

Mizener, Arthur. "Not in Cold Blood." *Kenyon Review* 13 (Spring 1951): 218–55.

Moore, Geoffrey. "Introduction." *The Penguin Book of Modem American Verse*. London: Penguin Books, 1954: 15–30.

Moore, Nicholas. *The Cabaret, The Dancer, The Gentlemen*. London: Fortune Press, 1942.

————. "A Short Note on the Writers." *Fortune Anthology: Stories, Criticism, and Poems*. London: Fortune Press, 1942.

————. *The Glass Tower*. London: Nicholson & Watson, 1944.

————. "Notes on Contributions." *Atlantic Anthology*. London: Fortune Press, 1946.

————. "Tambi the Knife." In *Tambimuttu: Bridge between Two Worlds*. London: Peter Owen, 1989: 57–64.

Morris, Tim. *Wallace Stevens: Poetry and Criticism*. Cambridge: Salt Publications, 2006.

Morse, Samuel French. "Introduction." Wallace Stevens, *Opus Posthumous*. New York: AlfredA. Knopf, 1957: xiii–xxxviii.

Mozart, Wolfgang Amadeus. Letter to Leopold Mozart, December 28, 1782. In *The Letters of Mozart and His Family III*. Ed. Emily Anderson. London: MacMillan, 1938.

Muldoon, Paul. *Why Brownlee Left*. Wake Forest, NC: Wake Forest University Press, 1980.

————. *The End of the Poem: "All Souls' Night" by W. B. Yeats: An Inaugural Lecture delivered before the University of Oxford on 2 November 1999*. Oxford: Oxford University Press, 2000.

Munson, Gorham. "The Dandyism of Wallace Stevens [1925]." In *The Achievement of Wallace Stevens*. Ed. Ashley Brown and Robert S. Haller. Philadelphia: J. B. Lippincott, 1962: 41–45.

Murphy, Shane. "Sonnets, Centos and Long Lines: Muldoon, Paulin, McGuckian and Carson." *Cambridge Companion to Contemporary Irish Poetry*. Ed. Matthew Campbell. Cambridge: Cambridge University Press, 2003: 189–208.

Nelson, Cary. "Literature as Cultural Studies: 'American' Poetry of the Spanish Civil

War." In *Disciplinarity and Dissent in Cultural Studies*. Ed. Cary Nelson and Dilip Parameshwar Gaonkar. New York: Routledge, 1996: 63–102.

Nicholson, Mervyn. "'The Slightest Sound Matters': Stevens' Sound Cosmology." *Wallace Stevens Journal* 18 (Spring 1994): 63–80.

Nietzsche, Friedrich. *The Will to Power* in *Complete Works of Friedrich Nietzsche*. Vol. XV. Trans. Anthony M. Ludovici. New York: Russell & Russell, Inc., 1964.

O'Brien, Sean. *Cousin Coat: Selected Poems 1976–2001*. London: Picador, 2002.

O'Driscoll, Dennis. *Troubled Thoughts, Majestic Dreams: Selected Prose Writings*. Loughcrew: Gallery Press, 2001.

Olson, Liesl M. "Stevens and Auden: Antimythological Meetings." *Wallace Stevens Journal* 27 (Fall 2003): 240–54.

O'Neill, Michael. *The All-Sustaining Air: Romantic Legacies and Renewals in British, American, and Irish Poetry since 1900*. Oxford: Oxford University Press, 2007.

Owen, Wilfred. *Complete Poems and Fragments*. Ed. Jon Stallworthy. New York: W. W. Norton, 1984.

Perloff, Marjorie. "Revolving in Crystal: The Supreme Fiction and the Impasse of the Modernist Lyric." In *Wallace Stevens: the Poetics of Modernism*. Ed. Albert Gelpi. Cambridge: Cambridge University Press, 1985.

Porter, Peter. "Introduction, Memoir and Critical Note." In Martin Bell, *Complete Poems*. Ed. Peter Porter. Newcastle upon Tyne: Bloodaxe Books Ltd., 1988: 11–30.

Pound. Ezra. "Eight Letters from Ezra Pound to Parker Tyler." Ed. George Bornstein. *Michigan Quarterly Review* 24 (1985): 1–17.

———. *Pound/Zukofsky: Selected Letters of Ezra Pound and Louis Zukofsky*. Ed. Barry Ahern. New York: New Directions, 1987.

Powys. Llewelyn. "The Thirteenth Way." *Dial* 77 (July 1924): 45–50.

Putnam, Phoebe. "Shall I uncrumple this much-crumpled thing? Wallace Stevens' Poetics of Sequence in 'Sea Surface Full of Clouds.'" *Wallace Stevens Journal* 31 (Spring 2007): 43–58.

Quinn, Justin. "A Second Look: His Damned Hoobla-Hoobla-Hoobla-How." In *Poetry Review* 90 (Summer 2000): 52–53.

———. *Gathered beneath the Storm: Wallace Stevens, Nature and Community*. Dublin: University College Dublin Press, 2002.

Ragg, Edward. *Wallace Stevens and the Aesthetics of Abstraction*. Cambridge: Cambridge University Press, 2010.

Raine, Craig. "Wallace Stevens, 1879–1955: A Centenary Essay." *Encounter* 53 (November 1979): 59–67.

Ramazani, Jahan. "Stevens and the War Elegy." *Wallace Stevens Journal* 15 (Spring 1991): 24–35.

———. *Poetry of Mourning: The Modern Elegy from Hardy to Heaney.* Chicago: University of Chicago Press, 1994.

Ransom, John Crowe. "Artists, Soldiers, Positivists." *Kenyon Review* 6 (Spring 1944): 276–81.

———. "The Rugged Way of Genius." In *Randall Jarrell, 1914–1965.* Ed. Robert Lowell, Peter Taylor, and Robert Penn Warren. New York: Farrar, Straus & Giroux, 1967.

Reddy, Patrick. "Politics." In *Wallace Stevens in Context.* Ed. Glen MacLeod. Cambridge: Cambridge University Press, 2017: 267–76.

Redgrove, Peter. *The Collector and Other Poems.* London: Routledge & Kegan Paul, 1959.

———. *Selected Poems:* London: Cape Poetry, 1999.

Reed, Henry. [Untitled Review of *The Necessary Angel* and *Opus Posthumous*]. *The Listener* 63 (April 14, 1960): 675–76.

Reeves, Gareth. "A Modernist Dialectic: Stevens and Williams in the Poetry of Charles Tomlinson." *Wallace Stevens Journal* 30 (Spring 2006): 57–85.

Rich, Adrienne. *What Is Found There: Notebooks on Poetry and Politics.* New York: W. W. Norton, 1993.

Richardson, Joan. *Wallace Stevens: The Later Years, 1923–1955.* New York: William Morrow, 1988.

Riddel, Joseph. *The Clairvoyant Eye: The Poetry and Poetics of Wallace Stevens.* Baton Rouge: Louisiana State University Press, 1965.

Riding, Laura, and Robert Graves. *A Survey of Modernist Poetry.* London: William Heinemann, 1927.

Ridler, Anne (ed.). *The Little Book of Modernist Verse.* London: Faber & Faber, 1941.

Riffaterre, Michael. *Semiotics of Poetry.* Bloomington: Indiana University Press, 1978.

Rogers, Arthur Kenyon. *A Student's History of Philosophy.* New York: Macmillan, 1932.

Rogers, Byron. *The Man Who Went into the West: The Life of R. S. Thomas.* London: Aurum Press, 2006.

Rosu, Anca. *The Metaphysics of Sound in Wallace Stevens.* Tuscaloosa: University of Alabama Press, 1995.

Rudd, Andrew. "'Not to the Bible but to Wallace Stevens'—What R. S. Thomas Found There." *P.N. Review* 30 (2004): 49–51.

Ruskin, John. *Works of John Ruskin, V.* Ed. E. T. Cook and Alexander Wedderburn. London: George Allen, 1904.

Russell, Bertrand. *The Autobiography of Bertrand Russell: 1914–1944.* Boston: Little, Brown & Co., 1951.

Santayana, George. *Interpretations of Poetry and Religion.* London: Adam and Charles Black, 1900.

Schlegel, Friedrich. From *Critical Fragments*. In *Critical Theory since Plato*. Ed. Hazard Adams. Fort Worth: Harcourt Brace Jovanovich, 1992: 429–32.

Schlesinger, Arthur. *The Age of Roosevelt: The Coming of the New Deal*. Boston: Houghton Mifflin, 1958.

Schmidt, Michael. *Lives of the Poets*. London: Weidenteld & Nicholson, 1998.

———. "Preface." *New Poetries II*. Manchester: Carcanet Press Ltd., 1999: 9–10.

———. "Wallace Stevens: Arranging, Deepening, Enchanting Britain." *Wallace Stevens Journal* 30 (Spring 2006): 52–56.

Schubert, Franz. "From Schubert's Diary," June 14, 1816. In *A Documentary Biography*. Ed. Otto Erich Deutsch. Trans. Eric Bloom. London: J. B. Dent & Sons Ltd., 1946.

Schumann, Clara. *Clara Schumann: An Artist's Life*. Vol. II. New York: Da Capo Press, 1979.

Schwarz, Daniel. *Narrative and Representation in the Poetry of Wallace Stevens*. New York: St. Martin's Press, 1993.

Serio, John. "Introduction." *Wallace Stevens: Selected Poems*. Ed. John Serio. New York: Knopf, 2011.

Shakespeare, William. *The Sonnets*. Ed. G. Blakemore Evans. Cambridge: Cambridge University Press, 1996.

Tony Sharpe. *Wallace Stevens: A Literary Life*. New York: St. Martin's Press, 2000.

———. "Final Beliefs: Stevens and Auden." *Literature & Theology* 25 (March 2011): 64–78.

Shelley, Percy Bysshe. *The Major Works*. Ed. Zachary Leader and Michael O'Neill. Oxford: Oxford University Press, 2003.

Shinbrot, Victoria. "The Lyric Element and the Prosaic World in 'The Idea of Order at Key West.'" *Wallace Stevens Journal* 29 (Fall 2005): 263–74.

Sidney, Sir Philip. "The Defense of Poesy." In *The Renaissance in England*. Ed. Hyder E. Rollins and Herschel Baker. Boston: D. C. Heath, 1968.

Sitwell, Edith. "The Rising Generation." *Times Literary Supplement*, September 17, 1954: i.

Smith, Stan. *Irish Poetry and the Construction of Modern Identity*. Dublin: Irish Academic Press, 2005.

Smith, Timothy D'Arch. *R. A. Caton and the Fortune Press*. North Pomfret: Asphodel Editions, 2004.

Solomon, Maynard. *Mozart*. New York: HarperCollins, 1995.

Spender, Stephen. "The Creative Imagination in the World Today." *Folios of New Writing*. (Autumn 1940): 145–160.

———. "American Diction v. American Poetry." *Encounter* 1 (October 1953): 61–65.

Stegman, Michael O. "Wallace Stevens and Music: A Discography of Stevens' Phonograph Record Collection." *Wallace Stevens Journal* 3 (Fall 1979): 79–97.

Stevens, Holly. "Flux." *Southern Review* 15 (October 1979): 771–74.

Stevens, Wallace. See "Abbreviations," p. xi.

———. "Letters to Ferdinand Reyher." Ed. Holly Stevens. *Hudson Review* 44 (Autumn 1991): 381–409.

———. "Six Stevens Letters." Ed. Jonathan Strange. *Wallace Stevens Journal* 18 (Spring 1994): 19–26.

———. *Wallace Stevens: Poems.* Selected by John Burnside. London: Faber & Faber, 2008.

Storrs, Richard S. *The Divine Origin of Christianity Indicated by Its Historical Effects.* Boston: Pilgrim Press, 1884.

Stubbs, Tara. *American Literature and Irish Culture, 1910–55.* Manchester: Manchester University Press, 2013.

Surette, Leon. *The Modern Dilemma: Wallace Stevens, T. S. Eliot, and Humanism.* Montreal: McGill-Queen's University Press, 2008.

Symons, Julian. "A Short View of Wallace Stevens." *Life and Letters To-day* 26 (September 1940): 215–24.

———. "Stevens in England." *Trinity Review* 8 (May 1954): 43–45.

Taylor, Dennis. "The Apparitional Meters of Wallace Stevens." *Wallace Stevens Journal* 15 (Fall 1991): 209–28.

Thomas, Dylan. *Collected Letters.* London: J. M. Dent & Sons Ltd., 1985.

Thomas, R. S. *Collected Later Poems: 1988–2000.* Highgreen: Bloodaxe Books, 2004.

———.*Collected Poems: 1945–1990.* Tarset, Northumberland: Bloodaxe Books, 2004.

Tomlinson, Charles. *Some Americans: A Personal Record.* Berkeley: University of California Press, 1981.

———. *Collected Poems.* Oxford: Oxford University Press, 1985.

———. "Wallace Stevens and the Poetry of Scepticism." *New Pelican Guide to English Literature.* Ed. Boris Ford. London: Penguin Books, 1988: 393–409.

———. "Words and Water [Interview]." In *Charles Tomlinson: Man and Artist.* Conducted by Alan Ross and Charles Tomlinson. Columbia: University of Missouri Press, 1988: 21–37.

Tompsett, Daniel. *Wallace Stevens and Pre-Socratic Philosophy.* New York: Routledge, 2012.

Valéry, Paul. *Oeuvres I* and *II* Paris: Bibliothèque de la Pléiade, Gallimard, 1973.

Van Vechten, Carl. *The Blind Bow-Boy.* New York: Alfred A. Knopf, 1923.

Vendler, Helen. "The Qualified Assertions of Wallace Stevens." In *The Act of the Mind: Essays on the Poetry of Wallace Stevens.* Ed. Roy Harvey Pearce and J. Hillis Miller. Baltimore: Johns Hopkins University Press, 1965: 163–78.

———. *On Extended Wings: Wallace Stevens' Longer Poems*. Cambridge: Harvard University Press, 1969.

———.*Wallace Stevens: Words Chosen Out of Desire*. Knoxville: University of Tennessee Press, 1984.

Virgil. *The Eclogues of Virgil*. Trans. David Ferry. New York: Farrar, Straus & Giroux, 1999.

Wain, John. *Professing Poetry*. London: Macmillan London Ltd., 1977.

Ward, J. P. *The Poetry of R. S. Thomas*. Mid Glamorgan: Poetry Wales Press, 1987.

Whitman, Walt. *Leaves of Grass*. Ed. Sculley Bradley and Harold W. Blodgett. New York: W. W. Norton, 1973.

Williams, William Carlos. "Poet's Corner." *New Republic* LXXXXIII, November 17, 1937, 50.

Williamson, Dennis. "Foreword." In *Wallace Stevens. Selected Poems*. London: Fortune Press, 1953.

Wootten, William. *The Alvarez Generation*. Liverpool: Liverpool University Press, 2015.

Wordsworth, Jonathan. "The Mind as Lord and Master: Wordsworth and Wallace Stevens."*The Wordsworth Circle* 14 (Autumn 1983): 183–91.

Wordsworth, William. *The Prelude*. Ed. Ernest de Selincourt. Oxford: Oxford University Press, 1933.

———. *Poems, in Two Volumes, and Other Poems, 1800–1807*. Ed. Jared Curtis. Ithaca, NY: Cornell University Press, 1983.

Wright, David. "Introduction." *The Mid-Century: English Poetry 1940–1960*. Harmondsworth: Penguin, 1965: 15–17.

Yeats, William Butler. "Introduction." *The Oxford Book of Modern Verse, 1892–1935*. New York: Oxford University Press, 1937.

———. In "Yeats as Anthologist" by Jon Stallworthy. In *In Excited Reverie: A Centenary Tribute to William Butler Yeats, 1865–1939*. New York: Macmillan, 1965: 171–92.

———. *The Poems*. Ed. Richard J. Finneran. New York: Macmillan, 1983.

———. "A Scholar Poet." In *Letters to the New Island*. Ed. George Bornstein and Hugh Witemeyer. London: Macmillan, 1989: 102–7.

INDEX

Prose